Mother of Writing

Mother of Writing

The Origin and Development of a
Hmong Messianic Script

William A. Smalley

Chia Koua Vang

Gnia Yee Yang

Mitt Moua, *Project Translator*

The University of Chicago Press
Chicago and London

WILLIAM A. SMALLEY, now professor of linguistics, emeritus, at Bethel College, was a missionary linguist in Vietnam, Laos, and Thailand between 1950 and 1977. He is the author of *Manual of Articulatory Phonetics*, and more than 120 scholarly articles.

The University of Chicago Press, Chicago 60637
The University of Chicago Press, Ltd., London
© 1990 by the University of Chicago
All rights reserved. Published 1990
Printed in the United States of America

99 98 97 96 95 94 93 92 91 90   5 4 3 2 1

Library of Congress Cataloging-in-Publication Data

Smalley, William Allen.
    Mother of writing : the origin and development of a Hmong messianic script /
William A. Smalley, Chia Koua Vang, Gnia Yee Yang ; Mitt Moua, project translator.
        p.   cm.
    Includes bibliographical references.
    1. Hmong language—Alphabet.   2. Hmong language—Writing.   3. Yang, Shong
Lue, d. 1971.   I. Vang, Chia Koua.   II. Yang, Gnia Yee.   III. Title.
PL3311.M5S6   1990   89-39956
495—dc20   CIP
ISBN 0-226-76286-6 (alk. paper)
ISBN 0-226-76287-4 (pbk.; alk. paper)

⊗ The paper used in this publication meets the minimum requirements
of the American National Standard for Information Sciences—
Permanence of Paper for Printed Library Materials, ANSI Z39.48-1984.

Contents

Tables

Illustrations

Figures

Plates (following page 118)

Acknowledgments

Support for writing this book and for the research behind it was provided through grants from the National Endowment for the Humanities and the Indochina Studies Program of the Committee on Southeast Asia (jointly sponsored by the Social Science Research Council and the American Council of Learned Societies, with funds provided by the Ford Foundation, the National Endowment for the Humanities and the Henry Luce Foundation), together with assistance from Bethel College.

Mitt Moua (Miv Muas ꞏꞏ) was project translator and made extensive comments on the drafts. Interviews were held with Chai Lee (Txais Lis ꞏꞏ), Yong Chue Yang (Ntxoov Tswb Yaj ꞏꞏꞏ), Ying Yang (Yeeb Yaj ꞏꞏ), Chia Long Thao (Txiaj Looj Thoj ꞏꞏ ꞏ), Shong Chai Yang (Shong Chai Yaj ꞏꞏ ꞏꞏ), Vang Geu (Vaj Ntxawg ꞏꞏ ꞏ), Hang Sao (Hang Choj ꞏꞏ ꞏꞏ), Yang Dao (Yaj Dos ꞏꞏ ꞏꞏ) and Lysao Lyfoung (Lis Choj Lis Foom ꞏꞏ ꞏꞏ ꞏꞏ ꞏꞏ). Pa Kao Her (Paj Kaub Hawj ꞏꞏ ꞏ ꞏꞏ) and Chai Lee arranged for survey questionnaires to be filled out in Thailand. Two hundred and twenty-seven people in all responded to the survey.

Yves Bertrais read a draft of Chapter 11 and contributed information which has been incorporated there. David Strecker read and commented on several chapters. He also supplied resources from his files, as did Margaret Lindley Koch and Michael D. Roe. Brenda Johns provided information, as did Jonas V. Vangay (Nas Vaj ꞏꞏ ꞏꞏ).

Rowena Fong, Kenneth E. Gowdy, James P. Hurd, James E. Koch, Margaret Lindley Koch, Donald N. Larson and Michael D. Roe read and commented on some chapters, Paul R. Spickard on the whole book.

The following individuals, constituting the board of the project, provided backing and encouragement: Cha Vang Yang (Tsav Vaj Yaj ꞏꞏ ꞏꞏ ꞏꞏ), Song Fue Yang (Soob Fwm Yaj ꞏꞏ ꞏꞏ ꞏꞏ), Pao Yang (Pov Yaj ꞏꞏ ꞏꞏ), Chong Khue Yang (Txoos Khwb Yaj ꞏꞏ ꞏꞏ ꞏꞏ), Thao Yang (Thoj Yaj ꞏꞏ ꞏꞏ), Wang Yee Yang (Vam Yis Yaj ꞏꞏ ꞏꞏ ꞏꞏ), Cher Pao Her

(Txawj Pov Hawj ꡝꡤ ꡝꡟ ꡝꡈꡲ), Sai Long Yang (Xaiv Looj Yaj ꡟA ꡠꡟꡈ ꡟꡳ),
Xia Mai Lee (Txhiaj Maim Lis ꡠꡲ ꡟꡰ ꡟꡈ), Ger Lee (Ntxawg Lis ꡠꡲ
ꡟꡈ), Tou Lee Her (Tub Lis Hawj ꡟꡲ ꡟꡈ ꡟꡈꡲ), Kao Lee (Kos Lis ꡟ ꡟꡈ),
Dang Her (Ntaj Hawj ꡟꡲ ꡟꡈꡲ), Long Yang (Looj Yaj ꡠꡟꡈ ꡟꡳ) and Eng
Yang (Eev Yaj ꡟꡲ ꡟꡳ).

Daniel R. Johnson alerted Smalley to the fact that the Pahawh Hmong
was being used in St. Paul, Minnesota, and introduced Smalley to the
Hmong co-authors. At Bethel College William Doyle, David Holter
and James Hurd answered questions about the use of computers; Mary
K. Anderson and Kathy L. Hart entered the survey data for computer
analysis; Carole Cragg provided special service in the library; Wayne
Roosa loaned equipment from the Art Department for making close-up
photographs.

The wordprocessing program which incorporates the non-English
characters used in this book was provided by JAARS, an affiliate of the
Summer Institute of Linguistics. The Southeast Asian Refugee Studies
Project of the University of Minnesota contributed information and use
of their files; they also loaned Pahawh Hmong rubber stamps held in
their collection.

To all of these people and institutions, our deep appreciation.

Introduction
Background for the Alphabet

It is rare in the history of the world (at most seven documented cases) that individuals who could not previously read or write any language devise a full-fledged writing system for their language, especially one symbolizing pronunciation rather than meaningful units like words. It is even more rare when that writing is an alphabetic system, representing sound units smaller than the syllable.

This is the story of Shong Lue Yang (Soob Lwj Yaj **ห็น ติก ลิง**), whose followers called him "Mother [Source] of Writing," and of his creation of an alphabet for, not one, but two quite unrelated languages. He also accommodated two significantly different dialects for one of the languages in the process. Furthermore, the alphabet he produced for that language, Hmong, was fully efficient, representing all of the sound contrasts, but with a structure notably different from that of any other writing system we have been able to locate.[1] He then went on to produce three successive revisions of his system, each simpler than the previous one, each capitalizing on increased linguistic abstraction.

We have an unprecedented look into the process of Shong Lue's creation through the eyes of his disciple and one of the authors of this book, Chia Koua Vang (Txiaj Kuam Vaj **ปิ๊ช ก๋ ลิเ**),[2] who documented the stages of development, discussing them with the creator and recording what he said in a notebook. Chia Koua has given us the opportunity to study and evaluate the development of Shong Lue's thinking about his language.

It is an opportunity that might easily have been lost, for the story of Shong Lue's alphabet is also the story of his death. His assassination at the hands of government agents was in large part the result of his invention of a Hmong writing system. He was hounded first by the Vietnamese communists and finally killed by Hmong of the anti-communist faction. Both sides accused him of aiding the other.

Chia Koua Vang and later Gnia Yee Yang (Nyiaj Yig Yaj **ปิ๊ช ห็ย ลิเ**),

1

another of the authors of this work, exercised extraordinary ingenuity and perseverance in seeking ways to type and print the new script, first carving individual wood block letters to use as stamps, then attempting to make a typewriter, and finally moving to the United States to find the technology which would enable them to reproduce "The Alphabet."

All these accomplishments were part of a larger movement in which hundreds of people flocked around Shong Lue Yang, not only to learn the alphabet from the Mother of Writing, but also to hear moral, ethical and religious teaching from the "Savior of the People." They believed, as Shong Lue himself believed, that he was a messenger from God. He was thus a messianic figure to many of the poor and uneducated, people whose ethnic memories included centuries of repression as a stateless minority, and who were now suffering from the prolonged disruptions of war and other severe cultural dislocation. He was also increasingly seen by others as a threat to the Hmong military establishment, which ultimately killed him.

The events connected with Shong Lue happened over the short space of twelve years between 1959 and 1971 in the Southeast Asian countries of Vietnam and Laos, where he started as a poor uneducated farmer growing mountain rice on unirrigated mountain slopes. He was ethnically of the minority Hmong people, his mother born of another minority group, the Khmu'.

Mother of Writing tells the story of Shong Lue Yang's writing system, its origin, development and use. It places his accomplishment among writing systems around the world (including other Hmong writing systems), and is the most complete account of any such development. It describes Shong Lue and his movement, how he understood his supernatural nature, the phenomenal response to his message by the poor and disenfranchised, his persecution and assassination. It deals with those who carry on the tradition, and touches also on how Shong Lue and the writing appear to Hmong non-believers.

This book is the product of collaboration between two Hmong men who have been promoting Shong Lue's writing for years and an American anthropological linguist with long-standing interest in the Hmong people. Much of it is written from the perspective of William A. Smalley, the linguist, who seeks to understand Shong Lue and his accomplishments in Western analytical ways, yet to be sensitive to the perspective of his Hmong co-authors as well. Because he is the one who writes in English, everything is inevitably filtered through his mind and recast to some degree in his thought patterns. Both Hmong authors, however, have questioned or criticized points of the book, helped by our associate and translator, Mitt Moua (Miv Muas **ᎭᏒ ᏋᏒ**).

The first two chapters were drafted initially by Chia Koua Vang, assisted by Gnia Yee Yang, and translated into English for Smalley by Mitt Moua. Smalley asked many questions for clarification and amplification, rewriting the chapters to enable Westerners to understand them better, but seeking to preserve as much as possible of the original perspective. The world view of Chapter 1 is essential to the story because it shows how Shong Lue and many of his followers understood his unusual gifts. Western readers not familiar with a wide range of non-Western world views may find a fascinating, perhaps troubling, new world there.

The Hmong

There are up to six million Hmong people in South China, North Vietnam, North Laos, and North and Northeast Thailand; since 1975 Hmong are also to be found in the United States (85,000), France (including French Guiana, 7,000), Canada (650) and Australia (350), having moved to these Western countries as refugees from some of the events recounted in Chapters 2 and 9 (Bliatout et al. 1988: 14). In whatever country the Hmong have lived, they have been a minority people, often struggling for survival, always striving to keep a Hmong identity and some form of independence, though not necessarily political independence.

The Hmong, along with several million other minority peoples in China, are called Miao by the Chinese. Other Miao languages are not mutually intelligible with Hmong,[3] but there are several different mutually intelligible dialects of the Hmong language, two of which are represented by Shong Lue's writing system.

The Miao peoples have been mentioned sporadically for centuries in Chinese annals,[4] with different attitudes expressed toward them at different times. In the eighteenth century antagonism between the Miao peoples and ethnic Chinese came to a head as some Hmong revolted against steady Chinese incursion into the areas where they lived, and against increasingly repressive Chinese rule. When their revolts failed, large numbers of the Miao moved southward within China, and in the nineteenth century thousands of Hmong began moving across borders into less densely settled areas of Vietnam, then Laos, and finally Thailand.[5]

The Vietnam-Laos Setting

The Hmong in Vietnam, Laos and Thailand are usually called Meo by the local populations and in older Western publications, a term which Hmong in the United States reject as pejorative, reflecting the concept of "primitives" generated by groups which have dominated them. The parts of these countries where the Hmong live are typically rugged mountain areas inhabited by a variety of ethnic groups. In Laos these peoples tend to be geographically stratified, with the Hmong occupying the higher elevations in the mountains, the Khmu' the lower elevations, and the Lao the river valleys, to mention only those peoples who figure importantly in Shong Lue's story.

The Lao are the most numerous people in the country (more than a million of them in the 1960's), although not the majority, and not even the most numerous in some of the provinces where the Hmong lived. For centuries they have been dominant over other peoples because of their more advanced technology and a stratified social system with a ruling class controlling the political and military structures. They belong to the same family of languages and cultures as the Thai on their western border, and as numerous smaller groups across South China and Southeast Asia. As valley-dwelling peoples many of them live in towns, others in smaller villages. They grow most of their rice in permanent paddies watered by rainfall, sometimes also by irrigation, like other lowland peoples in East and Southeast Asia.

The Khmu' are descended from inhabitants who lived in the area before the Lao filtered in and began to build up a few small city-states along the rivers in the thirteenth century. Their language is related to the Khmer of Kampuchea (Cambodia) and to languages of some of the hill peoples of Vietnam. They have been subject to the Lao for centuries, sometimes forced into feudal service. They tend to be poor, occupying economically less advantageous land in the mountains, and growing most of their rice on mountain slopes temporarily cleared of jungle. They live in small villages, although some individuals and families have moved into Lao towns to get work. There may have been 200,000 Khmu' in Laos at the time of Shong Lue. Other Khmu' lived in Vietnam, but not as many.

The Hmong in Laos when Shong Lue was teaching in the 1960's numbered 300,000 or more. They had settled on the higher mountain regions above altitudes occupied by the Khmu' because the land there was empty, and in some cases because it was suitable to their opium crop. They had brought many skills with them from China, notably

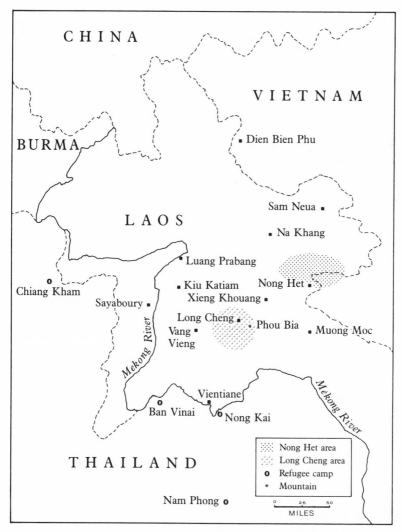

Fig. 1. Northern Laos, showing the two areas where Shong Lue Yang spent his life. All the events of Chapter 1 took place in the Nong Het area; those in Chapter 2 occurring after 1966 were in the Long Cheng area. Travel on foot along rugged mountain trails through the jungle made distances effectively much greater than the scale of miles would suggest to readers used to motorized transportation.

iron and silver craftsmanship, intricate needlework, and the ability to make guns. In technological resources, therefore, they were intermediate between the Lao and the Khmu'. Hmong agriculture normally included hillside dry rice, but many people also grew opium as their major source of cash, which helped some become prosperous.[6]

Some Hmong individuals, including Shong Lue Yang, themselves smoked opium. People who did so usually began at a time of severe illness or pain, but did not necessarily become addicted if use was not prolonged. Old and feeble people were more likely to be addicted. Some families produced enough opium so that regular use by one or two members did not drive them into poverty, but when the head of a household in a poorer family became addicted, the economic effects could be disastrous, even with the cheap prices for opium prevailing in the hills.

When the Hmong began to come into Vietnam and Laos in the nineteenth century, the French were well established in their colonial role, ruling at the lower levels through the local Lao and Vietnamese governmental administration but fully controlling the top levels of government. They were ousted from the area by the Japanese during World War II, but came back against the resistance of many Vietnamese after the war. That resistance continued to grow in Vietnam, and to develop in Laos until the colonial army was decisively defeated in 1954 at the Battle of Dien Bien Phu, Vietnam, close to the Laos border, about 250 miles from where Shong Lue Yang lived.

The North Vietnamese had long since been in control of the North Vietnam countryside, so the French evacuation of the cities and the garrisons after their defeat did not affect people like Shong Lue very much. However, the North Vietnamese then turned their attention more fully to eliminating the rival non-communist government in South Vietnam and the royalist government in neighboring Laos, where the North Vietnamese-supported Pathet Lao insurgents were already in control of some of the areas next to the Vietnam border. The North Vietnamese also supplied their forces fighting in South Vietnam over the Ho Chi Minh Trail, which ran through "neutral" Laos and Kampuchea.

North Vietnamese expansion of the war in Laos was countered by stepped-up U.S. military involvement there in the 1960's. Since foreign forces were supposed to be withdrawn from Laos after the 1962 Geneva Accords, the United States countered North Vietnam's presence in the country with its own covert action operated by the CIA. This developed into a major effort, largely led and fought by Hmong, with support from people in some of the other ethnic groups (including the Khmu') who had likewise been uprooted. How the Hmong became thus involved will be touched on a little later.

In 1959, therefore, when Shong Lue Yang produced his writing system and began his teaching, life was seriously disrupted for the Hmong in Vietnam and Laos. They had been a minority people there for more than a century, often discriminated against and treated with contempt. Earning a living was precarious. The Hmong were divided, as we shall see. War had been endemic in the region since the early 1940's; people were periodically in danger from enemy forces. As the decade of the sixties advanced, the situation got worse. Thousands of Hmong lost their lives both as soldiers and civilians. For those Hmong under the Royal Lao Government and allied to the Americans, large town-like conglomerations of displaced people were formed where refugees from scores of different villages could be protected more fully against enemy raids. Such was the disruption in the countryside that often even the rice they ate in these conglomerate communities had to be airlifted in.

Indigenous Hmong Leadership

The Hmong in Laos have not traditionally been a politically homogeneous people. Rather, they are loosely united by common language, many customs and a strong sense of ethnicity fostered by their rich folklore and mythology. The primary cohesive social units which do typically persist among them are large extended families. Although alliances of families are created through marriage and other means, a strong countervailing need for family independence renders these alliances fragile.

Each Hmong person is born into his or her father's clan, and should not marry someone from the same clan, even if they are not biologically related. People bearing the same clan name routinely feel some responsibility to each other (e.g., for hospitality and protection when they travel from place to place), and fellow clan members will cooperate temporarily under special circumstances, but this bond is not highly cohesive. The Hmong have neither tribal nor clan structure.

Over a village or a small cluster of nearby villages, the Hmong normally have a village headman, with corporate decision making led by an informal group of village elders. Above that there are higher layers of administration set up by the rulers of the country.

In addition to the headmen, other types of grass-roots leaders may have influence extending beyond their own village and family. These are people who have built personal reputations in one way or another, including shamans, other healers, foretellers, artisans, educated people,

people reputed to be wise, etc. Such people exert influence, but not necessarily any particular political power.

As we will see in what follows, however, from time to time leaders have arisen among the Hmong who have attracted a following. Sometimes leadership came from their unusual education or wealth, or their charisma. Sometimes authority has been given to them by the government, or people believe that they speak for, or otherwise represent, a deity. Particularly in time of adversity, when the Hmong are facing oppression, economic hardship, or cultural change greater than they can manage, such leadership may gain a very wide and intensely loyal following. The movements which build up around them draw upon the Hmong sense of ethnic identity to override the Hmong need for independence and bring at least some Hmong together in pursuit of at least a temporary common cause. Such leaders in effect become chieftains, or at least arbiters of morals and behavior, for segments of the Hmong population. A few such people figure in our story or in antecedent events.

The Revolt of Pa Chai

One man whose long shadow affected how some people perceived Shong Lue Yang was Pa Chai Vue (Paj Cai Vwj ꓯꓵꓑ ꓦꓲꓦ ꓔꓵ), who died in 1921, earlier in the decade in which Shong Lue was born. To the French colonists and the Lao, Pa Chai was the central figure in a rebellion against their authority. The French called the rebellion associated with him *La Guerre des Fous* 'The War of the Insane' (1919–1921)[7] because of magical beliefs expressed and the recklessness with which some of the Hmong fought, believing that God would protect them from bullets.

We summarize here one variant of the story of Pa Chai for comparison to that of Shong Lue.[8] According to this version, Pa Chai seemed to be a rather ordinary Hmong villager in Laos, but was unexpectedly and unwillingly taken to heaven one day at the summons of the Lord of the Sky and of the Earth (Lub Ntuj Lub Teb ꓡꓴꓭ ꓠꓔꓴꓲ ꓡꓴꓭ ꓔꓰꓭ). He entered a great palace of bricks shining like gold, where the Lord of the Sky and of the Earth told Pa Chai that he had been sent to earth from heaven to live with the Hmong and teach them a better way of life, but that he had not fulfilled his mission. The Lord of the Sky therefore sent Pa Chai back to earth to teach the Hmong to change their ways, to lead healthy, happy, prosperous lives.

After his return to earth, Pa Chai displayed magical powers which gave him enormous prestige. People around him urged him to use those powers to exterminate the Lao, whom they felt to be exacting onerous and unjust taxes, a situation which was creating great unrest among the Hmong people in Pa Chai's area. Pa Chai insisted that the Lord of the Sky had not told him to kill the Lao, but he nevertheless climbed a tree and disappeared for a while from its branches to go to consult with the deity, explaining how life had become intolerable for the Hmong and praying for help.

In spite of Pa Chai's moderation and the lack of any authorization from the Lord of the Sky, others continued agitating for revolt against the government. Then a Hmong who had been made a district headman by the Lao authorities betrayed this agitation to the French, who sent Vietnamese soldiers to suppress it.

Pa Chai, however, had enabled a gunsmith to make a magical gun with which his followers held off for two years all attempts to subdue them. The Hmong then mounted a counter-offensive in which they surrounded a government garrison and poisoned its water source, causing violent illness and forcing those enemy soldiers who were able to do so to flee. But some of the Hmong victors then brutally attacked the Lao people in the area of the conquered garrison, conspiring not to let Pa Chai know what they had done.

The Lord of the Sky was greatly displeased and withdrew his protection from the fighting Hmong, among whom there had as yet been no casualties whatsoever. The French assembled a counter-attack, and when Pa Chai performed ceremonies to request divine intervention, the omens showed that serious crimes had been committed by the Hmong soldiers, whose leaders then confessed.

Pa Chai and his immediate followers surrendered their arms to the French and hid in the jungle, but four Lao assassins led by one Hmong traitor found and beheaded Pa Chai. They carried his head off in a bag to collect bounty from the French, but in the three days they traveled, the head of the Hmong traitor was magically substituted for that of Pa Chai.

Pa Chai and Shong Lue

Pa Chai arose as a leader of a substantial number of people in a time of corporate distress, but his following did not encompass more than a minority of Hmong. Most stayed outside the struggle, many too far away even to hear much about it, others choosing not to join. This was also the case with Shong Lue Yang's movement.

Pa Chai's leadership was validated, in the understanding of his followers, by belief that he was a messenger from God, a role attested by his magical powers. Being a messenger from God was essential in the case of Shong Lue Yang as well, but his role was validated by his writing system and his perceived wisdom.

Pa Chai was an open threat to the authorities as leader of a rebel movement, and he was killed for it. Shong Lue's threat was implicit. He led no revolt, incited no revolution, but in his cryptic way he was critical of the authorities and gained a devoted following. Military leaders losing a war did not know what to make of him. Myths about God sending a writing system to the Hmong were associated with messianic kings who would come to rule the Hmong. Shong Lue never claimed to be a king, but he did claim to be a son of God, sent by God, and kings and gods are closely identified in Hmong legend. The leaders also feared his strange-looking writing could be an espionage code designed by the communists. So Shong Lue, also, was killed.

Other elements in the Pa Chai story important as background to Shong Lue, including parallels in their world views and in individual incidents, will become apparent later. But it seems clear that Shong Lue was perceived by some of his contemporaries as another Pa Chai, which colored their expectations of him. More than one Hmong person invoked Pa Chai when discussing Shong Lue with Smalley. Similarly, non-followers applied one term to both men's movements, calling them *Chao Fa*, 'Lord of the Sky' in Lao (Hmong: Cob Fab ᑎV ƏĈ). The term was first applied to the Pa Chai movement because the deity who summoned Pa Chai, and instructed him what to do, was *Lu Ndu Lu Te* 'Lord of the Sky and of the Earth' in Hmong.[9]

Shong Lue did not speak of coming from Lu Ndu but from Va (Vaj Ə̄C), another deity or (at least from Chia Koua Vang's perspective) another name for the same deity. Nor was there anything militant about Shong Lue or his movement. Nevertheless the label *Chao Fa* was attached to his movement also, first by the Vietnamese and then by others (including Hmong), and that label possibly contributed to fear on the part of outsiders that Shong Lue was about to lead a revolution, as Pa Chai had done. The militant image has been reinforced since the fall of Laos in 1975 (several years after the death of Shong Lue) by a continuing resistance movement led by some of Shong Lue's followers, also commonly called *Chao Fa*.[10]

Movements for Change

There come times in the history of a people when they long for a change in the intolerable situation they have been experiencing. Literature contains many outstanding expressions of such longing, from the ancient Jews captive in Babylon, in the spirituals sung by black slaves in the United States. Such feelings are also expressed in the tirades of Hitler and the fulminations of the Ku Klux Klan.

This longing may bring concerted effort to construct a more satisfying culture, an effort sometimes known as a "revitalization movement." Such movements may be "adoptive," in that they take over major elements from another culture; they may be "syncretistic," in mingling the new with the old; or they may be "nativistic," seeking to change life back to how it used to be, or to change it in ways that seem more in keeping with traditional cultural values.[11] The movements of Pa Chai and Shong Lue were nativistic movements in that sense.

Such movements have arisen all over the world where cultures clash, or where the physical or economic situation becomes intolerable, or where values are threatened by changes taking place in part of the culture, or where people feel that they are losing their roots and can no longer cope. The Plains Indian Sun Dance cult and Melanesian cargo cults are famous examples. But the movement in Iran under the Ayatollah Khomeini is also a nativisitic movement, as has been the movement to the right in the United States under Ronald Reagan after the disintegrating effects of Vietnam and Watergate and the changes in American mood and morality in the 1960's.

In the time of Pa Chai, the constraints of the government brought a longing for greater independence and justice for the Hmong. In the time of Shong Lue, the world around the Hmong was collapsing in the Vietnam War, intensifying their longstanding resentment over their domination by peoples of other cultures. Both men came with a message from God of how things should be.

Messages from a deity are frequent elements in nativistic movements. Sometimes the messenger is merely human, a "prophet" who hears from the deity and who transmits the message to the people. Such were the Old Testament prophets and others such as Muhammad and Joseph Smith. The prophet points to the better way, the way people should live.

In other nativistic movements the messenger is seen to be supernatural, or partly supernatural, originating in the spirit realm. Some remain spirit messengers, angels, although they may temporarily look like human beings or animals. Others are born as a human being but bring along some of the powers of the spirit world while they are living a human life. In the cases of Pa Chai and Shong Lue, the messengers did not even remember, at first, their supernatural origin.

Sometimes this supernatural messenger is understood to be the agent of salvation for the people, a "messiah," the one who will overcome the forces which are causing the intolerable situation and restore life to the way it should be. Messianic movements like that of Pa Chai may often take on political and military overtones, the changes to be brought about by overthrowing the rulers who created the intolerable situation. But even if there is no call for revolt, as in the case of Shong Lue Yang, such a vision of change often sounds threatening to people in power.

If the messenger is not the agent of salvation, the message may be of a messiah to come, the promise that at some time in the future a supernatural personage will bring about the envisioned utopia.[12] Movements built around a belief in a future messianic presence are sometimes called "millennial." There have been such movements in Thailand and Laos in recent Hmong history, some of them fostered by communist efforts to recruit Hmong to fight against the Lao government in order to establish a Hmong autonomous state with a Hmong king.[13] There is no evidence that Shong Lue Yang himself contributed to any such movement, but these movements may have colored the attitudes of some others toward him, and some of his followers may have moved in that direction.

Of course these categories are not watertight in human experience The same individual may be cast sometimes in the role of prophet and other times in that of messiah; the restored way of life may sometimes been seen as imminent, as a result of present events, and in the next moment be projected into the future. Nativistic movements are not unusual responses to cultural stress. Pa Chai and Shong Lue were both messiahs.

Unlike many nativistic movements, which are either "revivalistic" (seeking to bring back the imagined and glorified past), or "perpetuative" (seeking to preserve existing culture), there was a strongly "corrective" note in Shong Lue's message. It was rooted in traditional values, but he saw the present intolerable situation as being due, in part, to flaws within Hmong culture, particularly disunity and lack of cooperation. Like the great Old Testament prophets, Shong Lue saw the enemy within as well as without.

King or God?

We will see that Shong Lue Yang was considered politically subversive by many of his opponents. There was, and is, a widespread view that he was announcing a new king of the Hmong to take over Laos, a characteristic message of several Hmong messianic movements. Chia Koua

Vang and Gnia Yee Yang categorically deny any such political message, and their story contains no hint of such a point of view on Shong Lue's part.

The question is complicated by ambiguity in Hmong terms which refer both to rulers and to deities. We have already commented on this in relation to *Lub Ntuj Lub Teb* 'Lord of the Sky and of the Earth', who was invoked by Pa Chai and his followers. Shong Lue saw himself as a son of Vaj, whom he and his followers usually speak of as *Vaj Leej Txi* (ꓱꓯ ꓦꓵ ꓕꓦ), which they insist on translating as 'God'.

On the other hand, non-initiates to the movement Shong Lue started typically translate *Vaj* as 'king', and that is the definition given in dictionaries (Heimbach 1969: 398; Bertrais 1964; Lyman 1974: 355); but a semantic component of deity is to be seen in the use of *Vajtswv* (ꓱꓯ ꓪꓵ) 'God' by Protestant Christians. *Tswv* (ꓪꓵ) means 'Lord, owner, master' (Heimbach 1969: 361).

Another such term with double usage is *Huab Tais* (ꓦꓴꓩ ꓕꓭꓲ) or *Fuab Tais* (ꓦꓵꓸ ꓕꓭꓲ), defined as 'great ruler, emperor, legendary Hmong king, king, lord' (Heimbach 1969: 56; Bertrais 1964; Lyman 1974: 115). But this term, also, is associated with deity in such combinations as *Huab Tais Ntuj* (ꓦꓴꓩ ꓕꓭꓲ ꓕꓦꓲ) 'Lord of the Sky, God' (Bertrais 1964).

The Hmong world view apparently sees a close connection between gods and legendary Hmong kings, and this terminology we have been describing reflects that connection. Outsiders have regularly interpreted Shong Lue's *Vaj Leej Txi* to mean 'king', believing that he referred to a future Hmong royalty. Chia Koua and his associates, on the other hand, maintain that he made claims to divinity that had nothing to do with political kingdoms.

Externally Fostered Leaders

As we have seen, Hmong disunity was epitomized on one level by the lack of any permanent social structure above the village, and on another level by the occasional rise of charismatic leaders who would be followed for a time by one group or another. But on still another level it has been epitomized by the divisions between the higher political and military leaders who have emerged in the past fifty years, leaders fostered by external forces as well as internal ones.

Such leaders, whose influence extended more widely than local village and family-related units, or even clans, did not emerge from the grass roots primarily through Hmong processes, but were created to a significant degree from the top, especially through the action of external governments. Even the village headman, although often the choice of the villagers, was subject to approval by the Lao authorities. And when the first Hmong delegate was elected to the Lao National Assembly in 1947, it was only because the government decided to create the opportunity.

Three externally fostered Hmong leaders are important to the story of Shong Lue Yang, two of them not because of any direct involvement, but because rivalry between them contributed to the Hmong division and distress which engulfed him and his followers. These two were Touby Lyfoung (Tubnpis Lisfoom ꡤꡤꡦ ꡘꡨꡲ ꡘꡦꡲ ꡤꡦꡲ), allied to the French and the Royal Lao Government, and Faydang Lobliayao (Faiv Ntaj Lauj Npliaj Yob ꡤꡦ ꡘꡨꡲ ꡘꡤꡲ ꡤꡦ ꡤꡨꡲ), allied to the Vietnamese and the communist Pathet Lao.

In the late nineteenth century and early twentieth century, the French developed a policy of appointing Hmong chieftains to mediate between the government and the general Hmong population. The two dominant Hmong clans at the time were the Lor and Lee clans, and an important leader was appointed from each. As a result of a series of unfortunate events, however, bitter enmity and rivalry emerged between their successors.[14] When Touby Lyfoung (of the Lee clan) was given an important administrative position which Faydang Lobliayao (of the Lor clan) felt belonged to him and his family, Faydang turned against everything Touby was supporting.

During the Japanese occupation in World War II, Hmong associated with Touby assisted the fugitive French and later helped their reconquest of the area;[15] Faydang joined the resistance against the return of the French. After the war Touby became assistant to the Lao governor of Xieng Khouang Province, the major area of Hmong concentration in Laos, and he later had other important positions in the Lao government. The communist leaders in Laos gave Faydang and his Hmong followers an important place in their resistance movement.[16]

The majority of the independent Hmong villagers were not ideologically or emotionally allied to either of these leaders, but Touby, for example, gained a great deal of favor because of the way in which he was able to smooth the way toward more equitable treatment of the Hmong by the French and the Lao, and by the way he enabled Hmong villages to get schools and economic advantages (such as facilitating the sale of opium to the French government opium monopoly). It was therefore sometimes very helpful to be protected by Touby's umbrella. Many Hmong people also took pride in him and his accomplishments.

Touby Lyfoung and Faydang Lobliayao epitomize the many-layered but fluctuating divisions among the Hmong, although division is certainly not restricted to their family rivalry. At the same time, they both illustrate that large groups of Hmong people can unite, up to a point, under the right leader in times of sufficient need.

The other externally imposed national Hmong leader whom we shall mention is General Vang Pao (Vaj Pov ꓔꓶ ꓜꓲꓟ),[17] who figures more directly in the story of Shong Lue Yang. He had been a brave and able officer in the Lao army, and had risen rapidly because of his courage and ability in the fight against the Vietnamese and their Pathet Lao allies.

In 1961, when the United States entered the war in Laos more directly, Vang Pao and his men had been resisting the Vietnamese with almost no resources. Under U.S. prodding, the more effective Hmong forces were separated from the regular Lao forces and General Vang Pao was placed in command of the Second Military Region of Laos, which included Xieng Khouang Province, which bordered on Vietnam and was the heart of the area where the Hmong lived. He and his forces, supplied and paid by the United States, fought hard and often very effectively against the Vietnamese and Pathet Lao, suffering enormous casualties.

Fear of the Vietnamese, anger at loss of homeland and destruction of livelihood, opportunities for military and political power, the enormous quantities (by Laos standards) of money supplied by the United States, and hope of a better day to come united many thousands of Hmong behind General Vang Pao and the war effort he led. Some Hmong in the United States, particularly those who fought closely with him in the war, still look to him as the leader of the Hmong. Unfortunately, however, the Hmong military establishment was not immune to temptations of despotism, graft and unchecked power. General Vang Pao became a tyrannical opium warlord, and he was alleged to be aided in his opium dealings by the American CIA.[18] His administration increasingly became part of the problem for many of the Hmong, as we shall see.

These, then, were some of the people, events, structures and beliefs from which Shong Lue Yang emerged and acted. The Hmong saw themselves as weak, poor, put upon, divided, unable to maintain their independence, lacking in education and technology, unable to cope. They had intense pride in their ethnic identity, which was threatened.

According to Shong Lue Yang, they lacked two things. They lacked the knowledge of how to live harmoniously, both among themselves and with other people. And they lacked writing to validate their equality with other peoples. Shong Lue Yang, Savior of the People, Mother of Writing, believed he had come from God to meet both of those needs.

1

How the Alphabet Began:
A Believer's Perspective

One day, when Shua Yang (Suav Yaj ꘏꘨ ꘔꘪ) was a young Hmong orphan boy living with his grandparents, his grandfather took him out to
the cornfield, which had been cleared from the heart of the jungle in
typical Hmong fashion. Monkeys were regularly raiding the ripening
corn, so his grandfather told Shua to come there every day and drive the
monkeys off, just as other Hmong children do in Laos during the growing season.

Then one day while sitting there alone in the field, Shua fell asleep
and had a dream. Two young men came and spoke to him. "Have you
already taught the Alphabet (Phajhauj ꘪꘫ ꘬꘭), or not?" they asked.

"I don't even know how to read and write, so how can I teach any
alphabet?" he replied.

The two young men pressed him: "We already gave it to you."

"No, you haven't given me anything," he insisted.

"What do you mean we haven't given it to you? Look at your hands."

When he looked he found he was holding a book. The two young
men urged him again, "Don't delay any longer, but go and teach."

But he was bewildered: "I don't know anything about all this, so
how can I teach anything?"

"If we tell you to teach, then you can teach; hurry up and teach,"
they said. Then they disappeared.

Shua woke up in fear from what seemed like a nightmare, and returned home before dark.

In time Shua Yang grew up, married and had children. He eventually took the name Shong Lue Yang (Soob Lwj Yaj ꘏꘨ ꘫ꘭ ꘔꘪ), and
also bore the title "Mother of Writing" (Niam Ntawv ꘡꘢ ꘣꘤). He told
the above story to Colonel Yong Chue Yang (Ntxoov Tswb Yaj ꘏ꘐ ꘑꘒ
ꘔꘪ)[1] some years later.

On the fifteenth day of the fifth month (approximately May)[2] in the
year 1959, Shong Lue Yang finally began to receive the Pahawh[3] Hmong

16

and the Pahawh Khmu', the alphabet for the Hmong and Khmu' languages.[4] From the standpoint of the history and variety of writing systems around the world, this new Hmong writing system has remarkable features, which will be explored in subsequent chapters. From the standpoint of the modern history and development of those Hmong people who once lived in Laos, but are now scattered in France, Canada, Australia, China, Thailand, French Guyana and the United States (as well as in Laos), Pahawh was part of a singular complex of events all tied up in the trauma of the Vietnam War. And from the standpoint of a people's world views, belief systems and of movements to shape a people's self-understanding, Pahawh was part of a grass-roots nativistic and messianic movement in which God, the Spirit Va (Vaj **ɔc**), gave writing and knowledge to unlettered people through the prophet, Shong Lue Yang.

This chapter tells the story of how the Pahawh began, according to people who see Shong Lue Yang as a prophet, who believe that he held the key to all knowledge, and who perceive the Hmong and Khmu' writing systems to be gifts from God. Other perspectives will be included elsewhere in this book. But for now, here is an account by some students, neighbors and former associates of Shong Lue Yang, people who knew him and believe his claims.

Among these people, the most important to the telling of the story is Chia Koua Vang (Txiaj Kuam Vaj **ɐ̌ ɪɭ ɔc**), student of the prophet from 1964 to 1971. Shong Lue gave to Chia Koua the responsibility for preserving the record of what happened, and he has with him in the United States his notes made at the time, recording the events and Shong Lue Yang's teaching. This chapter is primarily his record, supplemented by others from time to time.

The Early Years of Shong Lue Yang

Shong Lue Yang was born as Shua Yang on September 15,[5] 1929, in Fi Tong (Fib Toos **ʌɛ̌ ɐ̌ɪ̌**; Lao: Huay Cha Ang)[6] a small Hmong village in Vietnam, over the border from the Nong Het (Looj Hej **ɐ̌ɪɪ ʊ̌ɪr**) area of Xieng Khouang Province, in Laos. His father, Chong Chi Yang (Txoov Cib Yaj **ɐ̌ɐ̌ ʌ̌ɐ ɔ̌ɯ**) was Hmong, his mother Kong (Koo **ɐ̌**) was born Khmu', and so had no clan name, but had been raised as a Hmong from childhood, in keeping with a common pattern of Hmong people adopting Khmu' children. She was the second wife of Chong Chi.

After Shong Lue was born, his parents soon adopted Ying Yang (Yeeb Yaj **ɐ̌ɯ ɔ̌ɯ**), who had been left an orphan by the death of Shong

Lue's uncle (his father's brother) and aunt. She was breastfed for a while by Shong Lue's mother and raised as his older sister. Then, according to her account,[7] first Shong Lue's father and then his mother died, leaving the two infants to be raised by their grandparents, who were extremely poor.[8]

Ying Yang says that as Shong Lue grew up, and prior to the main events in this chapter, he had only the farming skills of an uneducated Hmong villager, plus the skill of making and selling the type of basket which Hmong people carry on their backs (with straps to go over the shoulders). She insists that like almost all of their Hmong contemporaries, Shong Lue never had any education, nor any opportunity for education. As was usually the case in Hmong villages of the time, there were no schools close by where they lived, and nobody came to teach. Nor would the grandparents have been able to afford to send Shong Lue away to school even if they had wanted to do so. This picture of a typical poverty-filled Hmong childhood without formal education of any kind and without opportunity to learn to read or write any language is important for interpreting the significance and uniqueness of Shong Lue Yang's contribution within what is known of the history of writing worldwide (Chapter 10).

The picture is confirmed by Chia Long Thao (Txiaj Looj Thoj **ⴷ̌ ₤ⴑ ̄ⴈ ̄ⴑ̈r**),[9] who was one of Shong Lue's neighbors in the early years. Chia Long Thao remembers when Shong Lue was born, and then later when the Pahawh appeared to him. He knew when Shong Lue's family moved from Fi Tong to the village of Fi Kha (Fib Khav **Λ̌Ɛ̃ ⴑ⁄ⴄ̇**) in Laos, and then to Tham Ha (Thab Has **Ͻⴑⴕ ⴑ⁄ⴕ**), near Muong Long, back in Vietnam. He was also involved subsequently in events to be recounted in the next chapter, when Shong Lue was under attack by communist authorities who feared him. He insists that Shong Lue was a very poor man who never had the opportunity to go to school anywhere, in any country.

Another witness is Shong Chai Yang (Soob Cai Yaj **ⴑⴢ̈ ⴕ̇ⴄ ⴢⴑⴈ**),[10] a neighbor of the adult Shong Lue Yang, who knew him well. He says that in 1957, before the Pahawh was revealed, Shong Lue lived for a time at Pha Ta (Phaj Tam **Ͻⴈⴄ̃ ⴢ̌ⴑ̈**), very close to Fi Tong, where Shong Chai lived at the time. He verifies that Shong Lue was a very poor man.

Shong Chai Yang was aware when Shong Lue moved to Tham Ha, and remembers when the news of the Pahawh began to spread. He once had occasion to go to Tham Ha, which consisted of only a few houses. He said that there was no school there, nor had there ever been in the past, even in the surrounding areas. There was no one who would have known how to read and write, nor would there have been the opportunity for anyone to learn any writing system.[11] He is sure that Shong Lue himself did not know any writing system prior to the appearance of the Pahawh.

Others who knew Shong Lue later in life likewise say that in spite of his great knowledge, he was clearly not an educated person, not a person who had been to school. Colonel Yong Chue Yang indicates that Shong Lue did not talk as educated people do, nor could he have had any education from the Republic of China or anywhere else in the world, as skeptics sometimes suppose.[12]

Shong Lue Yang grew up and married Pang Xiong (Paj Xyooj ꗬ ꗛ); they had a number of children.[13] In due course, and in accordance with Hmong custom, his wife's family performed a ceremony (Npe laus ꚝꚈ ꖶ) in which an additional honorific name was prefixed to his original name of Shua Yang, making him Chia Shua Yang (Txhiaj Suav Yaj ꕮꙀ ꘕ ꗵ). These events took place before the Pahawh was revealed to him.

The Revelation of the Alphabet

According to Shong Lue Yang himself, as told to Chia Koua Vang in 1966 in Long Cheng, Laos, the revelation of the writing system took place in 1959, in his home village of Tham Ha, Vietnam. Shong Lue had prepared a new mountain rice field by clearing the jungle in the usual Hmong fashion, and during the fourth month, after the jungle had been cut and burned, he and Pang Xiong went to clean off the unburned residue, as Hmong farmers typically must do.[14] They also needed to build a small shelter for protection against the elements during the months when they would be working in the field and guarding it from birds and animals while the rice was growing.

On the morning of the third day of going out to the field in this fashion, Shong Lue told his wife that he was going to leave early to hunt squirrels around the field. She was to prepare breakfast and bring it along when it was ready.

So Pang Xiong prepared food and started out along the jungle path after her husband.[15] Halfway to the rice field, however, she was knocked unconscious by a whirlwind, lying there for almost half a day. She woke up a little after noon, and remembering her responsibility, raised the undamaged food basket to her back and continued on her way.

When she arrived at the field, Shong Lue was very upset. "How come you are so late?" he complained. "It's already afternoon! What's the point of coming at all at this late hour?" But when she told him what happened, he was afraid, and decided they should go home and consult a shaman to find out what the whirlwind was.

So at dawn the next morning, Shong Lue prepared for a ceremony to select the powerful shaman who could best determine what Pang Xiong had encountered the day before. As he sat down to perform the ceremony, he suddenly heard a loud voice speaking to him from the air:

You do not need a shaman. I am sending your two brothers to come to help you, that's all. You mustn't be afraid.

Beginning today, you must not sleep with your wife, and she must not go outside of the house to work in the fields until your two brothers are born. You must prepare a set of opium-smoking equipment made of *kulu* bamboo (kub lub **ᴜᴉ ᴜᴉᴜ**) so we can communicate.[16] Also build a round house or round temple (tsev kheej **ᕼᴉᴋ ᴠᴉᴋ**)[17] as a place to worship, and build a monument (pej thuam **ᴜᴍ̂ ᴉᴜᴉᴩ**)[18] beside it. Find candles and flowers to put inside the round place of worship as offerings. Make ink from the indigo plant, and paper from bamboo,[19] and have them ready. When that is done, people will come and bring you the Pahawh.

Shong Lue looked around quickly as he heard the voice, but saw nobody anywhere. He remembered an old saying that insanity begins this way, and became very fearful, wondering what it all meant. Suddenly he was slapped three times on the cheek, hard enough for him to see red stars flying around.

Again he heard the voice speaking to him from the air:

I am God, your Father (Vaj Leej Txi **ᕚᴄ ᕚᴉᴫ ᴉᴋᕓ**), who sent you to be born on earth as a human being. You are not crazy, but you must do what I tell you to do.

Shong Lue thought to himself, "I am so poor; if this is all true how can I ever do all of these things? I have no opium; my farming season is coming. If that time is lost, what will I feed my family for the year to come?"

Once more he heard the voice speaking to him from the air:

Don't worry about such matters. I will send three kings (peb tug vaj **ᴜᴍ̂ ᴉᴋᕼ̌ ᕚᴄ**) to come and help you to build the field shelter, plant the seed rice and weed the fields. Three days from now you just carry enough seed rice to the field and come back home. As for the opium, you only need to buy a little bit and it will last you forever.

So Shong Lue Yang decided to see if all this was true. When he woke up early in the morning on the third day, he carried a basket full of seed

rice to the field. There he found a small shelter made of earth already
built up in the rice field. Little yellow ants were still crawling slowly
down from it. He remembered what he had heard, so he left the basket
of seed rice in the small earth shelter, and returned home.

The next morning Shong Lue carried another basket of seed rice to
the field, and found that flocks of *pulika* birds (pum liv qag **ṳ̀m̀ ʌ̀ʌɪn ʉ̀ʀ̌**)[20]
were carrying away the grains of seed rice which he had left the day
before, and were flying all over the field. So he left the second basket of
seed rice in the small earth shelter and returned home.

Early the third morning, Shong Lue carried still a third basket of
seed rice to the field. Then he prepared equipment for smoking opium,
found wood and built up a round house and a monument, prepared
candles and flowers, and began to worship as he was told.[21]

After all of the instructions had been followed, beginning on the
night of the fifteenth day of the fifth month, in the year 1959, Shong
Lue began to smoke opium for the first time, using the equipment he
had made. He smoked until midnight; then, after his wife and children
were all asleep, suddenly two young men appeared in the bedroom
doorway.[22]

Shong Lue called out a greeting: "Are you here, the two of you?"

"Yes, we are here to teach you the Pahawh Hmong and the Pahawh
Khmu'," they replied. Shong Lue got up and brought in two low round
seats, and put them down next to his bed for the men to sit on. They
told him to get a pen and the paper he had made, so they could teach
him. He got his bowl of indigo ink and his pack of bamboo paper, but
didn't have a pen, so he asked what he should do. They told him to
sharpen a piece of bamboo into a pen. Then they took it, and with the
ink they wrote the Source Version of the Pahawh on the bamboo paper
for him.

They had been teaching him for just a short time when through the
bedroom doorway came a group of people in the black uniforms of officials, wearing medals made of gold. They brought candles and flowers
and kneeled down, bowing to the three who were sitting there. "We are
very happy to have you as the saviors of the people (cawm seej **ɪ̀v ʋ̌m̀**).
We bring candles, flowers and silver coins as offerings, to worship you."

They only stayed for a short while, but before leaving they said to
Shong Lue, "We couldn't bring with us all of the money we have for
you, so please come and get it."

They made an appointment, and told Shong Lue where he should
go; they told him to build a small thatch shelter there in which to wait

for them; and they would come to show him where the money was; then they left. Soon after that the two young men also left, disappearing through the bedroom doorway, and Shong Lue fell asleep.

The next day he went and waited, as he had been told, until those same people from the night before came to him, still dressed in black, with their medals of gold. They took him to a place where they pointed down to the ground and said to him, "Here is where the money is. Dig down and find it."

Shong Lue dug down and found a jar of silver bars buried a long time before in the way Hmong people who have wealth typically hide it. So he took the silver bars to pay for all his expenses. And Shong Lue realized that those people dressed in black had come from heaven (quam ntuj ꓧꓰꓼ ꓧꓴꓹ).

The two young men came to teach Shong Lue the Pahawh every night, always appearing after his wife and children had gone to sleep. Each night he lit his small round opium lamp and waited for the two young men to appear at the bedroom doorway, where they also disappeared again each night after the session was over.

They kept this up until one night when Shong Lue decided to pay special attention to just where the men came from, and how they came. After he lit his lamp, just before the two young men appeared at the door, he felt something walking across his feet from the other side of the bed, where his wife slept. So then Shong Lue Yang knew for sure that the strong whirlwind which had struck his wife on her way to the field that day was really the two young men, who entered her womb, and with whom she became pregnant at that time.

The men continued teaching Shong Lue the Pahawh until the beginning of the sixth month, when he was allowed to go back to inspect his rice field. He found that the seed rice had been planted and that the rice was coming up evenly all over the field. Then he knew for certain that the *pulika* birds had been there to plant his crop for him.

So he continued learning the Pahawh until the beginning of the seventh month, and again he was allowed to go back to see how the rice field was doing. He found no weeds interfering with the rice plants at all. As he took a good look around, he noticed that the weeds had been cut by mice, and knew for certain that the ants, the *pulika* birds and the mice were the three kings of which he had been told; so he returned home happy.

Shong Lue continued studying the Pahawh until the ninth month, the fifteenth day in the year 1959,[23] when his wife gave birth to twin boys.

The second morning after the twins were born, Shong Lue and his wife prepared a small traditional Hmong party to name their sons, and invited the wife's parents. The day when these in-laws arrived was a stormy one, with heavy rain and wind, so that it was very difficult for anyone to get about. It was typical in traditional Hmong life for some relatives to live several hours walk away, but the in-laws were nevertheless able to make it through the bad weather.

When they arrived at Shong Lue's house, and even before they had dried off, the mother-in-law walked over and sat down on the heavy horizontal bar to which the pestle for husking rice was attached. She began to scold the family angrily: "You two are so lazy that you haven't been going to work in the fields all this time but have just loafed at home. And on top of that, now you have twins! Don't you ever think about how you are going to feed your family?"

As she continued to berate Shong Lue and Pang, the faces of the twin boys turned blue. Shong Lue became very concerned and quickly picked up his bamboo pen, and with the indigo ink he wrote down a few of the Pahawh letters which the twins had taught him. He handed the paper to his father-in-law, since a Hmong son-in-law is not supposed to deal directly with his mother-in-law, and said, "Please show this to mother and see if she can read it; otherwise she should stop scolding."[24] The father-in-law looked at it and realized it was writing. He showed it to the mother-in-law, and she realized also that it was writing. So then she stopped scolding, and the twins' faces slowly returned to normal.

Early the next morning they had their celebration and named the twins. The older one was named Cha Yang (Tsab Yaj **ꬒꬲ ꬒꭒ**) and the younger Xa Yang (Xab Yaj **ꬒꜻ ꬒꭒ**). After the traditional celebration was over, the in-laws returned home.

A Message from Xa Yang

But the twins who had been born as sons of Shong Lue Yang and Pang Xiong did not live. First Cha Yang died, only seven days old. Xa Yang then lived for seven days more. Shong Lue was heartbroken, but he found a written message with a baby's footprint[25] on it, written to him by Xa Yang. It said,

It has been seven months and seven days since we came to stay with you.[26] We came this time only to find and help you. When the mother-in-law came and scolded us, my older brother Cha suggested that we should leave and hide because we are creating problems for you.

So that's why he left me alone with you for a while. Our duty was only to bring you the Pahawh, as God had authorized us to come down and do, so you could teach it to the Hmong and to the Khmu'. You must understand, and try not to miss us anymore.

This message is to let you know that the Pahawh for the Hmong and for the Khmu' is only being made available for a time now. The group that accepts the Pahawh will be blessed from now on, but if either group does not accept it, that people will remain downtrodden and poor, the servant to other nations for the next nine generations. After that the Pahawh will be brought back again.

You must also know that God has ruled that from now on the time for a generation will be eighty-five years. And God has ruled that since the Hmong writing system has been destroyed by other nations in the past,[27] the nations who keep destroying it and destroying the Hmong people will themselves be destroyed in return. But the nations that help to save the Pahawh Hmong and Pahawh Khmu' will be blessed by God.

From today on you will be able to remember all of the authority God formerly gave you, when he sent you to earth to be born as a human being, with the two of us to follow and bring you the Pahawh. God gave you that power so that you could save people. You must now go on to do what God has already given you the authority and the power to do.

When Shong Lue had finished reading the message which Xa Yang had left for him, it all came back. He remembered that God the Father had twelve sons, of which he was one, and that God had chosen three of them to come down to earth to teach the Pahawh to the Hmong and Khmu' peoples. And so from that day on Shong Lue Yang was totally awakened, knowing everything in the universe from the beginning to the end. He remembered also that his name had earlier been Shong Lue Yang (Soob Lwj Yaj ᏣᎴ Ꮣ Ꮿ), and that he had the title of Savior of the Common People (Theej Kaj Pej Xeem ᎥᎮ Ꮃ ᎤᎢ ᎥᎯ), a name and title which he then assumed for this life also. He began teaching the Pahawh Hmong to the Hmong and Pahawh Khmu' to the Khmu', as God had commissioned him to do. That story is told in the next chapter.

Xa Yang's written message was kept by Shong Lue, who brought it to Long Cheng in 1966 and showed it to Chia Koua Vang when the latter was studying the Pahawh Hmong and learning about its history. Chia Koua Vang was told to record and document this history for future use. Later on, when Shong Lue was arrested, he left the message with his wife in Long Cheng. Chia Koua does not know what happened to it when Shong Lue and his wife were murdered.

The Hmong authors of this book, participants in the legacy of Shong Lue Yang, insist that this chapter contains only the truth about the history of the prophet and the Pahawh Hmong. Any contrary information has been fabricated by outsiders who want to discredt Shong Lue Yang and his movement with false accusations. They feel that most Western-ers do not believe in supernatural power, merely practicing their re-ligion for political purposes; but they argue that Hmong people do believe in God even if they have never been told about Jesus Christ.

2

Spread of the Alphabet

The Pahawh Hmong which Shong Lue Yang introduced and continued
to improve was a remarkably original writing system, as we shall see in
Chapters 4–6, but there could have been many different responses
when he announced that God had revealed it to him. His neighbors, for
example, could have thought he had gone a bit crazy; they could have
ignored him; perhaps some of them did each of these. But enough
people believed him from the beginning, and enough people saw value
in a writing system and in the rest of his message, that a following began
to grow. Shong Lue Yang's claims must have resonated with needs
which many people had. Some of the historical and cultural reasons
why he may have been believable will be discussed in Chapters 7 and 12.

Shong Lue's success, his following, his message, the fact that his
writing system looked foreign, became a source of fear, however, first
to the communist authorities in whose area of control he lived, and then
to Hmong military authorities in the Royal Lao Government, into whose
area of control he later moved. The former tried to destroyed him, but
failed. The latter did not fail.

But even so, up to the very month of his death, Shong Lue's creative
genius continued. Over the years he revised the Pahawh Hmong three
times, each time increasing its efficiency and decreasing its difficulty.
And people continually flocked to him as his influence spread.

The Initial Reception

About September 1959, thirty-year-old Shong Lue Yang began to teach
the Pahawh to Hmong and Khmu' people, as he had learned it from
Cha Yang (Tsab Yaj **ƆK Ɔய**) and Xa Yang (Xab Yaj **ƆA Ɔய**), the twins
born to his wife, the two young men who visited him at night. He
taught at his own village of Tham Ha (Thab Has **Ɔᴙ ʉᴨ**), tutoring only
in homes and at the fields, where people were working or guarding their

crops, and responding only to those people who sought him out to learn. The people who learned the Pahawh, and others who looked on, called him Mother of Writing (Niam Ntawv **ɩɩʊ ɩɈʌ̌**), as some of them also called the writing system. This initial period of the introduction of the Pahawh lasted about four years.

Villagers from his own and surrounding communities, attracted by the stories they heard, came and questioned Shong Lue about who he was and about the strange phenomenon he represented. He answered questions of all kinds out of his complete knowledge and, when asked, foretold the future.

As time went on, more important people from both the Hmong and the Khmu' communities also came to question Shong Lue extensively about himself and about the Pahawh. And as he answered their questions, some of them came to believe that there was no one else who knew all that he knew.

Hmong people were quicker than the Khmu' to believe Shong Lue Yang was given his power by God, and that he had been sent to help them. How could a Hmong know about Khmu' history, traditions, and lore?

But Shong Lue seemed able to explain everything to the Khmu', too, so they set up a test to make sure of his legitimacy for them. As most Khmu' were heavy drinkers, they brewed a large quantity of rice beer, saying that if he would win a drinking contest they would believe him. Shong Lue agreed, and drank more beer than they did, and from then on they respected him as much as did the Hmong people.[1]

More and more Hmong and Khmu' people of the surrounding areas enthusiastically studied their respective Pahawh writing systems. Young people who were interested in learning would come to stay for a few days with Shong Lue in his own home, and he would teach them. He charged nothing, and fed them from what he had. Other followers also supplied food. Those who learned well enough went back to their homes and taught others there and at the fields. The word spread farther to the populations of surrounding areas, so that Hmong and Khmu' people who lived near the town of Muang Long (Muas Loom **ʊ̄R ɩ̍ɩʌ**), Vietnam (about three days walk), also came to learn.

But as the news kept spreading it was heard also by people in the communist government,[2] which was in control of Vietnam and of the area of Laos near the Vietnamese border. The communist authorities began to say that this Pahawh was part of a plot by the American CIA, which was supporting the non-communist forces in Laos. They spread the story that the two young men who had taught Shong Lue Yang the

Pahawh were really Americans who had hidden out in an underground bunker in Shong Lue's house and had taught him at night. They said that General Vang Pao (Vaj Pov ᦢᦰ ᦅᦲᧃᧃ), Hmong regional commander of the forces of the non-communist Royal Lao Government, had sent a Khmu' man who worked for him to lead these Americans to Tham Ha.

At the end of 1963 communist soldiers came to try to arrest Shong Lue at his home village. News of their intentions preceded the troops, however, and Shong Lue was able to escape, helped by Chia Long Thao (Txiaj Looj Thoj ᦓᦲᧄ ᦄᧃ ᦆᦲᧇ),[3] who took him off to his own village of Fi Kha (Fib Khav ᧚ᦰ ᦄᧇ) across the border in Laos. Pang Xiong and the children stayed at home in Tham Ha.

At Fi Kha, Shong Lue for the first time built a larger, communal round house and taught the people to worship in it. The earlier one in Tham Ha had been only for his own use. He also named twelve Hmong leaders, one each from different Hmong clans, to help in worship and in the teaching of the Pahawh. To these clan representatives he taught everything: worship, tradition, the future. They were in training to perform all of the functions he performed, and to know all he knew. They were to be dedicated to this responsibility, and were not to become soldiers or officials or anything else which would distract them from it. We do not know whether or not he also selected Khmu' representatives for parallel functions.

In addition, Shong Lue chose Hmong and Khmu' teachers to help with the increasing load of teaching the Pahawh Hmong to the Hmong and the Pahawh Khmu' to the Khmu'. These teachers concentrated exclusively on the Pahawh, leaving the other training to the clan representatives. They had no restrictions on them and were free to move about, become soldiers, etc. Of these Hmong teachers at Fi Kha, Pa Kao Her (Paj Kaub Hawj ᦄᧄ ᦺᦒ ᦆᦲᧃᧃ) remains one of the primary people leading the Pahawh Hmong movement and other current efforts which are to some degree legacies of Shong Lue Yang.

Shong Lue Yang also built a school in which to hold Pahawh classes at Fi Kha. Like other country schools in Laos, this was an open, thatched, one-room building with rough benches, all constructed by hand by the villagers. The teachers also began teaching the Pahawh at the nearby village of Fi Kham (Fib Kham ᧚ᦰ ᦅᦲᦷ). In all, about two hundred and fifty Hmong and Khmu' from Vietnam and from the Kiaw Ban (Kiaj Npas ᦆ ᦄᦲᧃᧄ) area of Laos came to learn the Pahawh in Fi Kha and Fi Kham. Many would come in periodically for instruction and return to their homes the same day to continue their regular work. They would bring their own notebooks[4] and a few new symbols would be added each time for them to take home and memorize.

These developments continued until early in 1964, when the communist government sent troops to Fi Kha village to try to get rid of Shong Lue once more. Like most Hmong villages, Fi Kha was located in a clearing in the jungle. The communist forces entered this clearing from all sides early in the morning. Shong Lue had already left.

One Hmong student and two Khmu' students, however, were killed. The Hmong student, living in Shong Lue's house, was not able to get away. The two Khmu' students were unfortunate enough to arrive unsuspectingly at the village from their home in the Kiaw Ban area just in time to be caught.

Shong Lue then hid in the jungle close to the village of Tham Ha, where he had lived when he received the Pahawh, and where his family was. His family joined him there in the jungle, where they were helped by villagers who brought them food.

During the time Shong Lue Yang was hiding, Wang Sao Thao (Vam Choj Thoj **ƏC ꝼꝫ ꝼꞽꞽ**), one of the twelve clan leaders who had been in training at Fi Kha, and Pa Kao Her, the teacher, went to the village of Pha Bong (Pham Npoos **ƏꝈ ꝼꝼꞽ**), Vietnam, built a new round house there, reinstituted worship and began teaching the Pahawh.

But this effort lasted only a month. In the second month of the year, the communist troops came and attacked there also. The villagers (including the Pahawh students gathered there) resisted, but as a result of the fighting Wang Sao Thao lost one of his eyes and many students were killed. The remainder escaped into the jungle, leaving in the village the wives and children, and any men who had not been involved in learning the Pahawh Hmong.

Fortunately, Special Guerrilla Unit 1 of General Vang Pao's army, consisting of four hundred men under the command of Youa Vang Lee (Ntsuab Vaj Lis **ꝼꝼꝈ ꝱC ꝼꝏ**), soon arrived in the area, looking for students of Shong Lue who were under attack, to protect them. As the SGU came into the area it split up into three sections, one of which came to Pha Bong.

The SGU had been sent out in response to an appeal for help which Shong Lue had sent to General Vang Pao's army some weeks before. Chia Long Thao (who had earlier rescued Shong Lue), Gnia Sau Her (Nyiaj Xauv Hawj **ꝼꞽꝱ ꝏꝴ ꝼꞽꞽ**) and Gnia Chao Her (Nyiaj Txos Hawj **ꝼꞽꝱ ꝼꞽꝟ ꝼꞽꞽ**) had gone to the army headquarters at Long Cheng (Looj Ceeb **ꝼꞽꝈ ꝟꝟ**). These three were older men with status in the area, and they were sympathetic to Shong Lue, although they were not his students. When a response was not immediately forthcoming from the military, they had returned home. The regiment had in fact started out early in 1964, soon after the Hmong New Year.

The government forces sent Wang Sao Thao to be hospitalized in Long Cheng. They also gathered together from different locations some of those people who were in danger because they had followed Shong Lue Yang, and took them to establish a new village of Kiaw Boua (Kiaj Npuam ꎵ ꈦꆄ), a little to the west in Laos, in an area under Royal Lao Government control.

In the meantime, Shong Lue Yang and his family had been found again by the communists in the jungle near Tham Ha. Again he managed to escape, as did his oldest son, Ge Yang (Zeb Yaj ꑈꑀ ꑇꑿ), but Pang Xiong (Paj Xyooj ꑇꆧ ꍊꑵ) and all the other children were captured.[5] Shong Lue and Ge continued hiding out for a time, but after nine months they were also brought safely to Kiaw Boua by Wang Houa Ber Yang (Vam Huas Npawv Yaj ꑉꑔ ꑖꑣ ꑈꆢ ꑿꑿ), one of the worship leaders at Kiaw Boua.

The Kiaw Boua Period

The population of Kiaw Boua included people who had been studying the Pahawh at Fi Kha, Fi Kham and Pha Bong. When Shong Lue Yang joined them, they asked him to begin teaching them the Pahawh again. He told them to find twelve new people from different clans who would learn to become leaders, for the previous twelve who had been in training at Fi Kha had been scattered.

Then in the fourth month, on the fifteenth day, in the year 1965, Shong Lue Yang introduced and began to teach the Pahawh Second Stage Reduced Version for the Hmong and the Khmu'. This revision of the writing system was (in the Hmong case at least) considerably easier than the Source Version, as we will see in Chapter 5. We know nothing about the Khmu' system, not having succeeded in finding anyone who knows it.

At Kiaw Boua Shong Lue built another school for teaching the Pahawh, and a round house in which the people could worship. People who were learning the Pahawh for general purposes studied the easier Second Stage Version. The twelve clan representatives learned both the Source Version and the Second Stage Version. This was because the Source Version was to be kept for sacred use in connection with worship in the round house, which the twelve were being trained to lead.

The word began to spread that the Mother of Writing had returned and was once more teaching the Pahawh. Hmong and Khmu' people flocked to Kiaw Boua village at an increasing rate, and many people learned the Second Stage well there. As in the earlier period, people would come and go, walking back and forth between their homes and Kiaw Boua in order to learn while they continued their farming and other work.

Two individuals who have remained important in the continuation of the Pahawh Hmong in more recent years entered the picture during this time. The first of these, Lor Moua (Lauj Muas ᾋᴨ ᾲR), was one of the students at Kiaw Boua. He and his sister, Bau Moua (Npaub Muas ᾋᾋ ᾲR), lived not far away at Ban Xong (Npab Xoos ᾋᾋ ᾲA), Laos. Shong Lue Yang married Bau Moua on January 15, 1965. Lor Moua has since become one of the leaders who have carried on Shong Lue's legacy.

The other important person who entered the picture during the Kiaw Boua period is Chia Koua Vang. He was a corporal in the regiment sent to rescue Shong Lue and his followers in 1964, and spent about ten months (much of the year 1964) on the expedition, several months of that at Kiaw Boua. Chia Koua did not become a student of Shong Lue at that time because he was busy with his military duties, but he did get someone to write out the tables of the Pahawh Source Version for him (before the Second Stage Reduced Version was in use). He made notations of the values of the Pahawh characters by writing the Romanized Hmong beside them, thus teaching himself to read and write in the system.

Kiaw Boua also became unsafe for Shong Lue. This time, however, the danger came not from the communist forces which had hounded him before, but from some Hmong leaders in the forces which were protecting him.

Shong Lue more than once had predicted the time and place of communist attacks and prepared people for them. At first this added to his stature, and was received with great appreciation by military officers. Because of Shong Lue's help of this kind, on several occasions General Vang Pao gave money to support him. At first the money was given directly, but one time the general sent it in the care of the commander of the forces in the area which included Kiaw Boua, someone who happened to be a relative of the general. But the officer kept the money for himself and became very angry when Shong Lue found this out and asked for the money. Two of the top officers then spread the word that Shong Lue was able to predict the communist attacks only because he was a communist sympathizer. They said he had a radio with which to communicate with the enemy, and that he gained his information about the attacks over this radio. They reported this story to their superiors, and seeds of suspicion were sown.

The Long Cheng Period

In early 1966 Shong Lue Yang had to make a trip to Long Cheng, the military center for the Hmong. His wife Bau Moua and his son Ge were along with him. But when he got ready to return to Kiaw Boua, he was denied the right to board the plane,[6] without explanation. In light of what had been happening, and after consulting with friends, he decided not to try to go back to Kiaw Boua.

Tens of thousands of Hmong and people from other ethnic groups lived in many small towns and villages around Long Cheng, displaced by the war and uncertain about the future. Shong Lue and his family joined them. He stayed for a while in the home of Colonel Yong Chue Yang (Ntxoov Tswb Yaj ၾၮ် ၮၬ ၁ဟ)[7] in Long Cheng, and after about a month moved to the village of Nam Ngua (Naj Gua ၁ဟ ၪဟဴ), close by. There once more he was recognized by the Hmong and Khmu' population as the Mother of Writing. Interest spread quickly among these displaced people. Hmong people from the nearby town of Phou Moc (Phwv Mum ၮၮၬ ၪၰR) especially came and asked him to teach them the Pahawh.

Shong Lue Yang's response was now more cautious, however. He did not build a school. The round house which he constructed for worship was a small one for his own personal use only. He assigned some young men as teachers for people who came and studied the Pahawh (still the Second Stage Reduced Version) in his house by day, but he did not do any teaching of this kind himself, nor did he train any clan representatives as leaders.

As it had been in earlier times, the teaching done by the young men was very informal. Gnia Yee Yang remembers his brother-in-law regularly leaving home early in the morning and walking for two hours to Nam Ngua. One of the teachers there would write out a line of one of the tables of characters for him, and tell him the values. He would then walk home to do his normal work, memorizing what he had been given, and practicing what he knew. He would return another day and get another line.

Chia Koua Vang was now assistant to the chief officer in the department where military personnel records were kept in Long Cheng, and he now had regular office hours, with work which was not very taxing.

When he approached Shong Lue, wanting to find out for himself what was true about this man and his writing, Shong Lue invited him to come and study at night, when the crowd was gone.

So Chia Koua became Shong Lue's primary disciple through the rest of the prophet's life. From early 1966 until Shong Lue sent him on an extended trip in April 1967, Chia Koua would walk regularly from Long Cheng to Shong Lue's house in Nam Ngua in the evening, after work. Shong Lue would light his opium lamp and talk.

Chia Koua learned the Second Stage Reduced Version of the writing system, as he had only known the Source Version before. Shong Lue also taught him religion, the future and numerous other things he had been sent from heaven to teach. It was during this period of regular contact with Shong Lue that Chia Koua kept notes on the most important things Shong Lue said.[8] Chia Koua asked many questions, and found that Shong Lue knew the answers to them all. Chia Koua told Smalley that he believed in Shong Lue because "he knew everything." Furthermore, Chia Koua told Smalley, "You studied a long time to get your doctor's degree, and you are very smart, but you do not know everything. Shong Lue had no education, but he knew everything by himself."

In his relations with people Shong Lue was pleasant, often smiling, but very retiring in disposition. He rarely talked unless asked a direct question; he never pushed his ideas. In a group he sat quietly and listened. When people asked him questions he would usually reflect for a few moments before answering.

And when people did ask him questions the response was often cryptic, oracular. People often came to him looking for ways to get rich, or to do things for which Shong Lue did not have much sympathy. When asked how they could get a lot of money, for example, Shong Lue might reply, "All the mountains and jungles are money." Chia Koua understood this to mean that people should use the resources they had.

On one occasion Chia Koua had bought a Thai lottery ticket, but had not told Shong Lue. Then Chia Koua had a dream in which he shot a deer. When he asked Shong Lue what the dream meant, Shong Lue replied, "If you don't win at the lottery you should get a shaman to help you." Chia Koua did win a prize; he understands Shong Lue's statement to show that the prophet knew he had a ticket without being told, and that he would win.

Shong Lue also had a sense of humor. Late one night in a group of people he asked how many wanted to become rich. Most raised their hands. Without saying anything more, Shong Lue went outside into the jungled and defecated. He came back and told the people that he had written the winning lottery number on the ground with his feces, and some people ran out looking for it.

If people did not pursue a cryptic statement, or took it to be literally true, this was indication to Shong Lue that they did not have insight. Insightful people probed to find what was behind the statement, what Shong Lue had in mind. For example, if he said, "I am a poor man, and have no money," an appropriate response might be "What do you need money for?" As the conversation continued, it might turn out that the statement had little or nothing to do with money.

For people whom Shong Lue felt to be self-serving, his answer to a question would be oracular, or it might simply be "I don't know." But for people who asked sincere and worthy questions, although he would first reply in the same cryptic way, Shong Lue would become more specific. Often his reply when pressed was to tell them how to find the answer. And if Shong Lue saw that they were working hard to find the answer, but were still unsure of what to do or think, he would discuss the issue with them directly.

So when Chia Koua would go to study he would question his way through the oblique answers, go out to investigate for himself and follow up Shong Lue's leads. He would then come back to tell Shong Lue of what he was finding. The farther he went, the more Shong Lue would talk it over with him, discussing, criticizing and making direct suggestions.

Chapter 8 includes the story of Chia Koua's search for ways of printing and typing the Pahawh Hmong under this kind of interaction with Shong Lue. Chia Koua also undertook the study of Hmong herbal medicine under Shong Lue's guidance, a subject in which he became very knowledgeable. He and his wife sold herbal remedies for brief periods in Thailand in 1974 and 1975 to pay for their attempts to find a place of refuge there in the face of the impending collapse of Laos.

As word of the Pahawh spread even more widely around the Long Cheng area in 1966, more and more Hmong and Khmu' people, civilians and soldiers, men and women, ten-year-olds and older people, people of all kinds, came from the surrounding areas to learn it. Younger people from as far away as the Na Kha (Na Kha ꗞꗞ) and Muong Moc (Moos Mauj ꗞꗞ) areas, far from Long Cheng (see Fig. 1 above), also came to learn the Pahawh.

The large numbers of people who kept coming to study disturbed some of the Hmong military leaders, however. Officials made the accusation that this writing was, or was based on, the Russian alphabet, and that it was part of a plot by the Chinese communists and the Russians to undermine the government.

These Hmong leaders were also disturbed by the other aspects of Shong Lue's life and teaching. They were suspicious of the religion and believed that the people were being misled. They were uneasy because so many people believed that the prophet had supernatural powers, such as the ability to predict the future. They interpreted him as a revolutionary, were concerned about what his message might lead to. The core of the Hmong establishment grew to fear him.

So Shong Lue Yang, who had been accused by the communist side of being a subversive supporter of the Royal Lao Government, was now arrested as a communist subversive by the Hmong military police of the Royal Lao Government. He was taken September 15, 1967, and imprisoned in the jail at Pha Khao (Pham Khom ꯀꯀ ꯀꯀ = Tsua Dawb ꯀꯀ ꯀꯀ), a nearby village. A son, Ba Yang (Npam Yaj ꯀꯀ ꯀꯀ), was born to Bau Moua soon after he went to prison.

The Final Period

Shong Lue was in prison for about three years. Many of his students now became afraid, and went underground. At first Chia Koua Vang was very cautious. Five or six times he communicated with Shong Lue by writing letters and baking them inside bread which he sent to the Mother of Writing. However, Shong Lue began to return his replies openly because a number of his police guards were among his followers and would transmit them. Then it became possible for Chia Koua to visit Shong Lue in prison, which he did many times. He would stay two days at a time, and continued learning from the prophet.

In August 1970, Chia Koua got a letter from Shong Lue in prison, but he could not understand much of it. The writing system was considerably different from what they were using. When he asked about it Shong Lue told him it was a new version of the Pahawh Hmong, the Third Stage Reduced Version. This revision involved considerable simplification from the Stage Two Version, and it shows greater linguistic sophistication. We do not know whether Shong Lue also revised the Pahawh Khmu' at that point.

Shong Lue had been in prison for about three years when he told Chia Koua he was going to be killed. He wrote a letter to his student in which the Pahawh numerals ꯀ ꯀ ꯀ '7 8 9' were all written backwards, as

Я Я Я. Chia Koua asked what this meant, and Shong Lue told him that it showed the three sons of God (the twin young men and himself) returning to God.

"Why?" Chia Koua protested. "We need you!"

"Yes," replied Shong Lue, "but the others don't want us. They want to kill us."

Chia Koua then carried the word back to Long Cheng, where he met with some of Shong Lue's other followers. One of them, Gnia Pha Her (Nyiaj Phab Hawj ɲɨ̌ ǯ ħɪɾ) devised a plan to rescue Shong Lue from prison, and on November 8, 1970, had him brought to his own village of Nam Chia (Naj Ciab ʒʊ ɯ∨), at the foot of rugged Phou Bia (Phu Npiab ṅǩ ɯǎ) Mountain. This is the highest mountain in the region, and as late as 1987 it was still a center of Hmong resistance against the present communist government. Others took his wife and two sons from Long Cheng to Nam Chia also.

At first Shong Lue and his family lived in a small hut in the jungle outside the village, and villagers supplied them with food. He built a small round house for his own personal worship, and in time the villagers built a larger one above the village for their use. One of Shong Lue's students in the supply office of the army gave Gnia Pha, Shong Lue's protector, a radio transmitter, and Chia Koua was able to communicate indirectly with Shong Lue by means of it.

Nam Chia was two days walk from Long Cheng, but at this time the military headquarters was unsafe because of communist attacks, and Chia Koua had moved his family to a safer place, which was only one day's walk from Nam Chia. So Chia Koua began visiting Shong Lue there, taking along Kao Lee (Kos Lis ʊ̌ ǎɯ), Shong Lue's nephew, son of his adopted sister Ying Yang (Yeeb Yaj ∨ɯ ʒɯ).

Shong Lue's mood was somber. He talked about the problems the Hmong people would have in the future, and about his returning to God. He said, however, that someone to take his place had already come to the world. In answer to questions about who this was, or where the person was to be found, he would only say, "You will know some day."

Shong Lue told Chia Koua that the country would be lost to the communists, and that he should plan to leave. He must take with him his notes, and preserve the Pahawh Hmong and all of the prophet's teaching.

During the next three months Shong Lue made still another revision of the Pahawh Hmong, resulting in the Final Version, which he gave to Chia Koua on January 21, 1971. He said this system would be easier to use in telegraphing, when that became possible. Once more it showed significant simplification over the previous stage.

Then, late in January, two men dressed as poor villagers came to Gnia Pha and gave him some money, saying that they wanted to go to worship with Shong Lue. Gnia Pha unaccountably let them know where Shong Lue was, and they visited him. Shong Lue, however, saw immediately that they were spies for the military authorities.

With his hideout exposed, Shong Lue moved into the village of Nam Chia. He did no teaching, but followers filled his house constantly. One day he pointed out two men in his house and told Chia Koua that they were the same government spies. Chia Koua wanted to take him away again, but Shong Lue said no. Instead, he gave Chia Koua a small packet of papers and told him to take them home, to keep them safe along with his notes and other things related to the movement. He told Chia Koua he should eventually take his family to safety out of the country.

Chia Koua took the packet home, but when he returned to Nam Chia, Shong Lue was dead. He believes that sending him off with the papers was Shong Lue's ruse to get him away from danger, lest he also be killed. Chia Koua still has the little packet of Shong Lue's papers, to which he has added some letters Shong Lue wrote to him earlier.

It was mid-February 1971[9] that Shong Lue Yang, Mother of Writing, Savior of the People, was assassinated at the age of forty-one. Gnia Pha had organized a cooperative fishing drive at a nearby stream, and most of the villagers had gone along. The crowd in Shong Lue's house went too, all but the Shong Lue family and the two spies. That morning Shong Lue made cryptic remarks to his wife, saying that she must not be afraid, that now was the time to go.

After the village was nearly empty, one of the spies said that he would go out and fix the bamboo conduit which brought water from a spring outside the village to the various homes in the village. The other said he had to go to the jungle (a euphemism corresponding to English "go to the bathroom"). It is believed that what they actually did was inform a party of five waiting assassins that the coast was clear.

About nine o'clock in the morning, two of the party of assassins came toward Shong Lue's house, while the others stayed on guard. As they came into the village, they found a neighbor man of the Her (Hawj ꗍꗏ) clan outside his home, sharpening his machete, and captured him. Then they went on and shot Shong Lue and Bau inside their home. Shong Lue's and Bau's three-year-old son, Ba (Npam ꒜ꓲ), darted to the jungle. The assassins shot at him, wounding him in the leg, but he managed to get away. Then they killed the neighbor they had been holding. Shong Lue's older son Ge was away from home, and was not injured.[10]

When the villagers heard the shots they came running back. Shong Lue and the neighbor were dead, but Bau Moua lived two days in the care of Joua Pao Yang (Ntsuab Pov Yaj ᑌᴋ ᑌᒪᐧᒪ ᔑᕽ), who also arranged the funeral. She was strong enough to tell what had happened, describing the assassins, who had been disguised as communist soldiers, carrying weapons of the type used by the communist troops.

All of the suspected assassins are known now, their identities learned in various ways. They were all soldiers in General Vang Pao's army. One who was a close relative of Chia Koua's wife told Chia Koua all about it after they all escaped to Thailand in 1975. Three have since died.

But what is puzzling about the events surrounding this assassination is the role of Gnia Pha. Was it just bad judgment which led him to tell the spies where Shong Lue was? Was it coincidence that he organized a fishing expedition the morning of the assassination? Is it possible that when he volunteered to rescue Shong Lue from jail he did it with other motives than the safety of the prophet? Chia Koua wonders. Gnia Pha was killed later as a soldier in battle.

Subsequent Events

After Shong Lue was assassinated, a student named Yong Lee Yang (Ntxoov Lis Yaj ᗅᵲ ᗅᒪ ᔑᕽ), who had been one of the twelve clan representatives at Kiaw Boua or Fi Kha, and so had been trained by Shong Lue as a leader, built a round house for worship and continued teaching the Pahawh Hmong in his own village of Houi Kinin (Haib Kees Nees ᕼᵲ ᔑ ᔑᕽ) in the Long Cheng area. Once more the Hmong people in the surrounding area gathered to study in increasing numbers, until there were five hundred of them. They studied the Second Stage Version, having no knowledge of the Third and Final Stages, which had been given to Chia Koua in the last weeks of Shong Lue's life. And by this time the Khmu' were no longer involved, having been frightened off by what had happened.

After a while Hmong people from Nam Theng (Naj Theem ᔑᕽ ᐧᑎᵲ) requested Yong Lee Yang to send two teachers to them. So he sent two of his students, Shoua Vang (Suav Vaj ᗅᐧᑎᵲ ᔑᑕ) and Kao Yang (Kos Vaj ᑌᵲ ᔑᕽ), to spread out the opportunity for instruction. As many as three hundred young people gathered at Nam Theng and rapidly learned the Pahawh Hmong.

This process of spreading the Pahawh Hmong continued until November 1971, when Yong Lee Yang was also killed in his Houi Kinin home. The assassins were dressed in the uniforms of government soldiers. They came early in the morning, armed with bazookas of the type supplied by the American CIA, weapons powerful enough to pierce tanks and blow up bunkers. With these weapons they killed not only Yong Lee, but also five other people, wounding sixteen as well. Then the next evening, at 4 P.M., two T-28 bombers, also of the type provided to General Vang Pao's army by the CIA, flew twice over the village and destroyed the round worship house.[11]

That disaster ended the spread of the Pahawh Hmong until the Royal Lao Government collapsed and Hmong people began to leave Laos, beginning May 14, 1975. The rest of the story of the development and spread of the system belongs to other times and places, and will be told in Chapters 8 and 9. Some contrary views about this history and its significance will also be summarized in Chapter 12. But with this much background on the short and troubled life and times of Shong Lue Yang, we turn next to his enormous intellectual achievement, the Pahawh Hmong.

3

The Sounds of Hmong

In order to understand how the Pahawh Hmong writing system works, and to appreciate the ingenious way in which it represents Hmong speech, it will be helpful first to understand a little about how Hmong pronunciation is structured.[1]

There are two major dialects of Hmong spoken in Laos and Thailand, and in the West. One is *Hmong Daw* (Hmoob Dawb ᲣᲗᲔ ᲒᲗᲘᲘ), typically referred to in English as White Hmong. The other is *Hmong Leng*, also spelled *Mong Leng* in English (Moob Leeg ᲣᲗᲔ ᲘᲘᲘ, pronounced Hmoob Lees in Hmong Daw). It is most often called Blue Hmong or Green Hmong in English. Some Hmong prefer to be called by their Hmong ethnic/dialect names in English (Hmong Daw or Hmong Leng/ Mong Leng) rather than by the English terms White or Blue/Green. We follow that preference in this book.

Most of what we say about the pronunciation of Hmong is equally true of both Hmong dialects, and we will often refer simply to "Hmong" in describing their common characteristics. When notable differences exist between them, we will specify the dialect.

The Tones

Hmong is a tone language. In this respect it is unlike English and most other European languages, but like Chinese languages, Lao, Thai and hundreds of other languages of Asia, Africa and the Americas. Being a tone language does not make it unusual, or difficult (for native speakers). It simply means that the sound system works differently from the non-tonal languages with which most Westerners are more familiar.

There are a number of different types of tone languages in the world, but generally speaking in Hmong each syllable has a distinctive tone. For example, the name of the writing system, *Pahawh Hmong,* has three syllables: pa-hawh-hmong. The first two of these syllables have tones that fall from a high position; the third remains high, without falling. The tones on these three syllables can be pictured as pa⼃ hawh⼃ hmongᴦ, with the vertical line in each case representing the full spoken voice range (high to low), and the line extending from it indicating roughly the contour of the tone, and its relation to the voice range. In actual speech, of course, a tone is spoken simultaneously with the rest of the syllable (especially with the vowel), but the symbol representing it in these examples is placed after the vowel for convenience.

A comparison with English will illustrate how the rise and fall of the voice is used differently in the two languages. English has a falling pitch on expressions like Oh! So! Good! That falling pitch sounds much like the tone on the syllables of the Hmong word pa⼃ hawh⼃. We could even represent such a fall in English pitch as Oh⼃, So⼃, Good⼃.

But the difference between this English intonation (as it is called) and Hmong tone is that the Hmong tone is intrinsic to the syllable, and the English pitch changes with different use. In English we can also say: Oh? So? Good? (Oh⼁ So⼁ Good⼁). If the same Hmong word *Pahawh* were said with rising tones, as in these last English examples, the first syllable would be pa⼁ 'tie' (pav Ʊꜝm̆) and the second hau ⼁ 'in, inside' (hauv ꙮᴦ). A different tone in Hmong potentially results in a different word, just as a different consonant or vowel potentially results in a different word in either Hmong or English. A different intonation in English results not in a different word, but in a signal that the word is being used in a different way, such as in a statement or question.

Table 1 shows a series of seven Hmong words, differentiated from each other by tone. These words illustrate and contrast the seven primary distinctive tones of the language. The last two of these tones are characterized by other sound distinctions in addition to the pitch contour, so that in those cases the distinctive tone consists of both pitch and the additional feature. Thus, the first five tones are simple tones, and the last two are complex.

Of the complex tones, tone ⼃ has a hollow, "breathy" sound to it, along with falling pitch. This "breathy" voice quality is similar to a voice quality sometimes interpreted as sultry or spooky when used in English. The breathiness is represented by the symbol ⼃ by the irregularity of the line descending to the right.[2] Tone ʟ, on the other hand, terminates suddenly with a sharp catch in the throat (a glottal stop), represented by the knob at the end of the horizontal line. Because such additional sound features occur in these two tones, the hearer does not

Table 1. An example of tone distinctions in Hmong. Of the spellings, the first column is the Romanized (or Latin) Popular Alphabet, the second Pahawh Hmong. Within the Pahawh Hmong written syllable the vowel is first, the consonant last.

Pronunciation	Meaning	Spelling
poⲅ	lump	pob ᲌᲌
poᴎ	female	poj ᲌᲌
poⲨ	to throw	pov ᲌᲌
poⲅ	pancreas	po ᲌᲌
poⱶ	thorn	pos ᲌᲌
poᴎ	grandmother	pog ᲌᲌
poⳑ	to see	pom ᲌᲌

have to depend on recognizing the pitch alone in order to distinguish them from other tones.

In addition to these seven primary distinctive tones (simple and complex), however, there is also another tone, much more rare, a variant of tone ⳑ, which occurs under certain grammatical conditions.[3] This eighth and limited tone is a simple tone, represented by Ⲩ. An example of its use in contrast to its counterpart ⳑ follows:

ti Ⲩ in the phrase nyoⲅ ti Ⲩ 'over there' (nyob tid ᲌Ă Ă)
ti ⳑ in the phrase nyoⲅ ti ⳑ ne ᴎ 'at your place over there' (nyob tim nej ᲌Ă Ă ᲌Ⲩ)

In the Romanized Popular Alphabet for Hmong, tones are symbolized by a consonant letter placed at the end of the written syllable. This can be seen in the Romanized spelling of the examples in Table 1. In this chapter we will continue to use symbols like ⲅ and ᴎ, as well as the Romanized tone spelling, to represent the tone configuration. This may both provide an aid to memory and help readers get accustomed to not reading the final consonant symbols as spoken consonants.

The Vowels

Hmong Daw has six simple spoken vowels, plus seven complex ones. The descriptions which follow should be taken only as rough approximations of how these vowels are pronounced. Symbols in square brackets[4] are phonetic symbols to help any reader who may understand them, but they may be ignored by others. The simple vowels are

i   similar to *see*. tiⲅ 'pile up' (tib Ă)
e   similar to *say*. teⲅ 'field' (teb ᲌Ă)

Table 2. Hmong Daw simple vowels, according to the position
in which they are made in the mouth

	Front	Central	Back
High	i	w	u
Low	e	a	o

w   [ɨ] roughly like *houses*, but with the lips rounded a little. twL
'buffalo' (twm 𝐭𝐨̃̈). Note that although the letter w represents a
consonant in English, it represents a vowel in the Romanized
Popular Alphabet.

a   similar to *father* as pronounced by many (but not all) speakers
of English. taꅐ 'inadequate' (tab 𝐚̃̈)

u   similar to *soon*. tuꅐ 'son' (tub 𝐔𝐧̃̈)

o   [ɔ] similar to *cot* for many speakers of English who do not pronounce that word with the same vowel as they use for *father*.
toꜛ rooꅐ 'hill' (toj roob 𝐚̃̈ 𝐔𝐔)

These six simple vowels are charted in Table 2 in an arrangement
analogous to the relative positions in which they are made in the mouth.
The vowels at the left are made with the hight point of the tongue at the
front of the mouth; those at the right have the high point of the tongue
toward the back of the mouth. The others are intermediate. The vowels
in the top row are made with the tongue closer to the roof of the mouth
(higher) than the ones in the bottom row. Not shown in the table is the
fact that the vowels /i/, /e/ and /a/ do not have rounded lips, while /w/,
/u/ and /o/ tend to have some rounding.

In addition to these simple vowels, there are two kinds of complex
vowels in Hmong, namely, nasalized vowels and vowel glides. Nasalized vowels are complex in that they are pronounced as simple vowels
but possess an additional feature of nasalization, where the sound comes
out through the nose as well as the mouth. Vowel glides are complex in
that they start with one vowel sound and end with another.

In Hmong Daw there are two nasalized vowels, [ɛŋ] and [oŋ]. In
their actual pronunciation they include a nasal consonant, [ŋ] like English *sing*, following the nasalized vowel. In the Hmong sound system,
however, that final sound does not function as a consonant when it
comes at the end of a syllable in this way, but serves to make the nasalization on the vowel clear. No other consonants occur at the end of
Hmong syllables, and because the [ŋ] is redundant with the nasalization
on the vowel, it does not have to be written if the nasalization is written.

For that reason, in the Romanized Popular Alphabet, nasalized vowels are represented without any [ŋ], but with a double letter instead:

teeΓ [tɛŋΓ] 'light, lamp' (teeb [illegible])
too↾ [toŋ↾] 'cooper, brass' (tooj [illegible])

There are five glided vowels in Hmong Daw, with the vowel /a/ involved in all of them, either as the starting point of the change in vowel quality, or the ending point. When /a/ is the starting point the tongue moves upward toward one of the vowels in the upper row; when it is the ending point the tongue moves downward from either of the two vowels in the upper row. In Romanized Hmong Daw the glided vowels are written with a sequence of two vowel letters:

ia roughly similar to *see a (cat)*. tiaΓ 'skirt' (tiab [illegible])
ua roughly similar to *sue a (man)*. tua↾ 'come' (tuaj [illegible])
ai similar to *tie*. tai⊢ 'fold' (tais [illegible])
aw [əɨ] (no helpful English analogy). tawΓ 'basket' (tawb [illegible])
au similar to some Canadian pronunciations of *about*. tau⊢ 'be able' (tau [illegible])

In the Romanized alphabet, then, all simple vowels are represented by a single vowel symbol, and all complex vowels are represented by a sequence of two vowel symbols, either a doubled vowel (for nasalization) or a sequence of two different vowel symbols, in which one of the two is the symbol a.

The vowel chart above can now be completed by adding the complex vowels, as in Table 3. The position of the glides on the chart, of course, reflects only one end of the glide. The other end is always /a/.

There are some significant differences between Hmong Daw and Hmong Leng vowels. The majority of regular correspondences in pronunciation are shown as follows:

Table 3. Hmong Daw vowels, simple and complex, as written in Romanized orthography. Doubling of the letter represents nasalization. The two vowel symbols used in transcribing each glided vowel indicate approximate end points of glides.

	Front	Central	Back
High	i	w	u
Low	e	a	o
Nasalized	ee		oo
Glided down	ia		ua
Glided up	ai	aw	au

Hmong Daw   Hmong Leng
   a   aa
   ia   a

This means that words with /a/ in Hmong Daw are regularly pronounced with /aa/ in Hmong Leng, etc. The aa represents a nasalized /a/ (pronounced [aŋ]) which occurs widely in Hmong Leng, but not in Hmong Daw. To show this same relationship between these vowels in another way,

Hmong Daw ia = a = aa Hmong Leng.

In other words, when Hmong Daw has a word with the vowel /ia/, Hmong Leng typically has a corresponding /a/, and when Hmong Daw has /a/ Hmong Leng typically has [aŋ]. Thus, the widespread Hmong clan names *Vang* and *Yang* are pronounced [vaˀ] and [yaˀ] in Hmong Daw, but (nasalized) [vaŋˀ] and [yaŋˀ] in Hmong Leng.[5]

The Consonants

The complexities of the Hmong sound system lie primarily in the consonants. As with the vowels and tones, there are both simple and complex consonants, but there are many more consonants than vowels, and more kinds of complexity. Hmong spoken consonants are, however, a marvel of symmetry, forming an intricate structure.

In presenting the consonants we will not yet explain the pronunciation values of the symbols or give examples (as we did for the vowels), in order not to obscure the system with too much detail. A table of values for the consonants is provided below on pages 48–50.

Simple Consonants. The simple consonants are displayed in Table 4 according to how they are produced in the mouth, from lips to uvula and

Table 4. Simple consonants in Hmong, as written in the Romanized Popular Alphabet. In this transcription, /ʔ/ (glottal stop, or catch in the throat) is not directly symbolized. The sound is indicated instead by the absence of a written consonant symbol before the vowel.

Lips	Teeth	Front Palate	Front Palate	Back Palate	Uvula	Vocal Cords
p	t	r	c	k	q	(ʔ)
m	n		ny	g		
f	x	s	xy			h
v	l	z	y			

the throat. There are two columns for "Front Palate" because a different part of the tongue touches the front part of the palate in each. The rows in the chart represent different ways of making sounds, which we do not need to go into now.[6]

Complex Consonants. In addition to the simple consonants, there are various types of complex consonants in Hmong. In Table 5, one of these complex consonants is much like a /t/, but has a simultaneous catch in the throat in Hmong Daw [ʔd].[7] In Hmong Leng, on the other hand, instead of this catch in the throat it is followed by a voiceless l, and pronounced [tL]. In either case it is here represented with the letter d, although some Hmong Leng prefer to spell it tl or dl.

Other complex sounds start like one or another of the simple consonants, but end differently. In such cases they are phonetically sequences of two different sounds, but they act as unitary, complex consonant phonemes in Hmong. Some of these complex consonant units end with an /l/. Others end with sounds like the sounds spelled s or sh in English. Table 5 also shows symbols for such complex consonants.

A different type of complex consonant in Hmong contains a puff of air through the mouth (aspiration) or nose (voiceless nasal) after or be-

Table 5. Some complex Hmong consonants added to the simple consonants of Table 4. The additions are in bold type.

Lips		Teeth			Front Palate	Front Palate		Back Palate	Uvula	Vocal Cords
p	**pl**	t	**d**	**tx**	r	c	**ts**	k	q	(ʔ)
m		n				ny		g		
f		x			s	xy				h
v		l			z	y				

Table 6. Complex Hmong consonants which include a puff of air (represented by h) as part of the consonant sound.

Lips		Teeth					Front Palate		Back Palate	Uvula	Vocal Cords
p	pl	t	d	tx	r		c	ts	k	q	(ʔ)
ph	**plh**	**th**	**dh**	**txh**	**rh**		**ch**	**tsh**	**kh**	**qh**	
m		n					ny		g		
hm		**hn**					**hny**				
f		x			s		xy				h
v		l			z		y				
		hl									

Table 7. The full set of Hmong consonants, as transcribed in the Romanized system. The complex consonants with pre-nasalization are shown in bold type. /'/ represents absence of initial consonant. Sounds in brackets are found only in Hmong Leng and will be discussed in the next section.

Lips		Teeth				Front Palate		Back Palate	Uvula	Vocal Cords
p	pl	t	d	tx	r	c	ts	k	q	(?)
ph	plh	th	dh	txh	rh	ch	tsh	kh	qh	
np	**npl**	**nt**	**[ndl]**	**ntx**	**nr**	**nc**	**nts**	**nk**	**nq**	
nph	**nplh**	**nth**	**[ndlh]**	**ntxh**	**nrh**	**nch**	**ntsh**	**nkh**	**nqh**	
m	**nl**	n				ny		g		
hm	**hnl**	hn				hny				
f		x			s	xy				h
v		l			z	y				
		hl								,

fore most of the consonants already discussed. This phenomenon almost doubles the number of consonants. The puff of air is represented by an h̲ included as part of the consonant symbol, as may be seen in Table 6.

The final type of complex consonant has a slight nasal sound preceding the other features. It is not always possible to hear the nasal when the consonant comes in a word spoken alone, but it becomes quite clear when following another word. This nasal consonant feature is represented by n̲ in the Romanized transcription, as may be seen in Table 7.

Syllable Structure

Most spoken Hmong syllables, then, consist of a consonant (simple or complex), followed by a vowel (simple or complex) with a simultaneous tone (simple or complex). This combination can be pictured as

CVᵗ

With thirteen vowels times fifty-nine consonants times seven tones, there are theoretically 5,369 such syllables in Hmong Daw. (The eighth tone adds a few more possibilities, of course.)

There are also, however, a very few words where Hmong syllables do not begin with any consonant at all. This lack of an initial consonant is represented with '̲ in the Romanized spelling. Such words only occur at the end of a grammatical expression of some kind, and although there are not many of them, some of them are used fairly frequently. A few examples follow:

Mus ua dab tsi 'o ᏁR ŴÀ ƎⱮ ÅK ᏰᏩ 'What are you going to do?'
Lawv 'e ᏇᎷ ᏯᏩ (expression of concern)
Txhob ua li ko 'auj ᏍᏘ ŴÀ ÅᎷ Ꮻ ᏰᏩ 'Stop it'

This much smaller number of syllables can be pictured as

V^t

This structure provides a few more potential syllables to those enumerated in the preceding paragraph.

Many of the potential syllables of Hmong are not actually used, however. Some consonants are very rare, occurring in only a few words. The consonant symbol g (representing /ŋ/ as in English *sing*, but occurring at the beginning of a few Hmong syllables), for example, is listed in only three words in one Hmong dictionary, and in no words in another. Also, there are not many cases were seven different words are distinguished only by the seven tones, as in Table 1. Most combinations of consonants and vowels are to be found with only two or three tones. The possible syllables which do not actually occur are potential sources for new words, however.

Pronunciation Values of the Romanized Consonant Symbols. With that overview of the consonant system, here follows a rough guide to the values of the letters in the Romanized system of transcribing Hmong consonants:

	(no written consonant symbol) [ʔ] similar to *oh-oh!*. iᒥ 'one' (ib ᏁÅ)
'	(no initial spoken consonant, not even [ʔ]). muᏞhoᏞ tuaᐸ 'oᐷ 'come again' (Mus ho tuaj 'ov ᏁR ᏰᎮ ᏁᏬ ᏰᏩ)
c	[t̪] very roughly similar to *jam*. ceᐸ 'leg' (ceg Ᏺᐯ)
ch	[t̪h] very roughly similar to *change*. cheᒥ 'sweep' (cheb ᏇᏋ)
d	Hmong Daw: [ʔd] roughly similar to English *do*. deᒥ 'distant' (deb ᏇⱮ)
	Hmong Leng: [tL] nothing similar in English. Sometimes spelled dl or tl.
dh	Hmong Daw: [ʔth] nothing similar in English. dhiaᒥ 'jump' (dhia ÅⱮ)
	Hmong Leng: [tLh] sometimes roughly similar to *climb*. Sometimes spelled tlh or dlh.
dl	see d
dlh	see dh

f   similar to *fat*. fiʟ 'to be acquainted with' (fim ʌč)

g   [ŋ] similar to *sing*. oʟ guʟ 'goose' (os gus ᴆiʌ ṅu̇)

h   similar to *hat*. huʟ 'call' (hu ṅⲓⲣ)

hl   [Ll] nothing similar in English. hliʟ 'moon' (hli ʌ4)

hm   [Mm] similar to *Hm!* hmooᒋ 'Hmong' (hmoob ᴃɛ̌)

hml   see hnl

hn   [Nn] nothing similar in English. hnaᒋ 'bag, sack' (hnab Ƨʜ)

hnl   [Mml] nothing similar in English. hnloʟ 'dented' (hnlos
        ᴆiʋ). Some people write hml or mlh.

hny   [Ññ] nothing similar in English. hnyaⲕ 'heavy' (hnyav ʋɛ̇)

k   very roughly similar to *gift*. keⲕ 'road' (kev ᴃ)

kh   similar to *cake*. khiʟ 'tie' (khi ʌʌ)

l   similar to *leave*. leⲕ 'mat' (lev ʜln)

m   similar to *man*. meʟ 'pen' (mem u̇ʀ)

ml   see nl

mlh   see hnl

n   similar to *now*. nuⲕ 'catch with a hook' (nuv ⲚU)

nc   [ñḍ] roughly similar to *enjoy*. nceⳊ 'post, pillar' (ncej ᴆu̇)

nch   [ñṭh] roughly similar to *can chew*. nchuaⲕ 'spill' (nchuav
        ᴡꞏ)

ndl   [ndl] (Hmong Leng only) similar to *candle*. ndluaⲕ 'throw
        out (liquid)' (ndluav ᴡč)

ndlh   [ntLh] (Hmong Leng only) similar to *mantle*. ndlhiⳊ
        ndlhuaⳊ 'sound of walking through mud' (ndlhij ndlhuaj
        ʌč ñč)

nk   [ŋg] similar to *anger*. nkawⳊ 'wasp, hornet' (nkawj ⲓⲥn)

nkh   [ŋkh] similar to *incongruous*. nkhauʟ 'crooked' (nkhaus ᴆⲘ)

nl   [ml] similar to *hamlet*. nloʟ 'statue' (nlom ᴆu̇). Some people
        write ml.

np   [mb] similar to *combine*. npeʟ 'name' (npe ḣã)

nph   [mph] similar to *compute*. nphauʟ 'turbulent' (nphau ᴆu̇)

npl   [mbl] similar to *emblem*. nploⳊ 'Lao' (nplog ᴆⲘ)

nplh   [mphL] similar to *complain*. nplhaiᒋ 'finger ring' (nplhaib
        ʜᴃ)

nq   [ŋg] nothing similar in English. nqeeᒋ 'thatch grass' (nqeeb
        ᴠu̇)

nqh   [ŋkh] nothing similar in English. nqhuaᒋ 'dried up' (nqhuab
        ᴎu̇)

nr   [ṇḍ] roughly similar to *can drink*. nroⳊ 'vegetation, weeds'
        (nroj ᴆč)

nrh   [n̥tʰ] roughly similar to *control*. nrhiav̌ 'look for' (nrhiav ᨠᨬ̇)

nt   [nd] similar to *endanger*. ntev̌ 'long' (ntev ᨳᨮ̌)

nth   [ntʰ] similar to *contend*. nthuav̌ 'open' (nthuav ᨓᨾ)

nts   [ndž] roughly similar to *and Zaza (Gabor)*. ntseˌ 'fish' (ntses ᨶ̄ᨩ)

ntsh   [ntšh] similar to *can chop*. ntshaiˌ 'fear' (ntshai ᨶᨲ̌)

ntx   [ndz] similar to *and Xerox*. ntxuav̌ 'wash' (ntxuav ᨓᨳ̇)

ntxh   [ntsh] similar to *ants here*. ntxhaiˌ 'daughter' (ntxhais ᨶ̄ᨲ̇)

ny   [ñ] roughly similar to *onion*. nyoˌ 'be at' (nyob ᨶᨲ̌)

ph   [pʰ] similar to *pan*. pheˌ 'evil, bad' (phem ᨳᨲ̌)

plh   [pʰʟ] similar to *plan*. plhuˌ 'cheek' (plhu ᨶ̇ᨾ)

q   [ḳ] roughly similar to *go*. quˌ 'old' (qub ᨓᨴ̌)

qh   [ḳʰ] similar to *coffee*. qhev̌ 'servant' (qhev ᨳᨦ)

r   [ʈ] nothing similar in English. riˌ 'carry on the back' (ris ᨩᨲ̄)

rh   [ʈʰ] roughly similar to *trough*. rhawv̌ 'tank, water tower' (rhawv ᨰᨲ̌)

s   [š] roughly similar to *ship*. siˌ 'try, test' (sim ᨳ̌ᨲ)

t   [t] roughly similar to *dip*. teˌ 'field' (teb ᨳᨲ̇)

th   [tʰ] similar to *tan*. theˌ 'pay' (them ᨳᨲ̇)

tl   see d̲

tlh   see d̲h̲

tsh   [tšʰ] similar to *change*. tsheˌ 'vehicle' (tsheb ᨳᨲ̇)

txh   [tsh] roughly similar to *fits him*. txhiv̌ 'redeem, ransom' (txhiv ᨳᨴ̇)

v   similar to *vat*. vaˌ 'garden' (vaj ᨛᨩ)

x   [s] similar to *see*. xov̌ 'to fence' (xov ᨵᨠ)

xy   [ɕy] roughly similar to *mash your (finger)*. xyooˌ 'bamboo' (xyoob ᨳᨯ̇)

y   similar to *yes*. yoˌ 'to be true' (yog ᨳᨴᨓ)

z   [ž] similar to *azure*. zeˌzoˌ 'village' (zejzog ᨳ̇ᨲ ᨳ̇ᨲ̇)

The most obvious difference in the pronunciation of consonants between Hmong Leng and Hmong Daw is that Hmong Leng does not
have the consonants /hm/, /hn/, /hny/ or /hnl/:

Hmong Daw	Hmong Leng
hm	m
hn	n
hny	ny
hnl	nl

This means that a Hmong Daw word beginning with /hm/ will be pronounced in Hmong Leng as beginning with /m/. So the very name of the people is pronounced with /hm/ by the Hmong Daw and /m/ by the Hmong Leng (thus the alternate spelling Mong Leng). Even someone who does not know the language can listen to Hmong people talking and pick out which dialect is being used, by noticing the presence or absence of the puff of air through the nose.

The other major differences in consonants between Hmong Daw and Hmong Leng are that speakers of the two dialects pronounce the sounds written as syllable-initial d and dh differently, and that Hmong Leng has an additional ndl and ndlh [8] which Hmong Daw does not have. These have been noted in Table 7 and in the descriptions of consonant pronunciations above.

Romanized Spelling	*Hmong Daw Pronunciation*	*Hmong Leng Pronunciation*
d	[ʔd]	[tL]
dh	[ʔth]	[tLh]
ndl		[ndl]
ndlh		[ntLh]

As the Romanized transcription was originally designed, the regular consonant differences were to be spelled the same way. Thus d was to be used for both [ʔd] in Hmong Daw and for [tL] in Hmong Leng, each group to read it in their own way. In many words the meaning would be the same. For example, *deb* ᴜⁱⁿ has the same meaning 'distant' in both dialects, but is pronounced [ʔdeꜜ] in Hmong Daw and [tLeꜜ] in Hmong Leng. Likewise, a word like /hmoŋꜜ/ in Hmong Daw and /moŋꜜ/ in Hmong Leng would both be spelled Hmoob.

This spelling feature of the Romanized system has been resisted by some Hmong Leng, however, on the grounds that the symbols in English or French stood for sounds more like the Hmong Daw sounds. Such people among the Hmong Leng tend to write the sounds as tl or dl and tlh or dlh. They are also the ones who prefer the alternate spelling of Mong. This issue concerning the Romanized transcription becomes especially interesting when we see in Chapters 4 and 11 how it is handled in the Pahawh Hmong.

Although these comparisons (and those of the vowels earlier) give the major systematic sound correspondences between the two dialects, there are many words which provide exceptions from them. There are also words in the two dialects with the same meanings which do not correspond in pronunciation at all (like "pavement" and "sidewalk" in British and American English). But in spite of such differences, speakers of Hmong Daw and Hmong Leng do understand each other, and if they can read well, they can normally read material written in the other dialect.

4

The Writing System

Shong Lue Yang developed the Pahawh Hmong writing system through four stages, all of which need to be described if we are to understand the process of its creation and the perception of language which lies behind it. The third of the four stages is being promoted as the current "standard" by the principal users of the writing outside of Laos and is the subject of this chapter.

The Vowel Symbols

Table 8 contains the basic Pahawh Hmong symbols for what Shong Lue Yang named *yub* or, as translated by users of the system, 'vowels'. To the right of the table of characters are the corresponding names of the individual symbols, written in Romanized Hmong. In the primary cases where Hmong Leng differs in pronunciation from Hmong Daw, the former is represented in brackets. The same Pahawh Hmong symbol is read differently by people of the respective groups, according to their dialect.

The "names" of the Pahawh Hmong symbols are more than arbitrary terms, however. In English the names for letters a, b, c, etc., (called "ay," "be," "see") sometimes bear little relation to the sounds they represent. The names for e and i ("ee" and "ai") are not to be heard in words like *bet* and *tin*, although they are in the second vowel of *extreme* and in *time*. The names for f and k ("ef" and "kay") are partly to be heard in *fill* and *kick*, but only the /f/ and /k/ parts, not the vowels pronounced along with them.

The Pahawh Hmong is much more consistent, and in some ways more complex than English in this regard. To take an example, the name for the character **V** (in the first line of the table) is *keeb*, and any word or any syllable pronounced /keeb/ is written simply as **V**. Thus **V** means 'yeast, leaven', and **ꓩ** /keev/ correspondingly means 'whole, solid'. In these cases the way the symbol is read is the same as the name

Table 8. Pahawh Hmong vowel symbols, names transcribed in Romanized Hmong. The Romanized transcription must be read in light of the information in Chapter 3. Note especially that the final b and v are not consonants, but represent the ⌐ and Υ tones, respectively. Transcriptions in brackets represent Hmong Leng pronunciation where that differs from Hmong Daw.

Ʋ	Ɔ	keeb	keev
∧	Ⴟ	kib	kiv
ฤ	◫	kaub	kauv
ᨕ	Ⴖ	kub	kuv
ʊ	Ⴌ	keb	kev
H	ᙁ	kaib	kaiv
Ⴘ	ᨓ	koob	koov
π	Ⴊ	kawb	kawv
ᨏ	Ɯ	kuab	kuav
ᨐ	ᨑ	kob	kov
ᛁᛁ	ᛆ	kiab [kab]	kiav [kav]
Ɔ	Ʊ	kab [kaab]	kav [kaav]
Ⴀ	Ⴑ	kwb	kwv

Table 9. Pahawh Hmong vowel symbols (Table 8) correlated with Hmong spoken vowels in Romanized orthography (Chapter 3). As they stand alone, the pairs of Pahawh Hmong symbols also represent tones ⌐ and Υ, and an associated initial /k/. Transcriptions in brackets represent Hmong Leng pronunciations corresponding to the Hmong Daw.

	Front	Central	Back
High	i	w	u
	∧ Ⴟ	Ⴀ Ⴑ	ᨕ Ⴖ
Low	e	a[aa]	o
	ʊ Ⴌ	Ɔ Ʊ	ᨐ ᨑ
Nasalized	ee		oo
	Ʋ Ɔ		Ⴘ ᨓ
Glided down	ia[a]		ua
	ᛁᛁ ᛆ		ᨏ Ɯ
Glided up	ai	aw	au
	H ᙁ	π ᨓ	ฤ ◫

of the symbol. As we shall see later, however, this is only true when the initial consonant of the pronounced syllable is /k/.

The Pahawh Hmong would therefore seem at this first glance to be a "syllabic" writing system rather than an "alphabetic" system. In an alphabetic system each individual phoneme, or some significant sound unit smaller than a syllable, is spelled with a different character, while in a syllabic system each individual syllable has its own character. To write the Romanized <u>keeb</u> is to write alphabetically, with one symbol for the initial /k/, another for the vowel /e/, a doubling of the vowel symbol to indicate the nasalization, and a final symbol <u>b</u> for the tone. **V**, however, seems at first to represent the whole composite of /keeb/, consonant, vowel and tone, all in one symbol. All of the Pahawh Hmong symbols in Table 8 work this same way. In addition to being the name of the symbol, each of the pronunciations at the right of the table is spelled in full by the corresponding single Pahawh Hmong character.

The spoken vowels described for Hmong pronunciation in the last chapter are shown again in Table 9, along with corresponding Pahawh Hmong characters, two for each spoken vowel. All the spoken vowels are represented in the Pahawh Hmong.

The Tone Symbols

In Table 10, however, we see that the version of the Pahawh Hmong which we are examining in this chapter is not a syllabic writing system. Smaller sound units than the syllable are individually represented. In six of the columns in Table 10 the tones are separately written as diacritics over the vowel characters. In contrast, in the other two columns the characters first seen in Table 8 indicate tone by lack of diacritics.

The truly unusual feature of the Pahawh Hmong vowel system which is clarified in Table 10 is that there are two classes of vowel symbols associated with two groups of spoken tones. Four of the eight Hmong tones are represented with vowel symbols of one class, the other four with vowel symbols of the other class. The names for these classes are *yub teeb* **ⴄⵏⵓ ⵖ⳦** 'beginning vowel' and *yub txauv* **ⴄⵏⵓ ⵁⵖ** 'following, replacement vowel'.

Each spoken vowel quality is represented in both classes of symbols. Which of the two symbols for a vowel is used to spell the vowel depends on the tone. In some cases the same tone mark occurs with both vowel classes; the ¯ , for example, represents ⵕ (j-tone) in **ⵖ** *keej* but ⵏ (s-tone) in **ⴃ** *kees*. The two-class system of vowel symbols reduces the number of tone diacritics required, but doubles the number of vowel symbols. The development and significance of this two-class system will be discussed in the next chapter.

In typical publications which introduce the Pahawh Hmong writing system, all eight tones are laid out as in Table 10, the type of display Shong Lue Yang initiated (without the Romanized transcription, of

Table 10. Tone writing in relation to vowels in Pahawh Hmong, with corresponding Romanized transcription. Tone values are shown at the top of each column. Pronunciations in brackets are Hmong Leng, where it differs from Hmong Daw.

Γ	L	ⱽ	ᐱ	Y	⊦	⊢	ᐱ
keeb	keem	keed	keej	keev	kee	kees	keeg
kib	kim	kid	kij	kiv	ki	kis	kig
kaub	kaum	kaud	kauj	kauv	kau	kaus	kaug
kub	kum	kud	kuj	kuv	ku	kus	kug
keb	kem	ked	kej	kev	ke	kes	keg
kaib	kaim	kaid	kaij	kaiv	kai	kais	kaig
koob	koom	kood	kooj	koov	koo	koos	koog
kawb	kawm	kawd	kawj	kawv	kaw	kaws	kawg
kuab	kuam	kuad	kuaj	kuav	kua	kuas	kuag
kob	kom	kod	koj	kov	ko	kos	kog
kiab [kab]	kiam [kam]	kiad [kad]	kiaj [kaj]	kiav [kav]	kia [ka]	kias [kas]	kiag [kag]
kab [kaab]	kam [kaam]	kad [kaad]	kaj [kaaj]	kav [kaav]	ka [kaa]	kas [kaas]	kag [kaag]
kwb	kwm	kwd	kwj	kwv	kw	kws	kwg

course). In some publications, however, the d-tone /ⱽ/ is not included in the table. It is treated separately because it occurs only in a few words, as a systematic alternate to the m-tone /L/.

There are no names for the individual spoken tones in Hmong except for the d-tone, which is referred to as *suab yuas* ⱎⱎ. This term is also used more generally for the category of tone itself. Hmong people also speak of tones descriptively as the voice going up and down. But there are names for all of the individual written diacritics in the Pahawh Hmong system, the Pahawh Hmong terminology being oriented toward visual symbols more than toward sounds.

Diacritic	Name		
(dot)	ÀV ᴜɜ̃	cim tub
–	ÀV Ḃ	cim kes
··	ÀV ɾɔ̃	cim taum
˅	ÀV ɓɯ̃	cim so

The Consonant Symbols

Table 11, in turn, displays the Pahawh Hmong consonants, called *las*. In some Pahawh Hmong publications the consonant symbols with diacritics (column 1) are presented first as the basic consonant symbols (as vowels are in Table 8 above); then the full table follows, as shown here.

In Table 11 each symbol is a unit, including its diacritic, and represents an individual Hmong spoken consonant, simple or complex. Unlike those in Table 10, the diacritics here have no independent value. They are like the dot on an i̱ in English.

This difference can be seen by comparing the columns and rows of Table 10 with those of Table 11. In Table 10 each column has one tone, the tone of each column different from those in each of the other col-

Table 11. Pahawh Hmong consonant symbols, with Romanized transcriptions. [ʔ] is the glottal stop, which is not written in the Romanized alphabet. Other pronunciations in brackets are Hmong Leng where it differs from Hmong Daw.

Sym 1	Sym 2	Sym 3			
ℂ	Ċ	Č	vau	nrau	fau
n	ṅ	ñ	nkau	ntxau	rhau
A	Ȧ	Ä	xau	[ʔ]au	nyau
V	V̇	V̈	cau	ntshau	txau
ɯ	ɯ̇	ɯ̈	lau	dau	dhau
				[dlau]	[dlhau]
K	K̇	K̈	ntsau	tsau	phau
Ҷ	Ҷ̇	Ҷ̈	hlau	zau	ntxhau
ʮ	ʮ̇	ʮ̈	rau	nphau	nphlau
Ж	Ж̇	Ӝ	hnau	khau	ntau
m	ṁ	m̈	plhau	tshau	pau
M	Ṁ	M̈	nthau	nplau	nkhau
Ж	Ж̇	Ӝ	chau	xyau	tau
U	U̇	Ü	nau	nqau	nqhau
℉	℉̇	℉̈	nlau	hnlau	gau
E	Ė	Ë	qhau	nyhau	hmau
ɼ	ɼ̇	ɼ̈	hau	thau	plau
Ħ	Ḣ	Ḧ	nchau	nrhau	npau
R	Ṙ	R̈	mau	txhau	qau
ɯ	ɯ̇	ɯ̈	yau	ncau	sau
ɤ	ɤ̇	ɤ̈	'au	ndlau	ndlhau

umns. Each row, furthermore, has one vowel sound. In Table 11, however, there is no common pronunciation feature to any column or to most rows. All the consonant diacritics do is reduce the number of basic consonant symbols which are required, without in themselves representing any linguistic feature.

One of the consonant diacritics, ˙ , is the same as one which occurs on vowels and is called by the same term, *cim tub* ꕶ ꕥ, but its function is very different in these two parts of the system. The diacritic not used also as a vowel diacritic, ˉ , is called *cim hom* ꕶ ꕺꕰ.

As with the vowels, the names of the consonant symbols sometimes represent full syllables. The word *tau* 'can, be able' can be spelled ꕭ, without an additional vowel or tone symbol for the /auꓩ/, for example. For this to be possible, the tone has to be ꓩ (unmarked in the Romanized), and the previous character must not be a vowel character, lest people read the combination as a single syllable instead of two.

In the following example the instances of ꕔ *rau* can be written as individual characters because there is no immediately preceding vowel character.

ꕔ ꕥꕰ ꕔ ꕥ ꕥꖇ rau tshais rau koj noj 'serve breakfast to you'

But the addition of the word ꘉ *kuv* before the first occurrence of *rau* causes the latter to be spelled ꕺꕔ, as in the next example. Otherwise the combination ꘉ ꕔ could be confused for ꘉꕔ *ruv* 'roof'.

ꘉ ꕺꕔ ꕥꕰ ꕔ ꕥ ꕥꖇ kuv rau tshais rau koj noj 'I serve breakfast to you' [Incorrect: ꘉ ꕔ ꕥꕰ ꕔ ꕥ ꕥꖇ]

The /auꓩ/ part of the various names for the consonants is not as fully inherent in the consonant symbol as the /k/ is in the vowel symbol, however. There is no separate consonant symbol at all for /k/, but there are separate /au/ vowel symbols with a full set of tones in each vowel class: ꕹ ꕯ (Table 10).

Whereas Table 10 shows that Shong Lue Yang was able to abstract tones from vowels, Table 11 shows only a consciousness of overall contrast between the consonants, not an awareness of the different features of the complex consonants. He did not isolate any consonantal pronunciation features like puff of air or pre-nasalization, discussed in the last chapter. In other words, /t/, /th/, /nt/, /nth/ are represented unambiguously and consistently as ꕭ ꕬ ꕫ ꕮ, and /p/, /ph/, /np/, /nph/ as ꕥ ꕦ ꕧ ꕨ, but the pronunciation parallels between /p/ and /t/, /ph/ and /th/, /np/ and /nt/, /nph/ and /nth/ are not captured in the Pahawh Hmong system. Each consonant symbol for single or complex spoken consonants has to be learned independently.

Table 12. Pahawh Hmong consonant symbols compared with spoken consonants of Hmong (Chapter 3)

Lips		Teeth				Front Palate		Back Palate	Uvula	Vocal Cords
p	pl	t	d	tx	r	c	ts	k (vowel)	q	(2)
ph	plh	th	dh	txh	rh	ch	tsh	kh	qh	
np	npl	nt	[ndl]	ntx	nr	nc	nts	nk	nq	
nph	nplh	nth	[ndlh]	ntxh	nrh	nch	ntsh	nkh	nqh	
m	nl	n				ny		g		
hm	hnl	hn				hny				
f	x				s	xy				h
v	l				z	y				
	hl									'

Table 12 shows that there is a Pahawh Hmong consonant symbol for every spoken consonant in Hmong Daw, except for /k/. /k/ is therefore consistently and unambiguously represented by lack of any consonant symbol, just as in the Romanized system there is no symbol for /ʔ/. In either case, so long as only one consonant does not have a symbol, there is no ambiguity in reading or writing.

As Table 12 also shows, the Pahawh Hmong has characters for the two extra spoken consonants in Hmong Leng, ndl ndlh ⊽ ⊽, as well as for all of the consonants of Hmong Daw and those common to the two dialects.[1] There is also a symbol ⊽ for no initial consonant (transcribed with ' in the Romanized), and Å for initial /ʔ/ (no consonant in the Romanized). As with the vowels and tones, the fit[2] with the spoken language is perfect.

Combinations of Vowels and Consonants

Individual Pahawh Hmong symbols and syllables follow each other from left to right across the page, like English. But an unusual feature is that within each syllable the written order does not follow the spoken

Table 13. Examples of Pahawh Hmong vowel and consonant combinations within syllables

Vowel	+	Tone	+	Consonant	=	Syllable	Meaning
ᵾ		(unmarked)		Ě		ᵾĚ	
oo		b		hm		Hmoob	Hmong
ᴫ		‾		ảᵢ		ᴫảᵢ	
ua		j		t		tuaj	come
ᴚ		(unmarked)		(unmarked)		ᴚ	
e		v		k		kev	road
ᴕ		·		ᴯ		ᴯᴯ	
i		(unmarked)		kh		khi	tie
ᴚ		(unmarked)		ᵬ		ᴚᵬ	
ai		b		nplh		nplhaib	finger ring
		(unmarked)		ῐ̆		ῐ̆	
au		(unmarked)		pl		plau	run away

order. The syllable has the vowel, with its tone, written first even though the consonant is spoken first:

> *Structure of the*   *Structure of the*
> *Written Syllable*   *Spoken Syllable*
> V^t kV^t
> V^tC CV^t
> V^tC V^t
> C $Cau\vdash$

In effect, the vowel is the nucleus, the heart of the written syllable, with the tone written as a diacritic on the vowel. The consonant, likewise, is appended, following the vowel nucleus as a satellite, a qualification of the vowel, unless it is the inherent /k/, which is not separately symbolized at all. On the other hand, the consonant is written alone if the vowel and tone are /au⊦/ and the symbol immediately preceding it is not a vowel. Table 13 shows some examples.

Pahawh Hmong written text is very compact. Its greater compactness than the Romanized is due to the fact that each consonant and each vowel, whether simple or complex, is represented with a single symbol, a characteristic not available from the smaller number of characters of the Roman alphabet. Tones are also written as diacritics rather than as symbols on the line. Here is one sentence written in both Pahawh Hmong and Romanized writing systems for comparison:

ᑐ ᑌ ᑎ ᑕ ᗅ ᕼ ᗰ ᗅᕮ ᗅᔑ ᑐ ᐯᗩ ᑎᔑ ᑐᛕ ᗰᒋ ᑌᕮ ᑕᒋ ᑫᛕᗷᛕ.

Yaj Soob Lwj twb pib kev cob qhia tib neeg nyeem tus Phaj hauj
Hmoob thaum 1959.

'Shong Lue Yang began teaching people to read the Pahawh
Hmong in 1959'.

Such, then, is the present "standard" version of the Pahawh Hmong.
It is an alphabetical system,[3] fitting the pronunciation of the Hmong
language perfectly, compactly and relatively efficiently. A number of
additional non-alphabetical symbols like numerals and symbols for clan
names will be described in Chapter 6.

Puzzling Interpretation

Most of Shong Lue Yang's work on the Pahawh Hmong, both that described in this chapter and what is to come, is easily interpretable in
the terms of Western linguistics, even when it departs from what Western linguists would be likely to do. There is one intriguing detail, however, which Smalley finds puzzling. This detail is not in the writing
system itself, but in how Shong Lue and the Hmong authors of this
book understand the relationship between the tones.

Figure 2 reproduces a type of diagram, first worked out by Chia
Koua Vang and repeated with variations in other Pahawh Hmong publications and manuscripts. The diagram explains the Pahawh Hmong
tone symbolization in relation to the spoken tones. The model displays
tones which occur with the written vowels of the first vowel class (described above) in order of ascending height, followed by tones on vowels
of the second class in order of descending height. The phonetic repre-
sentations of the tones from Chapter 3 are included in Figure 2 for
comparison.

Some parts of this model correspond well with the linguist's phonetic
perceptions, which are based largely on pitch. Starting with the lowest
tone pictured on the right side of the model, ᐱ (g-tone ¨ [on second-
class vowels]) is frequently called "low breathy" by linguists. It is
usually described as starting with low pitch and tapering off with an
additional "breathy" quality (although that is not how we pictured it in
this book for reasons described in Chapter 3). If the tone is perceived as
low, then the stair-step positions of the two tones preceding it in the
model also make good sense to the linguist.

The ᐱ (v-tone [no Pahawh Hmong diacritic on second-class vowels])
also makes sense from the standpoint of the final high point on the pitch
glide. Nor is ᐱ (j-tone ¯ [on first-class vowels]) a problem from the

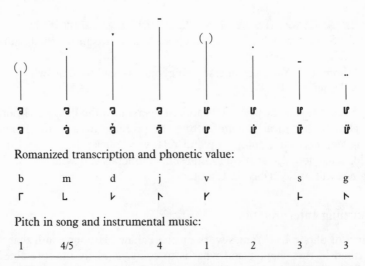

Romanized transcription and phonetic value:

b	m	d	j	v		s	g
⌐	L	⌐	⌐	⌐		⌐	⌐

Pitch in song and instrumental music:

1	4/5		4	1	2	3	3

Fig. 2. Model of relationship between Hmong spoken tones (after Chia Koua Vang 1976; Yang 1983), as described by Shong Lue and the Hmong authors, compared to Smalley's phonetic representation (Chapter 3) and typical musical pitches used for the respective tones in Hmong song and instrumental music (Catlin 1982: 178; 1986: 14). Musical pitch 1 represents the highest pitch, 4 or 5 the lowest, depending on whether a four or five pitch system is being used.

standpoint of the high start of the glide, although why the model would show the end point of a glide in one case and the beginning point in the other is a puzzle. In similar fashion, down the left side of the model, the next two stair-step tones fit in well, although the m-tone seems much too high in relation to the right side of the model. But placing ⌐ (b-tone [no diacritic on first-class vowels]) at the beginning, where it represents a medium-low tone, is incomprehensible to Smalley. Phonetically the pitch of this tone is the highest of all.

Adding to the puzzle is the fact that Shong Lue was a talented musician who played instruments like the *nraj pum liv,* a Hmong flute, so he was accustomed to musical notes as well as speech tones. Hmong song and instrumental music represent speech directly (though not always clearly) by transforming the speech tones of poems in loosely stylized fashion into notes of music.[4] Hmong people can translate such music directly into words more or less accurately, depending on the instrument, the type of music and their skill. They claim that every Hmong person can at least get the gist of what is "said" by the music.

In Hmong music ⌐ (b-tone [no Pahawh Hmong diacritic]) is typically sounded on the highest note of the musical system, and L (m-tone ˙) on the lowest. (There is variation between different occurrences of such tones in different contexts, so these generalizations represent statistical norms.) The ᴎ(j-tone ⁻), furthermore, is sounded at the fourth musical level down, which is the lowest level in a four-level system, or next-to-lowest in a five-level system, and the ⴸ(v-tone [no diacritic]) is sounded at the highest level. In both these cases the end point, not the beginning point, is represented by the note (or possibly upward glide is "high" and downward glide is "low"). At any rate, the music corresponds rather well to the Western linguists' phonetic interpretation of the spoken tones, and makes it even more difficult to understand why Shong Lue, an acute observer, described some of the tones as he did.

Discussion of this question with the Hmong authors has not clarified this question for Smalley. They find no problem with the model, saying that it represents the way they hear the tones. Perhaps some other feature than pitch is the salient one to them, at least on some of the tones, and the ordering of the tones is completely or partially dependent on it.

But the writing system described in this chapter does not depend on such interpretations. The contrasts are all represented. Furthermore, this is not the Pahawh Hmong that Shong Lue Yang first began to teach, which was different in some very significant ways. In the next chapter we offer a description of the first system and its evolution to what we have described here, and to one more still later system. This progression shows the development of Shong Lue Yang's linguistic understanding.

5

Evolution of the Writing System

To speak of the development of the Pahawh Hmong as occurring in four stages may be a bit misleading. To be more precise, there were four stages of development in the writing of vowels and tones; for the consonants there were only two stages. All of the stages in the vowels and tones show progression in simplification, and some show progression in linguistic abstraction; the consonant stage changes, on the other hand, involve simplification alone.[1]

There is a big difference in appearance between the Source Version (1959) of the Pahawh Hmong and the other versions which followed. The vowel tables of the two middle versions, in turn, look more alike than do any other pairs. These two are also grouped together in Hmong terminology, both being called *Pahawh Njia* (**ɔ̌ǩ ɑ̄ᴦ ᴜᴋ** Phajhauj Ntsiab), which implies an alphabet reduced in number by selecting the best and most essential (Table 14). Linguistically, however, the major

Table 14. The four versions of Pahawh Hmong

Date	Hmong Name	English Name
1. 1959	**ɔ̌ǩ ɑ̄ᴦ ɔ̌m̂** Phajhauj Paj 'flower, origin, source alphabet'	Source Version
2. 1965	**ɔ̌ǩ ɑ̄ᴦ ᴜᴋ ṻṁ ᴍÀ** Phajhauj Ntsiab Duas Ob 'kernel, heart, essence alphabet, Stage Two'	Second Stage Reduced Version
3. 1970	**ɔ̌ǩ ɑ̄ᴦ ᴜᴋ ṻṁ ᴜm̂** Phajhauj Ntsiab Duas Peb 'kernel, heart, essence alphabet, Stage Three'	Third Stage Reduced Version
4. 1971	**ɔ̌ǩ ɑ̄ᴦ ừŘ** Phajhauj Txha 'bone, hard core, important, essential alphabet'	Final Version

step in the development of the systems comes between the Second Stage (1965) and Third Stage (1970) Reduced Versions.

The Source Version

The Source Version, which Shong Lue Yang began to teach in May 1959, is called the *Pahawh Pa* (Phajhuaj Paj ꗶꗂ ꖳꖲ ꗶꖶ) in Hmong. *Pa* means 'flower', implying the 'original', the 'source' system, that from which the fruit comes. Referring later to the Source Version, Shong Lue said that you cannot eat the flower, but it must come before the fruit.

Table 15, showing the Source Version symbols for vowels and tones, is laid out in exactly the same arrangement as Table 10 in Chapter 4, which has the corresponding vowels and tones of the Third Stage. Major differences in appearance and structure between the two systems are immediately apparent on comparison.

The most basic structural difference is that every symbol in the Source Version was an individual unit representing a combination of vowel plus tone, whereas in the Third Stage tones were abstracted from vowels and written separately by use of diacritics. The symbols for the ninety-one combinations of vowel plus tone in the Source Version all had to be individually memorized. This means that the Source Version was a fully demi-syllabic system, with one unitary symbol representing the vowel-tone part of the syllable and another representing the consonantal part. It was thus slightly more like a syllabic system than is the version described in Chapter 4.

In the Source Version there was not yet, therefore, any division of vowels into two classes. The diacritics which were used (all dots except for two cases of underlinings (Ụ kus and Ụ kooj) helped to distinguish symbols, but did not represent any linguistic feature in themselves. There were sometimes similarities of shape between some of the symbols in a given row (symbols representing the same vowel quality), but the variations were not consistent from row to row. Subsequent versions like the Third Stage looked very different because they did not have this multitude of inconsistently different symbols.

Another difference between the Source Version and the Third Stage Version is that the d-tone was not included in the Source Version. As explained in Chapter 3, the d-tone occurs in relatively few words in Hmong speech. It is somewhat predictable on grammatical grounds, so that its omission is neither surprising nor particularly serious. Most writing systems are incomplete in some ways. All other vowel-tone combinations were represented in the Source Version.

Table 15. Vowel-tone symbols of Source Version (1959) of Pahawh Hmong. The d-tone was not written at this stage.

⌐	L	Ⴑ	↖	Ⴑ	⊢	⊦	↖
keeb	keem	keed	keej	keev	kee	kees	keeg
kib	kim	kid	kij	kiv	ki	kis	kig
kaub	kaum	kaud	kauj	kauv	kau	kaus	kaug
kub	kum	kud	kuj	kuv	ku	kus	kug
keb	kem	ked	kej	kev	ke	kes	keg
kaib	kaim	kaid	kaij	kaiv	kai	kais	kaig
koob	koom	kood	kooj	koov	koo	koos	koog
kawb	kawm	kawd	kawj	kawv	kaw	kaws	kawg
kuab	kuam	kuad	kuaj	kuav	kua	kuas	kuag
kob	kom	kod	koj	kov	ko	kos	kog
kiab [kab]	kiam [kam]	kiad [kad]	kiaj [kaj]	kiav [kav]	kia [ka]	kias [kas]	kiag [kag]
kab [kaab]	kam [kaam]	kad [kaad]	kaj [kaaj]	kav [kaav]	ka [kaa]	kas [kaas]	kag [kaag]
kwb	kwm	kwd	kwj	kwv	kw	kws	kwg

In spite of the radical differences in appearance and in structure between the two systems, however, there are also important similarities. For example, the tradition of displaying the vowels in columns according to tone, and the order of these columns, began with the Source Version. It is clear that Shong Lue Yang had perceptually isolated the tones from the vowels right from the start, even though he did not write them separately in the first version of his alphabet.

The conventions for naming vowel symbols, furthermore, began with the Source Version. The names were then carried over as the names for corresponding symbols in later versions. Using the vowel-tone symbols to represent full syllables for those syllables that begin with /k/ also started with the Source Version, as did writing vowels before consonants of the same syllable.

Table 16 shows the consonants of the Source Version in the same arrangement as Table 11 in Chapter 4, again the arrangement used by Shong Lue Yang from the beginning. The shapes of the symbols in a row were not yet regularized. There was sometimes similarity of shape between some consonants in a row, but not as much as in the vowel-tone symbols. The sixty consonant symbols, like the ninety-one vowel-tone symbols, had to be individually memorized.

In discussing the Third Stage Reduced Version, we mentioned that the transcription of vowels and tones showed more linguistic abstraction and ingenuity than did the transcription of consonants. The diacritics on the consonants served simply to reduce the number of basic consonant symbols required, whereas those on the vowels consistently represented tone. Although this advantage did not begin in the Source Version—where in neither group did symbols represent any linguistic feature below that of individual consonant (simple or complex) or individual vowel-tone—the structure of the vowel-tone table was more sophisticated than that of the consonant table even at that point. This was because there was good linguistic reason for rows and columns representing the combinations of vowels and tones, but not for those representing the consonants.

Table 16. Consonant symbols in Source Version (1959) of Pahawh Hmong

			vau	nrau	fau
			nkau	ntxau	rhau
			xau	[ʔ]au	nyau
			cau	ntshau	txau
			lau	dau	dhau
				[dlau]	[dlhau]
			ntsau	tsau	phau
			hlau	zau	ntxhau
			rau	nphau	nphlau
			hnau	khau	ntau
			plhau	tshau	pau
			nthau	nplau	nkhau
			chau	xyau	tau
			nau	nqau	nqhau
			nlau	hnlau	gau
			qhau	nyhau	hmau
			hau	thau	plau
			nchau	nrhau	npau
			mau	txhau	qau
			yau	ncau	sau
			ʼau	ndlau	ndlhau

The Source Version is the only stage of the Pahawh Hmong no longer in use in its entirety by anyone, so far as we know, although some people who learned it, like Pa Kao Her, one of the original teachers of the Source Version, still occasionally use individual symbols from it when writing in another version. All the other systems are still in use by different people.

But the system is not considered obsolete by those who carry on the traditions established by Shong Lue Yang. It is still the "source" in more than a historical sense. As subsequent systems were developed, Shong Lue himself saw all of them as latent within the Source Version. He told Chia Koua Vang, furthermore, that in the future the Source Version should be used for sacred purposes, in connection with prayers, sacred writings and traditional history. It should be taught and preserved in the worship center, the *tsev kheej*, the round building in which worship was to be conducted. None of this is being done at the present time, but Shong Lue's instructions are remembered and preserved as a hope for the future.

The First Revision: The Second Stage Reduced Version

In April 1965, just six years after he began to teach the Source Version, Shong Lue Yang made public the first revision of his writing system. This stage he called *Pahawh Njia Dua O* (Phajhauj Ntsiab Duas Ob ꘜꘝ ꘞꘟ ꘠꘡ ꘢꘣ ꘤꘥), which we have rendered in English as the Second Stage Reduced Version. *Njia* means 'essence, heart of the matter, kernel'. *Njia* is reached by selection among alternatives, thus 'reducing' the range. *Dua* means 'step, stage' in a process like cutting down a giant tree by cutting out one notch at a time. So in this 'second stage' Shong Lue selected from among the many symbols of the Source Version, reducing the number needed.

Visually and mnemonically the Second Stage Reduced Version is considerably simpler and more regular than the Source Version, but linguistically it is virtually the same. The number of vowel-tone symbols has been reduced from seven to two in each row (Table 17); the diacritics are also simpler, reduced to three in number, and placed in one uniform position above the basic symbols instead of being scattered around in different positions. The two basic symbols in each row were usually selected directly from the seven symbols of the corresponding row in the Source Version, sometimes modified in the transition. In a few cases they were taken from another row or were new.

But the diacritics of the Second Stage Reduced Version are still not independent tone markers. Different diacritics (or no diacritic) do not

Table 17. Vowel-tone symbols of Second Stage Reduced Version (1965) of Pahawh Hmong

Γ	L	ν	⌐	Y	⊢	⊦	⌐
keeb	keem	keed	keej	keev	kee	kees	keeg
kib	kim	kid	kij	kiv	ki	kis	kig
kaub	kaum	kaud	kauj	kauv	kau	kaus	kaug
kub	kum	kud	kuj	kuv	ku	kus	kug
keb	kem	ked	kej	kev	ke	kes	keg
kaib	kaim	kaid	kaij	kaiv	kai	kais	kaig
koob	koom	kood	kooj	koov	koo	koos	koog
kawb	kawm	kawd	kawj	kawv	kaw	kaws	kawg
kuab	kuam	kuad	kuaj	kuav	kua	kuas	kuag
kob	kom	kod	koj	kov	ko	kos	kog
kiab	kiam	kiad	kiaj	kiav	kia	kias	kiag
[kab]	[kam]	[kad]	[kaj]	[kav]	[ka]	[kas]	[kag]
kab	kam	kad	kaj	kav	ka	kas	kag
[kaab]	[kaam]	[kaad]	[kaaj]	[kaav]	[kaa]	[kaas]	[kaag]
kwb	kwm	kwd	kwj	kwv	kw	kws	kwg

consistently represent any tone, as a glance down any column will show. Also, in any row the division of vowels and tones between the two basic symbols is not always the same. In rows 3, 5, 7, 12 and 13, for example, the first symbol appears three times, the second symbol four, while in the other rows there are four symbols of the same shape first, followed by three of another.

The d-tone became available in the Second Stage Reduced Version, although it was not included in the vowel-tone tables. It was added when Chia Koua was learning this system. He already knew how to write Hmong in the Romanized system, with its d-tone, and asked Shong Lue Yang about how to write that tone in Pahawh Hmong. Shong Lue told him to use ˅ as a diacritic over the basic vowel of the left-hand set of vowels on each line.

The way in which the d-tone was written as a genuine diacritic is remarkable at this point because it was apparently the first tone to be written thus consistently, unless the Third Stage was already evolving in Shong Lue's mind. Shong Lue also showed Chia Koua where the d-tone would go in the table of vowels and tones, exactly as it appeared later in the Third Stage. However, when Chia Koua raised the question of including the d-tone in the table at the Second Stage, Shong Lue told him it was not to be included, but was to be treated as something extra.

Certainly not everyone learned how to write the d-tone at this stage. As we shall see in Chapter 8, when Chia Koua taught the Second Stage to Chai Lee (Txais Lis ꯁꯦ ꯑꯦꯟ), he neglected to teach him how to write it. As Chai Lee used the system, he sensed a need for the d-tone and devised his own way of marking it with a ꞉ after any syllable which has such a tone.[2] For him ꯁꯦ꞉ would be *ntawd* 'there' and ꯁꯦ꞉ would be *tid* 'over there'. Without the ꞉ the first of these examples would be *ntawm* 'there' and the second *tim* 'over there'. Chai Lee's way of writing this tone does not fit the system of writing the other tones in any version of Pahawh Hmong. It treats it more like an additional feature overlying the other tones. There is some linguistic validity to this, as the d-tone words generally have counterparts with other tones, as in the example above. In Shong Lue's writing, however, as in the Romanized transcription, the d-tone is symbolized as a separate tone.

There is no need to reproduce here the table of consonants for the Second Stage Reduced Version, as it is virtually identical with that of the Third Stage Reduced Version consonants (Table 11 of Chapter 4). These consonants were even more systematically simplified from the Source Version than were the vowels, because only one symbol was used for each row, and the diacritics were made consistent to each column, even though they had no independent meaning.

The only difference in consonants between the two stages in Chia Koua Vang's notes is that the Second Stage Reduced Version did not include the last line of the consonant table we have seen in both the Third Stage Reduced Version and the Source Version. There are only nineteen rows instead of twenty. In the Third Stage Reduced Version this missing row includes the symbol ꯕ ' (representing absence of initial glottal stop), plus the symbols ꯕ ndl and ꯕ ndlh (representing two consonants of Hmong Leng not found in Hmong Daw). Chia Koua believes that the exclusion was an oversight as he collected the information, and that these symbols already existed. Symbols for these sounds are to be found in the Source Version.

As in the case of the vowels, the Second Stage Reduced Version consonants were often selected from the Source Version consonants of the same row. But again, this did not always happen. Some symbols do not seem similar to anything in the corresponding row of the older version. Appearance of printed forms may be deceptive, however, and we do not have all the handwritten variants to compare.[3]

Chia Koua learned the Second Stage Reduced Version in Long Cheng after Shong Lue Yang moved there in 1966 and he went to study directly under Shong Lue for the first time. He was surprised to find that what Shong Lue was now teaching was different from what he had recorded in Tham Ha. By this time nobody was using the more difficult Source Version anymore.[4]

Changes in the Third Stage Reduced Version

In August 1970 Chia Koua Vang received a letter from Shong Lue Yang, written in prison, in a new version of the Pahawh Hmong which Chia Koua could not read. Chia Koua asked Shong Lue about the writing and noted down his explanation. This new version was the Third Stage Reduced Version, as described in detail in Chapter 4. Because at that time followers of Shong Lue Yang were being persecuted, most did not dare admit knowing any form of the system. There was therefore no general attempt to teach this new version, but Chia Koua was charged with preserving it and passing it along whenever that would be possible.

From a linguistic standpoint the development of the Third Stage Reduced Version was a far greater advance than was the Second Stage Reduced Version, although the earlier changes paved the way by rendering the vowel-tone table more regular.

The big change, of course, was in the independent indication of the tone. The separation of tones from vowels was a major step in the direction of a more abstract writing system representing directly more individual features of the spoken language. It also made memorization of the alphabet much easier. Instead of having to remember 91 symbols for vowel-tones (104 with the d-tone), the learner had to remember 26 vowel symbols (for 13 vowels), plus 4 tone diacritics.

In order to accomplish this reform, two simple but critical changes had to be made (Table 10). First, whereas the basic symbol in the v-tone column of the Second Stage Reduced Version sometimes matched the symbols to its left in the row, and other times matched the ones to its right, it was now made consistent, always matching the symbols to the right. The individual diacritics (and lack of them), likewise, were made to correspond consistently with the tone columns, and were no longer scattered all over the table. The second change was the recognition of the d-tone as being completely parallel to the other tones. These changes may have been stimulated by Chia Koua's questions.

There was no corresponding change in the consonants. They were already visually consistent in the previous version, although not in a way that would suggest a systematic correspondence with features of pronunciation.[5]

The Final Version

Only five months after Chia Koua recorded the Third Stage Reduced Version, Shong Lue Yang told him about still another major simplifica-

Table 18. Vowel and tone symbols of Final Version (1971) of Pahawh Hmong

Γ	L	ν	↖	ⲅ	ⲅ	⊢	↖
ᴠ	ᴠ̇	ᴠ̈	ᴠ̄	ᴠ̂	ᴠ̇	ᴠ̇	ᴠ̈
keeb	keem	keed	keej	keev	kee	kees	keeg
Λ	Λ̇	Λ̈	Λ̄	Λ̂	Λ̇	Λ̇	Λ̈
kib	kim	kid	kij	kiv	ki	kis	kig
�	ᴅ̇	ᴅ̈	ᴅ̄	ᴅ̂	ᴅ̇	ᴅ̇	ᴅ̈
kaub	kaum	kaud	kauj	kauv	kau	kaus	kaug
ᴜ	ᴜ̇	ᴜ̈	ᴜ̄	ᴜ̂	ᴜ̇	ᴜ̇	ᴜ̈
kub	kum	kud	kuj	kuv	ku	kus	kug
ᴜ	ᴜ̇	ᴜ̈	ᴜ̄	ᴜ̂	ᴜ̇	ᴜ̇	ᴜ̈
keb	kem	ked	kej	kev	ke	kes	keg
ʜ	ʜ̇	ʜ̈	ʜ̄	ʜ̂	ʜ̇	ʜ̇	ʜ̈
kaib	kaim	kaid	kaij	kaiv	kai	kais	kaig
ʜ	ʜ̇	ʜ̈	ʜ̄	ʜ̂	ʜ̇	ʜ̇	ʜ̈
koob	koom	kood	kooj	koov	koo	koos	koog
π	π̇	π̈	π̄	π̂	π̇	π̇	π̈
kawb	kawm	kawd	kawj	kawv	kaw	kaws	kawg
ɴ	ɴ̇	ɴ̈	ɴ̄	ɴ̂	ɴ̇	ɴ̇	ɴ̈
kuab	kuam	kuad	kuaj	kuav	kua	kuas	kuag
ɯ	ɯ̇	ɯ̈	ɯ̄	ɯ̂	ɯ̇	ɯ̇	ɯ̈
kob	kom	kod	koj	kov	ko	kos	kog
ᴊᴊ	ᴊᴊ̇	ᴊᴊ̈	ᴊᴊ̄	ᴊᴊ̂	ᴊᴊ̇	ᴊᴊ̇	ᴊᴊ̈
kiab	kiam	kiad	kiaj	kiav	kia	kias	kiag
[kab]	[kam]	[kad]	[kaj]	[kav]	[ka]	[kas]	[kag]
ꓚ	ꓚ̇	ꓚ̈	ꓚ̄	ꓚ̂	ꓚ̇	ꓚ̇	ꓚ̈
kab	kam	kad	kaj	kav	ka	kas	kag
[kaab]	[kaam]	[kaad]	[kaaj]	[kaav]	[kaa]	[kaas]	[kaag]
τ	τ̇	τ̈	τ̄	τ̂	τ̇	τ̇	τ̈
kwb	kwm	kwd	kwj	kwv	kw	kws	kwg

Table 19. Diacritics of the Final Version

Diacritic		Name
.	ȦV ᨀ̃	cim tub
ˎ	ȦV ᨀ̃	cim so
˗	ȦV ᨁ	cim kes
^	ȦV ᨆ̇	cim khav
˵	ȦV ᨆ̃	cim suam
ː	ȦV ᨀ̇	cim hom
··	ȦV ᨀ̃	cim taum

tion in the vowels (Table 18). This was in January 1971, about a month before the prophet's assassination. The new version was called *Pahawh Tsa* (ᨀ̌ ᨁ ᨆ̇ Phajhuaj Txha). *Tsa* means 'bone, basic, essential', reflecting further reduction of the Second and Third Stage Reduced Versions. We call it the Final Version.

In this Final Version Shong Lue eliminated the vowel classes by increasing the number of vowel diacritics, so that there are only thirteen vowel symbols to remember, plus seven tone diacritics (Table 19). The consonants, again, were not changed.

But the Final Version, in spite of its greater simplicity and the fact that it was produced by Shong Lue Yang shortly before he died, is nowhere in use for formal purposes. When Shong Lue gave it to Chia Koua he told him it would be needed in the future for telegraphy (like Morse code). The people who know it do use it sometimes for rapid writing, as when taking notes, and refer to it in English as "shorthand."

Concluding Comparisons

Table 20 provides a summary comparison of the numbers of different symbols required for representing the consonants, vowels and tones of the four systems.

Here follow brief samples of connected text of each of the four versions.

Source Version: ꯱ꮃꯂ ꯮꯭꯱ ꓕꭹꭱ ꮢꯆꯔ꯱ ꯱ꓞꮬꮖ꯱ꮃꓐ ꓕꓒꭲꭱꭳꮃ ꮬꮢ ꓕꯔ ꮀꓩ̌ꭲꮃꯔ꯱
ꭱꮒꮬ ꭲ꯴꯲ ꯱ꓕꭲꮃ ꯶꯭ꮬꯆꮖꓐ ꯱ ꯱꯴.

Second Stage Reduced Version: ꮢꮃ ꮬꮀ̃ ꭱꭲꭹ, ꮦꯔ ꮢ̇ ꮀꓩ̃ ꮮꭱ, ꮢ̌ ꮬ꯴ ꮃꮢ̃ ꮬꯔ
ꮒꮢ ꮦꭱ ꮬꯔꯔ ꮬꭱ ꭱ꯴ ꮀꮖ̃ ꯴ꭱꭱ꯴.

Third Stage Reduced Version: ꮢꮃ ꮬꮀ̃ ꭱꭲꭹ, ꮮꯔ ꮢ ꮀꓩ̃ ꮦꭱ, ꮢ̌ ꮬ꯴ ꮃꮢ̃ ꮬꮖ
ꮒꮢ ꮦꭱ ꮬꯔꯔ ꮬꭱ ꭱ꯴ ꮀꮖ̃ ꯴ꭱꭱ꯴.

Final Version: ꮢꮃ ꮬꮀ̃ ꭱꭲꭹ, ꮮꯔ ꮢ ꮀꓩ̃ ꮦꭱ, ꮢ̌ ꮬ꯴ ꮃꮢ̃ ꮬꯔ ꭱꭲꭹ ꮢ̌ꭱ ꮬꯔ ꮬꭱ
ꭱ꯴ ꮀꮖ̃, ꯴ꭱꭱ꯴.

Table 20. Number of symbols in each system of Pahawh Hmong

Sounds	Source Version	Second Stage Reduced Version	Third Stage Reduced Version	Final Version
Vowels	91	91 (26 basic)	26	13
Tones			8 (4 diacritics)	8 (7 diacritics)
Consonants	60	19 × 3	20 × 3	20 × 3

Romanized: Yaj Soob Lwj, Theej Kaj Pej Xeem, tau raug tua hauv nws tsev thaum ob hlis ntuj 1971.

English: Shong Lue Yang, Savior of the People, was assassinated in his home in February 1971.

6

Punctuation, Numerals and Other Symbols

In previous chapters we have described the Pahawh Hmong systems for writing consonants, vowels and tones. But as with most other writing systems, there was need for various other symbols as well. Some of these are not much different from parallel features in other languages, but others are quite different.

Punctuation Marks

Strictly speaking, in most languages punctuation marks represent sound features like intonation, pauses and phrasing; or they show the boundaries of grammatical groupings; or they may indicate whether a sentence is to be interpreted as a statement, question or exclamation.

In English, for example, a written sentence often starts with a capital letter and ends with a period, thus marking its boundaries, visually separating it from preceding and following sentences. A sentence may also contain one or more commas, marking the boundaries of phrases or other smaller grammatical groupings. Space between words also typically represents a linguistic boundary—the borders of a word—although it is not often thought of as a punctuation mark by users of English. Parentheses or brackets, when used, enclose more optional groupings. A question mark at the end of a sentence not only indicates a boundary, but also that the sentence has the force of a question, and sometimes that it should be said with a rising English question intonation as well.

Not all of the non-alphabetical symbols in English writing are punctuation marks in this sense, of course. Nobody thinks of numerals or of arithmetic signs like − and + as punctuation, for example. Symbols like %, $ and & are not punctuation either; in fact, we do not seem to have a general term to cover them in English.

The Pahawh Hmong system has a miscellaneous group of symbols called *vos* ꘙꘙ by Shong Lue Yang. Many of them are punctuation marks,

75

Table 21. Pahawh Hmong punctuation marks

Symbol	Hmong Name		English Equivalent
.	ᴔᴄ ᴣᴎ	vos rwg	.
,	ᴔᴄ ᴠᴣᴎ	vos cheem	,
;	ᴔᴄ ᴊᴎ	vos twv	;
:	ᴔᴄ ᴇᴠ ᴟᴟ	vos txooj sua	:
?	ᴔᴄ ᴙᴎ	vos thom	?
ᴤ	ᴔᴄ ᴣᴎ ᴠᴠ	vos tshab ceeb	!
(	ᴔᴄ ᴣᴎ	vos tab	(
)	ᴔᴄ ᴟᴙ	vos txhais	)
(	ᴔᴄ ᴧᴇ	vos qhib	(
)	ᴔᴄ ᴟ	vos kaw	)
—	ᴔᴄ ᴨᴠ ᴠᴄ	vos cawb veem	—
-	ᴔᴄ ᴙᴄ	vos nrug	-
"	ᴔᴄ ᴧᴎ	vos piv	"
ꜧ	ᴔᴄ ᴟᴄ	vos nrua	(reduplicate)
꞉	ᴔᴄ ᴣᴟ	vos seev	(singing, chanting style)

others not, like the English examples above. Because they are grouped together in the Hmong classification, we will describe them in the same section here but deal with the different types separately.

Punctuation was not used in the Pahawh Hmong Source Version, but it became well established during the time when the Second Stage Reduced Version was being used. Chia Koua Vang does not know exactly when it was added, but in 1969 he wrote to Shong Lue in prison and asked him questions like "What can we use for the ends of sentences?" "What sign can we use for percent?" and "What do we call it when we put together three posts [sides of a triangle]?" With a few exceptions which will be noted, the symbols shown in Tables 21, 22 and 28 were Shong Lue's reply. With them came new Hmong words he coined to label them.[1]

Unlike the alphabet characters we have seen, most of the true punctuation symbols (Table 21) are obviously derived from other languages; three, however, are unique in form, more typical of the Pahawh Hmong. Chia Koua does not know why Shong Lue did not create his own symbols for more of the punctuation, following his practice on almost every other part of the system.

Furthermore, other than himself, Chia Koua knows of no students or associates of Shong Lue Yang at that time who knew how to read and write in any other system or in any other language. Pa Kao Her, for example, learned to read and write Lao after this time, as an officer in the army. The people with education were not generally the ones who learned the Pahawh Hmong.

It seems obvious, however, that someone who knew some other language like French, or who knew the Romanized Hmong, taught punctuation to Shong Lue. (There is not much punctuation used in Lao, and what it has is borrowed largely from French.) Shong Lue adopted not only the functions from other languages, but also most of the symbols themselves. Unlike the few Pahawh Hmong consonant and vowel symbols which have the appearance of letters from other alphabets, but which do not have the same values they have in other alphabets, the punctuation marks match both the form and function of other systems.

Two of the symbols in Table 21 were not in Shong Lue's list of non-alphabetical symbols sent to Chia Koua, however. The question mark was added by Youa Ze Vang (Ntxuaj Zeb Vaj ꟄꟂꟃ ꟄꟅ ꟆꟇ), then a young student of the prophet, who became one of the primary teachers of the Pahawh Hmong in Laos, beginning in 1976 after the collapse of the war. He taught many Hmong who were hiding from the victorious Vietnamese (and from the communist Lao government) in the rugged Phou Bia Mountain area (Chapter 9). Also, where Table 21 has ꟊ for the exclamation point, Shong Lue's original list had !, a Western symbol like the other punctuation marks. It was Pa Kao Her who introduced the form shown here in 1985.

It should be noted also that Chai Lee and his students at the Hmong temple in the Ban Vinai refugee camp in Thailand sometimes use other symbols than those of Table 21 for period, comma and other common punctuation marks.[2] It is possible that some users of the Pahawh Hmong want to eliminate the few non-unique elements from the system.

As for those symbols in Table 21 which do not have English parallels, Ɤ is written to indicate that the syllable which precedes it is to be repeated. There is a similar device in the Lao and Thai writing systems.

ꟌꟍꟋ tsuag tsuag 'hurry, hurry'

꞉ is used to indicate a singing, chanting style of recitation, or a very strong intonation contour, with long, slow changes of voice pitch. In the first example below, it is written at the end of a line of a song or poem. (We have not undertaken a translation of the difficult poetry.)

꟎꟏ Ꟑꟑ ꟒ꟓ ꟔ꟕ Ꟗꟗ Ꟙꟙ Ꟛ ꟛ Ƛ꟝꞉.
꟞꟟ ꟠꟡ ꟢꟣ ꟤꟥ ꟦ ꟧꟨ ꟩꟪ ꟫ ꟬꟭꞉.
꟮꟯ ꟰ ꟱ꟲ ꟳ ꟴ Ꟶꟶ ꟷꟸ ꟹꟺ ꟻꟼ꞉.
Tsoom me yes sawv los nreg kev kawm txuj
peb lub neej yuav kawm ua txoj kev zoo
xyaum kom tau kawm kom yog mus zoo zus.

Second, when ꞉ is used to represent speech which has strong intonation contours, it is written after any phrase on which the contours may come:

ꓱꓮ ꓵꟷ꞉ ꟷꓮ ꟷꞧ ꞓꞟ ꞎꞟ ꟷꓮ ꓱꞟꞧ ꓮꓘ ꞧꟷ ꞏꞧꞬ꞉

Ab yuad! ob hnub no nej ua dab tsi lawm 'os?

'(introductory exclamation)! What have you been doing all this time?'

Third, ꞉ is characteristically used for indicating intonation rhythms in a traditional form of chanted speech called *kwv txhiaj* ꓵꞧ ꟷꞧ. The example is again left untranslated:

ꓥꞟ ꓵꟷ꞉ ꓮꞧ ꞓꞟ ꟷꞟ ꞓꞎ ꞎꓬ ꞎꞟ ꟷ ꞓꞎ Ɡꓘ ꞟꓘ ꞓꞎ ꞓꞟ ꞟꞧ ꞓꞟ ꟷꞟ ꟷꞟ
ꞟꞟ ꞎꞎ ꞟꞟ ꞓꞟ ꟷꞟ ꓮꓘ ꓮꞟ ꞓꞟ ꞧꞟ ꓮꞧ ꞎꞟ ꞓꞟ ꟷꓘ ꞎꞟ ꞟꓘ ꓮꓮ ꞎꞟ ꞟꞧ
ꓮꞟ ꞎꞟ ꞟꞟ ꞟꞟ ꟷꞟ ꞓ ꞟꞟ ꟷꓮ ꞟꞟ ꓮꞓ ꞟꞓ ꟷꓬ ꞟꓘ ꟷꞟ ꟷꓮ ꓮꞟ ꞟꓮ ꞟꓘ ꞓꞟ ꟷꞟ
ꟷꓰ ꞟꞟ ꞟꞟ ꞓ ꟷꞟ ꓮꞟ ꞟꓘ ꞓꞧ ꞟꓘ ꞟꞟ ꞧꞧ ꞟꟷ ꞟꞟ ꞟꞟ ꞟꓘ ꞓꞟ ꟷꞟ ꞟꟷ ꓮꓘ
ꞟ ꞓꞎ ꓬ ꟷꞟ ꞧꞧ ꓮꓘ ꞟꞎ ꞓꞧ꞉

Nib ye! me nkauj Hmoob cas zeej leej kav zeej tswb tsav tsheej nkauj huab tais yuav kav laj pem ceeb rov los poob ntsib li dheev nkawm me noog paj tsawb noog tsum xib ya tsaws li ntua ntiaj teb ces kaum liaj es yuav fi xov tib nruj nraws rau ib tsoom nkauj Hmoob nyob ntiaj teb kom leg cim tsoos maj tsoos ntuag mus thawm niaj ces tsoom nkauj Hmoob thiaj ntsib tau txoj kev nyob mus tsim txiaj mog.

The other symbols in the *vos* category, those which do not relate to the information or the structure of the text, are logographs. These symbols represent full words and are used for brevity and convenience in Pahawh Hmong, as a few such symbols typically are in other alphabetic writing systems. Note that a logograph does not represent pronunciation on any level, unlike alphabetical or syllabic (and even sometimes punctuation) symbols. Instead it represents a word, no matter how the word is pronounced in a language. In some cases the same logograph may represent words of the same meaning in different languages, as do

Table 22. Pahawh Hmong symbols of *vos* category that are not punctuation marks

Symbol	Hmong Name		English Equivalent
/	ꞓꞟꞓ ꞟꓮ	vos cav	/
ꓴ	ꞓꞟꞓ ꞎꞓ	vos feem	%
=	ꞓꞟꞓ ꞎꓘ	vos tseeb	=
ꞵ	ꞓꞟꞓ ꞟꞟ	vos thiab	&
•	ꞓꞟꞓ ꞎꓘ	vos ntsua	•
→	ꞓꞟꞓ ꞟꞟ	vos taw	→
ꭩ	ꞓꞟꞓ ꞟꞟ	vos lub	' (shorthand for *lub;* classifier)

Arabic numerals (1, 2, 3, etc.) in countless languages. Pahawh Hmong logographs in the *vos* category are listed in Table 22. Note also that most of these characters are used in restricted ways, as in English, where we would write *25%* but not *twenty-five %*.

ᔐ, one of the symbols in Table 22, was not created by Shong Lue, but was added by Pa Kao Her. It is apparently modeled after &. Only one of the symbols in Table 22 does not have an English counterpart. ᗡ is used as a substitute for ᙙᙙ *lub*, the most common grammatical classifier in the Hmong language. It is used in text in the same way that % is a substitute for *percent* in English (or for ᙙᙙ ᙙᙙ *vos feem*) in Hmong.

ᗡ ᙙᙙ   lub npe 'a name'

Numerals

The numeral system of the Source Version was significantly different from that of later versions of Pahawh Hmong. Like the Greek and Roman numeral systems of earlier civilizations, the Source Version does not have a zero (Table 23).

In the Source Version the numerals are logographic,[3] representing spoken words, but they are not arithmetic. Because of the lack of a zero and of relative positions indicating multiples of ten, they do not stand for mathematical combinations. Thus, when expressing larger numbers, ᙙᙙ ᙙ is 'forty-one' not '4 × 10 + 1'. English '41', on the other hand, can represent either words or mathematical combinations, de-

Table 23. Numerals in Pahawh Hmong Source Version. Multiples of 10 from 50 to 90 follow pattern shown for 30 and 40.

Value	Numeral	Hmong Word	
1	ᙛ	ᙛᙛ	ib
2	ᙛᙛ	ᙛᙛ	ob
3	ᙛ	ᙛᙛ	peb
4	ᙛ	ᙛᙛ	plaub
5	ᙛ	ᙛᙛ	tsib
6	ᙛ	ᙛ	rau
7	ᙛ	ᙛᙛ	xya
8	ᙛ	ᙛᙛ	yim
9	ᙛ	ᙛᙛ	cuaj
10	ᙛᙛ	ᙛ	kaum
20	ᙛᙛ	ᙛᙛ ᙛᙛ	nees nkaum
30	ᙛᙛ	ᙛᙛ ᙛᙛ	peb caug
40	ᙛᙛ	ᙛᙛ ᙛᙛ	plaub caug
100	ᙛᙛ	ᙛᙛ ᙛᙛ	ib puas
1000	ᙛᙛ	ᙛᙛ ᙛᙛ	ib txhiab

pending on the way in which it is used. Illustrations of some combinations are to be found in Table 24.

In the Stage Two Reduced Version of the Pahawh Hmong, the essential zero (called *zauv* 🔲) was added, and a modern arithmetic system adopted (Table 25). This fundamental change was undoubtedly made on the model of Lao or French, but just how Shong Lue learned these things is not known. This system has continued to be used without modification through subsequent versions.

Shong Lue Yang called the numerals of Table 25 *zauv tab* 🔲. But there is also another kind of Pahawh Hmong notation for larger numbers, called *zauv txooj* 🔲. It follows and elaborates on the non-arithmetic Source Stage numeral system, though it does not use many of the actual symbols of that system.

Table 24. Examples of more complex numbers in Source Version of Pahawh Hmong

Value	Representation	Literal Translation
10	ɰ	ten
11	ɰʮ	ten one
12	ɰꟼ	ten two
32	ꟽꟼ	thirty two
34	ꟽᴛ	thirty four
63	ᴅꟽ	sixty three
77	ʋᴀʋ	seventy seven
101	ʮꟻʮ	one hundred one
202	ꟼꟻꟼ	two hundred two
332	ꟽꟻꟽꟼ	three hundred thirty two
144	ʮꟻᴘᴛᴀᴛ	one hundred forty four
1,036	ʮꟽꟽᴅ	one thousand thirty six
2,194	ꟼꟽʮꟻᴘᴋᴀᴛ	two thousand one hundred ninety four
4,890	ᴛꟽʮꟻᴘᴋᴀ	four thousand eight hundred ninety
10,100	ɰꟽʮꟻ	ten thousand one hundred
25,000	ɰʮᴘꟽ	twenty five thousand
150,000	ʮꟻʮᴀꟽ	one hundred fifty thousand

Table 25. Numerals and examples of arithmetic combinations in Second Stage Reduced Version and subsequent versions of Pahawh Hmong

0	o	10	५०	100	५००
1	५	11	५५	101	५०५
2	3	12	५3	212	3५3
3	஡	32	஡3	332	஡஡3
4	⅄	34	஡⅄	144	५⅄⅄
5	3	50	3o	500	3oo
6	ᴄ	63	ᴄ஡	236	3஡ᴄ
7	ᴙ	77	ᴙᴙ	726	ᴙ3ᴄ
8	⅄	85	⅄3	481	⅄⅄५
9	ᴋ	91	ᴋ५	692	ᴄᴋ3

Table 26. Non-arithmetic symbols for words for larger numbers in Pahawh Hmong

Numeral	Hmong Word		English Meaning
ꘀ-ꘗ	ꘒꘀ	cua	ones
ꘁ	ꘓꘀ	caum	tens
ꘈ	ꘒꘌ	pua	hundreds
ꘈꘁ	ꘖꘙ	txhiab	thousands
ꘉ	ꘐꘊ	vam	ten thousands
ꘉꘁ	ꘜꘗ	ntsuab	hundred thousands
ꘋ	ꘛꘀ	roob	millions
ꘋꘁ	ꘕꘌ	tw	ten millions
꘏	ꘖꘀ	neev	hundred millions
꘏ꘁ	ꘚꘌ	taw	billions
ꘐ	ꘝꘀ	ruav	ten billions
ꘐꘁ	ꘀ	kem	hundred billions
ꘔ	ꘗꘌ	tas	trillions

Table 27. Examples of arithmetic and non-arithmetic Pahawh Hmong numerals

Number	Arithmetic System	Non-arithmetic System	
10	ꘐ꘠	ꘐꘁ	one ten
20	ꘓ꘠	ꘓꘁ	two tens
100	ꘐ꘠꘠	ꘐꘈ	one hundred
200	ꘓ꘠꘠	ꘓꘈ	two hundreds
110	ꘐꘐ꘠	ꘐꘈꘐꘁ	one hundred, one ten
210	ꘓꘐ꘠	ꘓꘈꘐꘁ	two hundreds, one ten
1,000	ꘐ, ꘠꘠꘠	ꘐꘈꘁ	one thousand
2,000	ꘓ, ꘠꘠꘠	ꘓꘈꘁ	two thousands
10,000	ꘐ꘠, ꘠꘠꘠	ꘐꘉ	one ten-thousand
20,000	ꘓ꘠, ꘠꘠꘠	ꘓꘉ	two ten-thousands
120,000	ꘐꘓ꘠, ꘠꘠꘠	ꘐꘈꘁ ꘓꘉ	one hundred-thousand, two ten-thousands
210,000	ꘓꘐ꘠, ꘠꘠꘠	ꘓꘈꘁ ꘐꘉ	two hundred-thousands, one ten-thousand
1,000,200	ꘐ, ꘠꘠꘠, ꘓ꘠꘠	ꘐꘋꘓꘈ	one million, two hundreds
2,000,100	ꘓ, ꘠꘠꘠, ꘐ꘠꘠	ꘓꘋꘐꘈ	two millions, one hundred

Before Shong Lue Yang, the Hmong language included words for numerical units up to 'ten thousand'. Some other languages in the area have words not only for 'hundreds', 'thousands' and 'millions', etc., as in English, but also individual words for 'ten thousands', 'hundred thousands', etc. Shong Lue coined such terms above 'ten thousand' for Hmong as well, and gave each a symbol in Pahawh Hmong (Table 26).

The Stage Two way of writing numbers in Pahawh Hmong (the *zauv tab* ꘍ꘀ ꘗꘌ) corresponds to the familiar worldwide arithmetic system, although with unfamiliar symbols; the Source System works more like Roman numerals, without a true zero. It is not possible to do conventional arithmetic with the earlier system. In Table 27 examples of numbers are compared in the two systems.

The advantages of the earlier system are that larger numbers can be written in a condensed way in text, as demonstrated in Table 27, and that it follows more directly the word sequence of the spoken language.

Other Symbols

Symbols for Arithmetic Functions. The symbols for arithmetic functions are called *xyeem* ꝏꞇ. Although the form of these logographs in Hmong is different than in other languages, the function is the same (Table 28). Chia Koua Vang learned about these arithmetic symbols along with the punctuation marks in the letter from Shong Lue described earlier.

Symbols for Periods of Time. Time periods are designated by symbols called *zwj* ꞇꓸ, which means 'time' (Table 29). Except for the last two of these symbols, Chia Koua learned them when he learned the Second Stage Reduced Version. The other two were supplied by Pa Kao Her, who either learned them from Shong Lue Yang or designed them himself.

These symbols for periods of time are used in dates and other time references in text. In the example which follows, the text is first written with all words spelled out in full. Then the same sentence follows with the symbols for periods of time and some other logographs substituting for spelled-out words. (The various logographs in Table 30 all appear in this example.)

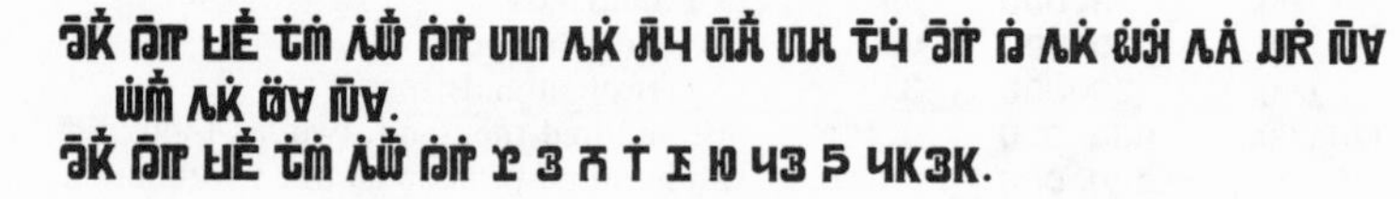

ꓱꓗ ꓳꓵ ꓴꓰ̌ ꓔꞟ ꓥꟗ ꓲꞟ ꓳꟿ ꓥꓗ ꓓꓴ ꓴꞟ ꓴꓧ ꞇꓸ ꓱꓵ ꓕ ꓥꓗ ꓶꓵ ꓥꓮ ꓳꓮ ꓰꓨ
ꟿꓲ ꓥꓗ ꓳꓦ ꓰꓨ.
ꓱꓗ ꓳꓵ ꓴꓰ̌ ꓔꞟ ꓥꟗ ꓳꟿ ꓔ ꓳ ꓙ ꓔ ꓯ ꓲ ꓮ ꓦꓳ 43 ꓝ ꓮꓗꓮꓗ.

Table 28. Symbols for arithmetic functions

Symbol	Hmong Name		English Equivalent
ᵌ	ꝏꞇ ꓮꓵ	xyeem ntxiv	+ (plus)
ꓸ	ꝏꞇ ꓳꓵ	xyeem rho	− (minus)
ꓸ	ꝏꞇ ꓳꓲ	xyeem tov	× (times)
ꓺ	ꝏꞇ ꓧꓰ̌	xyeem faib	÷ (divided by)

Table 29. Symbols for periods of time

Symbol	Hmong Name		English Equivalent
ꓝ	ꓰꓵ	xyoo	year
ꓷ	ꓮꓸ	hli	month
ꓴ	ꞇꓸ ꓳꟿ	zwj thaj	date
ꓲ	ꓴꓧ	hnub	day
�	ꟿꓮ	ntuj	season

Table 30. Logographs in sample sentence (p. 82)

Symbol	Substitute for		Meaning
ℐ	барш	lub	'classifier'
З	ʌќ	tsib	'five'
ह	åч	hli	'month'
∳	ᴃᴀ̊	ntuj	'season'
Ɪ	барх	hnub	'day'
ℍ	ʈ̄ч ɜ̂ᴘ̂	zwj thaj	'date'
ч	ʌᴀ̊	ib	'one'
Ϸ	ɛ̀ɜ̀	xyoo	'year'
к	ᴨ̃ᴠ	cuaj	'nine'

Table 31. Logographs for clan names. The first fourteen were designed by Shong Lue Yang, the last four by Chia Koua Vang. The logos apply equally to Hmong Daw and Hmong Leng.

Symbol	Substitute for		English
ᚠ	ɜ̃ɯ	Yeeg	Yeng
ᚸ	ᚫᴧ	Lis	Lee
ᛖ	ᴼᴧ	Lauj	Lor
衾	ᴇᴊ̇	Xyooj	Xiong
ᚱ	ᴛ̃ᴦ	Hawj	Her
Ꜧ	ᴡ̃ʀ	Muas	Moua
ᚦ	ᴏ̃ᴘ̂	Thoj	Thao
ᚁ	ɔᴋ́	Tsab	Chang
ᛖ̃	ɜ̇ᴀ̇	Khab	Khang
ᛖᴤ	ɜ̂ᴦ	Ham	Hang
ᚪ	ɜ̂ᴄ	Vaj	Vang
ᚯ̊	ɜ̃ɯ	Yaj	Yang
ᚼ̈	ṫ	Kwm	Kw
ᚥ	ʈ̄ᴄ	Vwj	Vue
ᚨ̃	ᴠ̃ᴍ́	Tsheej	Cheng
ᛗ	ᴇ̇	Koo	Kong
ᚩ̃	ɜ̂ᴇ̆	Faj	Fang
ᚠ̈	ᴛᴋ́	Tswb	Chue

Phaj Hauj Hmoob tshwm sim thaum lub tsib hlis ntuj hnub zwj
    thaj kaum tsib xyoo ib txhiab cuaj pua tsib caug cuaj.
'The Pahawh Hmong has existed since May 15, 1959'.

Translated literally, the last part of this sentence reads:

' . . . since ¦ classifier fifth month ¦ season date one five [fifteen] ¦
year one nine five nine'

Logographs for Clan Names. Shong Lue Yang also designed logographs for clan names (Table 31). According to Hmong custom, men and women from the same clan cannot marry each other, and are restricted in their behavior in each other's presence. They are perceived to be like brothers and sisters so far as the appropriateness of sexual contact is concerned, with considerably more restrictions than exist in a sibling relationship in the West. For example, men and women of the same clan should not throw the ball to each other at the Hmong New Year, a custom potentially leading to courtship; neither should they spend time alone together.

A Hmong myth tells of twelve married sons in a family. God (Vaj **ꓱꓛ**) told the father that no two descendants of any one son should marry each other. This was to avoid the concentration of supernatural power in one family. Intermarrying would multiply that power and enable one family to dominate other families. The Lao and the Thai kings, for example, will marry a 'sister' (by Hmong classification) and increase their power, strengthening the dominion of their family. For the Hmong, however, the descendants of each son were to marry descendants of other sons, and the power would be spread out among all of the Hmong people. No family could then dominate. Children, both boys and girls, were counted as descendants of their father, not their mother, in this reckoning, and the lines of descent were symbolized in clan names.

Shong Lue Yang designed the clan logographs to be sewn into garments or worn as badges, or posted on desks or doors to identify a person's clan. This would enable people to behave appropriately. Such identification was needed in the resettlement camps in Laos to which many Hmong people had fled for protection from the communists. In those surroundings they did not know all of their neighbors, much less other people they met.

It is also sometimes hard to identify a person's clan even if you have heard the person's name. Order of given name and clan name is not fixed. Somebody called *Vaj Yaj* **ꓱꓛ ꓱꘄ** 'Vang Yang' might belong either to the *Vang* clan or the *Yang* clan, depending on which order is being used. Under conditions where strangers are regularly encountered, it is awkward to have to ask constantly what the other person's clan is.

There are more clan names in Hmong than the twelve of the myth, however. Shong Lue considered these other clans to be offshoots of the ones listed. For any such names, substantially the same symbol was used, with minor modifications in the logograph to show that it was a variant. Chia Koua recorded fourteen examples in all from Shong Lue, and he himself designed four more, as seen in Table 31. Shong Lue told him that all of the additional symbols which would be needed should be derived from the basic twelve, with modifications by adaptation and recombination.

The clan name logographs have never been used for their intended purpose. Only a few of the close students and associates of Shong Lue even knew about them when they were designed. Shong Lue was then under suspicion by the authorities, and put in prison, so he did not teach groups of people in Long Cheng. The clan name logographs are therefore considered to be ready for use at some future time when Shong Lue's teaching will prevail.

7

How Did Shong Lue Yang Do It?

Shong Lue Yang's own account of his supernatural origin, of how he created the Pahawh Hmong and the source of his message, was told in Chapter 1. But even for such people as the Hmong contributors to this book, who believe this account in some literal sense, the question of how Shong Lue created his writing system still persists on another level. They are puzzled, for example, by why Pahawh Hmong punctuation is much like that of other languages, although very little else in the system has any significant resemblance to other ways of writing. And a supernatural explanation for the writing system does not detract from their wonder at Shong Lue's genius or at the scope of what he did.

Other Hmong, who do not believe in Shong Lue Yang as a supernatural phenomenon, are nevertheless very proud of the writing system as a Hmong creation, and wonder how he managed it. Still others do not believe that Shong Lue Yang could have produced the writing himself. Some have ascribed his work, including the writing system, to a communist plot to undermine the Lao government and the Hmong military effort in the war. Others insist that Shong Lue must have had a well-concealed education. Some say the writing system must have come from Tibet; or that it is the Pollard system once used for Hmong in China. The speculation goes on.

Most Westerners are not likely to accept a supernatural explanation, either. The educated Western world view requires that we understand Shong Lue Yang's accomplishment in terms of psychological processes, historical influences, linguistic structures and cultural patterns. In this chapter, therefore, we will explore some of the potential influences on Shong Lue and the probability that his work derived from them.

Shong Lue Yang's Original Setting

The villages where Shong Lue grew up and lived when he began his teaching were not far from Nong Het (Looj Hej ꯁꯟ ꯎꯤꯔ), a town in

Xieng Khouang Province, Laos (Figure 1, Introduction). The area straddled the border with Vietnam. Like most Hmong communities at the time, these villages were in remote and mountainous locations, accessible from towns like Nong Het only by walking or riding horseback through the jungle on precipitous trails. They were nevertheless subject to many varied influences.

The Nong Het area is important in Hmong history. It was one of the earliest areas where Hmong settled in Laos.[1] Through it passed a road the French had built years before from Vietnam to the provincial capital of Xieng Khouang in Laos. This had brought outside influences into the area for many years, but in the time of Shong Lue the road had fallen into disrepair and was unsafe for travelers as a result of endemic warfare.

Two powerful Hmong families had emerged in the Nong Het area, one of them the family of Touby Lyfoung, for many years leader of the pro-French, pro-Lao government faction among the Hmong, and the other the family of Faydang Lobliayao, leader of the pro-Vietnamese, pro-Pathet Lao faction. General Vang Pao, Hmong military leader under the Royal Lao Government during the war, was also from Nong Het area, as were Pa Kao Her and Chai Lee, who have figured prominently in this book. Lor Moua as well is in this group. Thus, many Hmong leaders have come from around Nong Het (see Appendix).

Ever since 1939 there had been a school in Nong Het, attended primarily by Hmong children; and some members of the important Hmong political families had also gone to be educated in Hanoi, Saigon and France. The majority of Hmong in the villages around still could not read or write any language, however, and it is possible that there were no literate individuals at all in the villages where Shong Lue lived and began his teaching. Nevertheless, education and writing were known and valued and, Smalley assumes, would most certainly have been observed in some form by Shong Lue Yang.

But a Hmong like Shong Lue would not have needed to know about the school in Nong Het, about an educated Hmong elite, or to have actually seen writing to be aware of these things. Hmong tradition includes tales about why the Hmong did not have writing although peoples around them did. The Hmong words *sau* 'write' and *ntawv* 'paper, writing' are not recent borrowings, but go back many centuries in Hmong vocabulary.[2] There were also tales of former Hmong writing systems used and lost in ancestral China. Writing in Chinese was sometimes part of Hmong amulets and charms.[3] Writing had been associated with messianic movements in the Hmong past, including the Pa Chai movement; and in Shong Lue's time there were people who foretold the future, who said that supernatural beings would at some time provide writing for the Hmong. Messianism also produced the Sayaboury script for Hmong on the Western side of Laos (Chapter 11).

The anthropologist Jacques Lemoine gives a good picture of the place of writing in the world view of many Hmong:

> This lack of any ability to write on the part of the great majority of the Hmong did not in the least show any lack of interest. On the contrary, no doubt struck with the importance placed on written documents by the Chinese administration, the Hmong dreamed of a writing system to fall from heaven as their very own. This theme recurred constantly through the different messianic movements. . . .
>
> According to the messianic myth, a king would be born, or already had been born to unite the Hmong and deliver them from subjection to other peoples. The king or his prophet did not fail to announce that writing had been revealed to him. That in itself was the sign of the heavenly commission.[4]

Although remote, the Nong Het area was a communication crossroads at which several cultures met. The Hmong were the most numerous people in the area, primarily rural and mountain-dwelling, geographically the least accessible to outsiders of all the ethnic groups of northern Laos. Ethnic Lao, the politically dominant people in the country, lived in the towns and along some of the river valleys. Vietnamese settlers were steadily encroaching into the Laos side from across the border; many bureaucrats in the French/Lao government offices in the towns had been Vietnamese, and such people also remained in these small towns as merchants and skilled workers.

The Chinese presence was important, too. The Hmong are conscious that their original homeland was China, and a significant portion of their trade was done either with traveling Chinese traders or in stores owned by Chinese merchants in the towns. Many Hmong had a special relationship with traders from Yunnan Province, China, men who traveled the hills in horse caravans or occasionally settled in Hmong villages to operate small stores. Chinese traders of both types bought opium and other products from the Hmong, selling them manufactured goods, salt and other necessities.

Surrounding Nong Het in every direction there were other minority peoples also, among them some Tai-speaking ethnic groups. Tai is the name of the language family which includes the Thai languages and dialects of Thailand, Lao dialects of Laos and Thailand, and languages spoken by a number of other groups in these two countries plus China, Vietnam, India, Burma and Malaysia. Some of the smaller Tai-language groups (along with Lao) were located not very far from Nong Het.

Still another important group of people in the area were the Khmu', from whom Shong Lue's mother originally came, and for whom he also created the Pahawh. Their language is related to Khmer (Cambodian) and some of the "Montagnard" languages of Vietnam.

And then there were the French, whose military and political presence was dominant in the area during Shong Lue Yang's younger years, from the end of World War II until the Vietnamese finally defeated them in 1954 at Dien Bien Phu. By 1959, when Shong Lue began to teach, there were probably few French nationals living in the area, but the French language was still there, as educated individuals from any ethnic group would have studied French, and some of them would have taken their education in French.

In addition to this direct meeting of cultures and languages, there was more indirect communication of other kinds in the Nong Het area. War brought military goods from all over the world. They were stockpiled and distributed and scattered and abandoned all over the area as military fortunes rose and fell. The lettering on them was in languages as varied as Chinese, Russian, English, French, Vietnamese and Czechoslovakian.[5]

The Writing Systems in Shong Lue Yang's Setting

It is very clear, then, that Shong Lue Yang had plenty of opportunity to know about writing, to observe writing (although he could not read), and to notice the shapes of letters in other languages (although he could not write). He most certainly did not re-invent the idea of writing. His writing system, however, shows remarkably little significant resemblance to any of the systems already in the area.

The Roman systems in the area formed one group. Vietnamese writing, for example, not only uses Roman letters (and modifications thereof), but is also organized in much the same way as writing in Western languages. The primary difference is in the Vietnamese representation of tone, for which accent marks above or below the vowel are used.

The Romanized writing system for Hmong had probably not yet reached the Nong Het area by 1959, when Shong Lue produced the Source Version. As we have seen, the major structural difference between the Romanized Hmong and Vietnamese is in the way the Hmong tones are represented by consonants at the end of the syllables, instead of as diacritics over or under the vowel symbol.

As we also saw earlier, in the course of its development each successive stage of the Pahawh Hmong became a little bit more like the

Roman system (particularly like Vietnamese, and many other such tone languages around the world) with respect to the way in which tones were written above the vowels. By the Final Version each tone had a different accent mark, and each vowel a different basic symbol. In the writing of consonants and the order of consonant and vowel symbols, however, all versions of the Pahawh Hmong remained significantly different from the Roman type.

Chinese is the second of the major writing systems in the area. Chinese is a logo-syllabic system which represents syllables and words (or other meaningful linguistic units) in symbols that are partly syllabic and partly logographic.[6] But in spite of the importance of Chinese culture to the Hmong people, Shong Lue's work shows no more tendency toward logographic structural principles than do other alphabetic writing systems of the world that include logographic writing as a secondary feature. In its logographic writing Pahawh Hmong is more like Vietnamese, French or Lao than like Chinese. It shows no logo-syllabic characteristics whatsoever.

The third major type of writing system in Shong Lue's environment, and perhaps the most prevalent, was the Tai type, exemplified in Lao and the ethnic Tai languages near Nong Het and adjacent areas. This system is alphabetic, but it is organized in a sufficiently different way from the Roman group so as to require some explanation.

In addition to the shapes of the letters, Tai writing systems[7] differ from Roman systems in how they represent vowels and tones. The basic order of writing in Tai-language systems is left to right, but that order applies primarily to the consonants. Individual vowels are written somewhere in an orbit around the particular consonant or consonant cluster which precedes them in pronunciation.

The following examples show how this works, although not all the syllables shown represent actual Lao words. The Lao consonant ຂ (one of the consonants representing /kh/) is followed by the vowel for /aa/ as in ຂາ, preceded by the vowel for /ee/ as in ເຂ, has the vowel for /ii/ above it as in ຂີ, and the vowel /ɔɔ/ before and above it as in ເຂີ, etc. The consonant symbol (or symbols in the case of a consonant cluster) thus provides the core, the reference point, the nucleus of the written syllable, with vowels written after, before, above or below it, or in various combinations of some of these positions. Each spoken vowel has its fixed place in writing, but different vowels do not have the same place.

The Pahawh Hmong is fascinatingly similar to this, and fascinatingly different. Right from the Source Version, the Pahawh Hmong vowel has been the core of the syllable, and the consonant has been written as a satellite after it, even though the consonant precedes in speech. The one written consonant position in Pahawh Hmong is used for all consonants except /k/, which is inherent in the vowel symbol. To put this more simply, the Pahawh Hmong treatment of syllables is somewhat like that of the Tai languages, but it reverses the core roles of consonant and vowel symbols.

The other big difference between the Tai-language writing systems and Roman ones is in the complicated way Tai-language symbols represent the tones. The complexity is due to changes in the pronunciation of tones and consonants down through the centuries, without corresponding modifications in the writing.

Tones in a typical Tai-language writing system are represented in part by three different classes of written consonants. The tone depends on the type of initial consonant, written with or without a tone diacritic, and other details. In Lao, for example, a spoken /kh/ consonant is written ຂ to represent that consonant plus one tone, and ຄ to represent the same consonant plus another tone. The following examples show how a series of five different tones is written in Lao, using two of the consonant classes. The pronounced consonants and vowels are always /khaa/, and the raised numbers at the end of each syllable in the Roman-letter representation symbolize the five respective tones:

ຂາ	ຄາ	ຄ່າ	ຂ້າ	ຄ້າ
khaa[1]	khaa[2]	khaa[3]	khaa[4]	khaa[5]

The Pahawh Hmong in the Third Stage Reduced Version, but only in that version, is reminiscent of this Tai-type system in that there are two classes of vowel symbols (again, not consonants as in the Tai languages) related to the writing of tone. The spoken vowel /a/, for example, is represented as ꓷ with high tone, but as ꓲ with rising tone.

To summarize, the Pahawh Hmong system is reminiscent of, but also contrary to, the Tai-language writing system. In the Tai system there are consonant classes representing tone; in the Pahawh Hmong Third Stage Reduced Version there are vowel classes representing tone. In the Tai-language systems the consonant symbols are the nucleus of the written syllables, and the vowel-tone symbols are written as satellites to them; in all the Pahawh Hmong systems the vowel-tone symbols are the nucleus of the written syllables, and the consonants are written as satellites to them. The vowel classes, of course, developed later in the Pahawh Hmong, and were not part of the Source Version.

Although there are some similarities, the Pahawh Hmong system differs in profound ways from all of the writing systems which might have had an influence on Shong Lue. Clearly the Pahawh Hmong is not modeled directly on any of them, although features of it may have been influenced by them at later stages. It may be significant that the Source Version, Shong Lue's first creation (so far as we know), is less like either the Roman or the Tai-language system than are the later stages.

Influences on the Source Version

Of the three types of writing in Shong Lue's environment, the Roman and Tai systems are alphabetic, the Chinese logo-syllabic. And although the Pahawh Hmong system rapidly became more efficiently alphabetic as it was changed, it started with some characteristics reminiscent of a syllabic system, a type of writing system different from any of these others in the area.

But it never was a truly syllabic system, in which each individual symbol represents a full syllable. If the writing of the Hmong words *Phajhauj Hmoob* were syllabic, for example, the written sequence would consist of three symbols, one for each syllable, rather than of the six symbols (plus tone diacritics) actually used. In a syllabic system, symbols would represent the pronounced syllables, not the meaningful words (as in logographic systems). In English, for example, if 2 were a symbol in syllabic writing rather than being logographic, it would represent not only 'two', but also 'to' and 'too', and would be the first syllable of 'Tudor'. Perhaps it would even appear as part of 'tomb'.

Instead, most symbols in the Source Version of the Pahawh Hmong represent half a syllable—the consonant half or the vowel half. It is demi-syllabic. Only symbols for syllables beginning with /k/ or ending in /au/ actually or potentially represent full syllables. The Source Version of the Pahawh Hmong therefore is an alphabetic system, but with a different kind of alphabet than the Roman or the Tai, based on a different level of the sound system.

Demi-syllabic systems do exist elsewhere in the world, including the Pollard script for Hmong Bo in China (Chapter 11), but there were no such writing systems in the area around Shong Lue. Chinese linguists tend to see the phonology of Chinese and other languages demi-syllabically. It may be that Shong Lue and these linguists were both responding to some psychological reality in the structure of languages of the area.[8]

The order of elements within the syllable is another indication that Shong Lue Yang's perception of the function of writing was close to syllabic in the Source Version. The fact that consonants follow vowels in writing although they precede them in speech may indicate that he perceived the syllable as a unit, and the consonant as modifying the vowel core of the syllable.

As we shall see in Chapter 10, syllabaries often preceded alphabets in the history of writing systems, so it is not surprising that a tendency toward syllabic features is to be found in the Source Version. In fact, this tendency lends credence to the view that Shong Lue invented the system rather than adapting it from something else. That the Pahawh Hmong is not syllabic may be due to the fact that more than 5,000 symbols would have been required to differentiate all of the syllables of Hmong. By writing consonants and vowels separately Shong Lue reduced the number of symbols needed for the Source Version to 151.

So it seems likely that although Shong Lue's Source Version was inspired by writing of various kinds around him, ones which he could not read, it was not modeled after them. Rather, in a process anthropologists call "stimulus diffusion," Shong Lue was stimulated to perceive the possibility of writing Hmong as he saw other languages being written around him. But he invented his system of writing independently of those existing systems. The Pahawh Hmong was based on Shong Lue's folk linguistics, his perception of the Hmong language. In this perception the half syllable (or perhaps the whole syllable at first) was the salient sound unit.

It seems highly probable, also, that most (if not all) of the shapes of the characters themselves were independently invented, and not modeled after the characters seen in the writing systems of the area. However, some of them, as has been frequently noted, bear resemblance to letters in the Roman, Tai-language and Russian alphabets. Since the resemblance to Russian letters has fed speculation that the system was part of a communist plot, we will look at that similarity more closely.

Six of the basic shapes of the Source Version bear resemblance to Russian letters. They are the vowels ♎ (ki), Ƅ (kai), Г (kawj) and Т (kwm) and the consonants Н (hnau) and М (nthau). In one of these cases the sound represented by the Hmong symbol is also similar to that of the corresponding Russian symbol, if we disregard the tone in Hmong: ♎ is pronounced /i/ in both. In another case there is partial similarity: Н is pronounced /hn/ in Hmong Daw and /n/ in Hmong Leng and Russian. Thus, six of the basic Source Version consonants and vowels (a few more if ones with diacritics are counted) show a resemblance in form to Russian and two also show a similarity of pronunciation.

But three of the "Russian" symbols in the Source Version (**T H M**) also resemble English, and one of them,**H**, also has a phonetic resemblance to English as well as to Russian because of the /h/ part of the Hmong Daw pronunciation. On top of this, there are five more Source Version symbols which look like English and not Russian: **J** (kej), **W** (kais), **D** (rau), **R** (mau) and **L** (tau). So eight of the basic Source Version characters look like English, and one of these has similarity of pronunciation. If diacritics are discounted there are a few others which look like English, like **U** (kus). So the argument that the Pahawh Hmong derives from Russian, based on the similarity of letters, as advanced by some of those who feared Shong Lue and oppose the writing system, is weaker than an argument would be for an English source or for French or Vietnamese, which have long been in the area and look like English.

But even if Shong Lue consciously took some symbols that he saw in the world around him, or was unconsciously influenced by such shapes, such inspiration was only the beginning of his development of the individual characters. Take, for example, the following symbols for w /i̠/, with its respective tones:

$$\text{ᴜ} \quad \text{T} \quad \dot{\text{T}} \quad \text{J} \quad \text{.ᴜ} \quad \text{ᴛ̅} \quad \text{ᴖ̣}$$
(k)wb   (k)wm   (k)wj   (k)wv   (k)w   (k)ws   (k)wg

One of these symbols looks like an English <u>T</u> (and the symbol for a Russian /m/). Two others look like a <u>T</u> with diacritics. Three others have been modified by a foot in one direction or another on the <u>T</u>.

An even more interesting line is

$$\text{P̣} \quad \text{ᴨ} \quad \text{P̣} \quad \text{·ᴤ} \quad \text{ᴨ̣} \quad \text{ᴨ̀} \quad \text{ᴡ̈}$$
(k)uab   (k)uam   (k)uaj   (k)uav   (k)ua   (k)uas   (k)uag

Here the first symbol looks like a <u>?</u>, but when diacritics are removed the symbols are all basically the same. They are oriented in different directions with one leg absent or positioned in different ways.

Similar families of shapes occur sporadically in other lines as well. These suggest that Shong Lue Yang often devised characters by modifying others, rather than seeking to borrow many characters from existing systems.

Chia Koua Vang once asked Shong Lue about the shapes of the characters in Pahawh Hmong. Shong Lue replied that if you examined all of the languages of the world you would duplicate somewhere every character of the Pahawh Hmong, that all possible shapes are to be found somewhere. He was implying that there is a limited number of possible configurations for a letter, and that it was not surprising that some symbols in a different system would look alike.[9]

For a theory of influence to be convincing, the similarities must in some way be consistently patterned, or must require some other explanation than coincidence. An example of such a case would be one in which both the forms and their use or pronunciation values were the same as in another writing system. There is no such consistent pattern to indicate that the Pahawh Hmong symbols were taken from other languages, except for some of the punctuation. Even where there is a resemblance in a few letters, the resemblance does not seem greater than chance. In very few cases does the resemblance in form correspond to a resemblance in pronunciation.

A point of view about writing which is prevalent in Southeast Asia is that each different language should have an identifiably different writing system. From this perspective, even Vietnamese, although it has Roman letters, looks different from Western languages because of symbols like ư and ơ, and diacritics that combine to give configurations like ồ or ặ. Various Tai languages also look different from each other because of the different shapes of the characters, even though they work in much the same way.

Shong Lue shared the view that writing systems for different languages should be different. He said God (Vaj **ᕆᏂ**) had a different writing system for each language, but some people had not received their writing system from God, and so they borrowed a writing system from another people. In his view, the world was divided into two parts. In Asia, many (but not all) peoples were given their own writing systems; but in the other part of the world, in Europe, most peoples did not receive their own writing system, but took systems from each other instead.

The value of the Pahawh Hmong, to many of its advocates, is partly in that uniqueness, whether they believe in its supernatural origin or not. To them the Romanized writing of Hmong is useful for some people and some purposes, but it is not Hmong.

A different kind of evidence that Shong Lue was not following an existing model when he developed his writing system comes from the numerals in the Source Version. It seems likely that a literate person, or anyone following the model of another language, would feel the need for a zero. The Source Version numerals, as we have seen, are not arithmetic symbols, but logographs representing existing words for numbers in Hmong. The numerals **UU** and **UU** for '10' and '20', for example, are unitary numerals representing the Hmong words *kaum* **UU** 'ten' and *neesnkaum* **UU** 'twenty'. The Hmong words for 'thirty' *peb caug* **MV** ('three tens'), 'forty' *plaub caug* **TV** ('four tens'), etc., include a word for 'tens', but the words for 'ten' and 'twenty' are different words entirely.

Possible Influence of Khmu'

Given the fact that documented cases of new writing systems developed by non-literate people are normally syllabic, if they are not logographic, one of the questions raised by the development of the Pahawh Hmong is how Shong Lue managed without a true syllabic stage. There is an intriguing possibility that Shong Lue's creativeness may have been enhanced by his simultaneous development of a writing system for Khmu' with one for Hmong.[10]

Syllabic writing is easier for the non-literate to invent than alphabetic writing because it does not require analytical separation of spoken vowels from spoken consonants, or perception of some kind of structure within the syllable. The Source Version of the Pahawh Hmong, however, does separate vowel-tones from consonants, and the vowel-tone chart which Shong Lue taught demonstrates that he had conceptually isolated the tones from the vowels even if he had not done so graphically.

If Shong Lue was working on the writing of Khmu' and Hmong at the same time, the differences between the two languages may have helped him make the analytical separation because Khmu' has two relevant structural differences from Hmong. Khmu', in contrast to Hmong, does not have a tone system, and Hmong, in contrast to Khmu', does not have syllable-final consonants. These differences could have helped Shong Lue sense phonological categories where the inventors of other writing systems, working on only one language, had not done so. The two languages, perhaps, did not allow the same orthographic solutions at every point, forcing Shong Lue to notice the internal structure of the respective syllables. We lack crucial evidence for such a theory, however, because we have no idea what the Pahawh Khmu' was like, or whether it showed equivalent perception of Khmu' phonology to what the Pahawh Hmong shows of Hmong phonology.

Possible Influence of Religious Pseudowriting

There may have been another important influence of a different type on Shong Lue as he produced the Source Version. The Hmong have a tradition of pseudowriting practiced by certain people who foretell the future and who are considered to have supernatural knowledge. Such individuals are called *shau* (saub ꓔꓵ), which is also the name of a Hmong creator deity, perhaps another name for Va (Vaj ꓨꓵ). The foretellers, as we shall call them, are not considered to be divine but are empowered by the deity.

Foretellers are not the same as the healing shamans called *neng* (neeb ꓦꓵ) or sometimes *shau neng* (saub neeb ꓔꓵ ꓦꓵ). They have no healing function. But people in trouble or uncertainty ask them for guidance or for information about the future.

These foretellers sometimes build small round buildings in which they perform their rituals and do their foretelling. When asked to predict the future, they go into a trance, and in this trance some of them make marks on paper. Some of these marks look like writing, others more like circles and wavy lines. When they come out of the trance they "read" the writing, giving the prediction. However, after a few days they are no longer able to read what they "wrote" on any particular occasion. An example of the pseudowriting of a Hmong foreteller is shown in Figure 3.

Both Hmong authors of this volume have relatives who are foretellers, and who do this writing. Both have questioned their relatives closely, and are convinced that the foretellers cannot do simple things which genuine readers and writers can do. They cannot give the values of any symbols, cannot write anything from dictation, cannot tell what any sequence of characters means when taken at random in what they have written, cannot pronounce anything pointed out to them on the page. In other words, they cannot read or write.

The phenomenon is reminiscent of glossolalia, or "speaking in tongues," which occurs in some forms of Christianity.[11] Glossolalia, of course, is typically oral rather than written. The glossolalist produces fluent, speech-like utterances which sound like a foreign language. There are people who claim to interpret the message of the glossolalist, but nobody can break it down into words, or explain what the different parts mean. It gives the illusion of language, but is not.

The Hmong authors of this book insist that Shong Lue was not a *shau*, not a foreteller in the traditional sense. Nevertheless, he did pre-

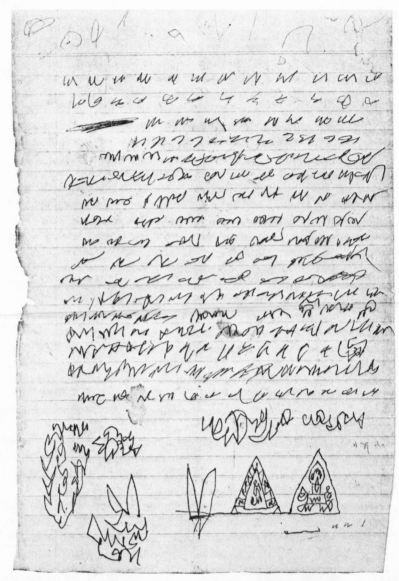

Fig. 3. Pseudowriting by Dia Lor (Diav Lauj ꯅꯤ ꯁꯤꯅ), a foreteller now living in Fresno, California

dict the future, and he also built round buildings in which to worship. One great difference, of course, is that he used genuine writing, accurately and consistently representing speech.

Another reason why Shong Lue's students do not consider him to have been a foreteller in the traditional sense is that they say he was never crazy. Foretellers generally gain their powers through a period of illness or disorientation, in which they say things which seem strange to the people around them. Later, when what they say is interpreted to come true, people believe that they are actually foretellers.

But craziness is often in the eye of the beholder. People hostile to Shong Lue Yang sometimes considered him crazy, and he himself wondered if he was going crazy when Va spoke to him from the air.

It seems far more fruitful to search for the influences on Shong Lue in the Hmong cultural tradition of the foretellers than to look for them in the writing systems of Shong Lue's neighbors or the Russians. We certainly do not know enough to offer a complete picture, but it would seem that the foreteller provided a model for Shong Lue, although he advanced far beyond that model in representing speech by marks on paper and in his general perceptions of the Hmong plight.

Influences on the Other Versions

Shong Lue Yang revised the Source Version in four separate ways to produce the Second Stage Reduced Version. In two of these ways influence from another language or other languages seems highly likely. In the two others it does not seem so probable.

As was shown in Chapter 5, to produce the Second Stage Shong Lue simplified the Pahawh Hmong by reducing the number of basic symbols for the vowel-tones and the consonants. He did this by use of diacritics which served to differentiate between different values for a single basic symbol, although the diacritic in itself did not consistently represent any linguistic feature. As a result of this revision, the number of shapes to remember was reduced, but the system itself was not changed.

These changes seem to have been made simply because the new system was easier. The need for simplicity that probably produced the half-syllable representation in the Source Version probably also led to this Second Stage Reduced Version. The system did not become more like that of any other languages in the area.

Shong Lue's punctuation symbols, however, are the same both in form and in function as punctuation in other languages. This is conclusive indication that some other language was used as a model at this point, although Chia Koua does not know how Shong Lue learned of punctuation in other languages.

This applies to the new arithmetically based numeral system introduced in the Second Stage as well. It has a zero, and the zero has the shape of zero in Roman-symbol and Tai systems. The numbers from ten on up are constructed in the fashion of arithmetic systems elsewhere, also.

But the non-arithmetic system was also modified and expanded, not only by adding numerous symbols for larger numbers, but also by coining new Hmong words, in multiples of ten, for those numbers above ten thousand up to trillion. Hmong previously had such terms only up to ten thousand. Here Lao and other languages in the area that have similar words could well have provided a model, but these languages, so far as we know, do not have any additional written numeral systems beyond the regular arithmetic ones. The extra set of numerals for the Roman numeral-like symbols again seems to be Shong Lue's invention.

In the Third Stage Reduced Version, the significant change was the separation and systematization of vowels and tones. Each tone was now given its own consistent representation by a diacritic (or lack of one), and the representation of vowels was regularized to two consistent vowel symbol classes. As a result of doing this Shong Lue (probably unwittingly) changed the fundamental structure of the writing system.

This change brought the Third Stage a step toward the way of representing tones found in most Roman systems which symbolize them (as in Vietnamese), and a step toward the Tai-language system as well, except that in the Tai languages the writing of tone is related to the consonant rather than the vowel, as was discussed above.

But here again, the system is not yet like Vietnamese, and the difference from the Tai system is a major difference. Rather than being modeled after either of these, a more likely reason for the change is again simplification. Once Shong Lue had the vowel-tone table of the Second Stage, the changes to produce the Third Stage meant minor adjustments, although the structural effect was radical.

It must be emphasized that Shong Lue had isolated the spoken Hmong tones from the very beginning, although he had not symbolized these tones as such. Symbols in the Source Version and the Second Stage Version represented vowel-tone combinations. But the tables which he used to teach those systems were organized by tone as well as by vowel quality. The innovation in the Third Stage Version was not the recognition of the tones, but their independent symbolization.

And the Final Version followed almost immediately, every vowel and every tone now always represented with the same symbol. There were no longer any classes of vowels reminiscent of the classes of consonants in the Tai languages, and the basic system of writing vowels and tones had become just like Vietnamese, although the characters were not the same. But again, the individual changes were minor simplifications, logical developments, although the structural effect was significant. There seems no reason to believe that Shong Lue must have been following a Vietnamese model.

After the Second Stage there was no further development in the representation of consonants. The initial simplification of the consonants did not lead later to a separating out of consonant features. Maybe if Shong Lue had listed the simple consonants in one column, and the corresponding ones with the puff of air in another, and the ones with the preliminary n-quality in a third, for example, he would ultimately have seen the economy and simplicity of separating those features in the writing and would have represented them independently in a consistent way. We should also remember that before he died Shong Lue had been making revisions of the Pahawh Hmong at an accelerating rate. Perhaps if he had lived he might have found a key to the simplification of the consonants, too.

How Did Shong Lue Yang Do it?

As best we can evaluate the evidence, Shong Lue Yang created the Pahawh Hmong system himself.[12] Although without education, he apparently possessed extraordinary insight and ability to analyze speech. His linguistic sense might fairly be called genius. He also felt very strongly the importance of Hmong ethnicity, Hmong differences from other people, and a desire for unity among Hmong groups. As in earlier messianic movements, writing was to him a symbol of identity and of a place in the modern world, as well as a useful means for communication.

Shong Lue was certainly familiar with the pseudowriting of the foretellers, and with the existence of the real writing of other people around. Although he was not a standard foreteller, Shong Lue adopted some of their trappings, including the round building for ritual and the marks on paper.

Shong Lue took ingredients in his own culture and an idea from outside, synthesized them into something new and kept working on them, refining and simplifying the resulting system. In doing so he borrowed directly a few elements like punctuation and the decimal arithmetic number system, but not much more. As he went along, he also coined a number of technical terms for parts of his system and for numbers which were not previously available in Hmong. The ultimate product of his creativity was the Pahawh Hmong, Final Version.

8

From Handwriting to Wordprocessing

Part of the motivating force behind the Pahawh Hmong is a strong desire to have a writing system which is unique in origin and appearance. Shong Lue Yang said that God wanted every people to have their own system, and some who support the Pahawh Hmong feel that the Hmong are culturally cheated if they have to use one adapted from other languages.

Part of the price of a unique writing system, however, is the initial lack of any way to type or print it. Everything has to be written by hand unless special equipment is made. This was normal in the ancient world, but it is a severe handicap today. Chia Koua Vang and Gnia Yee Yang have worked for years to overcome the technological problems of typing and reproducing the Pahawh Hmong.

As recounted in Chapter 2, the people whom Shong Lue had attracted as his followers were uneducated villagers like himself. Chia Koua likewise had no formal education, but he did have a wider background than most of those who learned the Pahawh Hmong. He had taught himself to read and write Lao in 1961, when he was a soldier in the jungle, getting others who knew Lao writing to help him. Then he had taught himself the Romanized Hmong in 1962 in Vientiane, where he stayed for about a week in the Catholic hostel for Hmong students, on his way to a military training program in Thailand. He had learned the Source Version of the Pahawh Hmong in 1964 on the expedition to find and rescue Shong Lue. After that he had been appointed to work in one of the military offices in Long Cheng.

So in 1966, when the controversial Shong Lue Yang found it wise to live in Nam Ngua (Naj Gua ᦀᦵ ᦵᦁᦰ), just outside Long Cheng, twenty-one-year-old Chia Koua approached him, wanting to learn the truth about him and the Pahawh Hmong. Shong Lue must have sensed that this man could go farther than most of the villagers who had flocked around, because he invited Chia Koua to come and be tutored alone at night. As it turned out, in doing so he kept his legacy alive after his assassination, and ensured that someone would develop ways of typing the Pahawh Hmong.

From Handwriting to Movable Type

As Shong Lue's student, Chia Koua soon raised the inevitable question: "Would it be possible to make books in the Pahawh Hmong?"

Shong Lue told him that indeed it was possible, that Chia Koua should first learn how to draw, that he should draw the Pahawh characters on blocks of wood and carve them. Eventually he could make them of brass and steel. Chia Koua then began to practice drawing objects, animals and people. He also began to search for a way of making wood blocks on which to carve the letters.

In 1967, after Shong Lue was arrested, Chia Koua took Kao Lee (Kos Lis ꖀ ꕤꖀ), Shong Lue's nephew, with him into the jungle, where he cut down a "spoon wood" tree (ntoo diav ꕮꕎ ꕤꖌ) with his machete. They carried home a section of the trunk about eighteen inches long and five inches across.

No saw was available, so still using his large machete and his traditional wood-cutting techniques, Chia Koua cut a cross-section out of the trunk to give him a disk about one and a half inches thick, with smooth, flat surfaces on the top and bottom. He then divided the disk by placing the sharp edge of the machete across one of the flat surfaces at about half-inch intervals and striking the back of the machete each time with a heavy object. The wood split easily and smoothly with the grain.

The resulting blocks were seven millimeters square at the ends and seventeen millimeters long. These Chia Koua shaved down, leaving the seven millimeter square surface on one end, but tapering the sides until the other end nearly came to a point. He then drew the Pahawh Hmong letters on the larger end, backwards of course, so that after having been carved and inked they would print out correctly on paper.

Chia Koua then carved each of the sixty-two letters, diacritics and numbers of the Second Stage Reduced Version on the end of a separate block, spoiling only about half a dozen blocks in the process. The whole project took him about two months, fitted in among his other duties.

Working for about a month in late 1967, Chia Koua produced his first book, a primer.[1] He laid it all out by hand, drawing the pictures; then, inking each symbol (letter or diacritic) on an ink pad one at a time, he stamped it carefully on the paper at the proper place. Only one copy of this booklet was made, but it was used later in teaching the Pahawh Hmong.

Toward a Typewriter

But even as Chia Koua Vang was carving wood type for the Pahawh Hmong, he and Shong Lue were already discussing more efficient ways of reproducing the characters. Chia Koua examined typewriters in the office where he worked, to figure out how they were made, and eventually decided to experiment with constructing one out of wood. He first tried to carve a platen, but it did not come out very well.

Shong Lue saw that making a typewriter was too difficult, and gave Chia Koua 100,000 kip (approximately $200 at the time)[2] to buy a Lao typewriter to adapt instead. So Chia Koua sent his wife, Sai Yang Vang (Ntxhais Yaj Vaj ꞏꞏꞏ), a schoolteacher in Houei Hong (Haib Hoos ꞏꞏꞏ), to Vientiane for a Lao typewriter, which cost about 80,000 kip (approximately $160); the rest of the money was spent for travel costs and the expenses of adapting the typewriter. The money was part of a sum of 160,000 kip (approximately $320) which Colonel Lia Ma Vang (Liaj Mas Vaj ꞏꞏꞏ) had given Shong Lue to help promote the Pahawh Hmong.

Now began the task of making Pahawh Hmong characters for the typewriter. Chia Koua decided that he wanted to be able to use the machine for both Pahawh Hmong and Lao, so he needed not only to make new characters, but also new type bars (the arms which move up when a key is pressed). He could then partially dismantle the typewriter when he wanted to switch between the two, and mount one set of type bars or the other as needed.

Chia Koua considered and discarded more than one way of making the letters themselves. He could not figure out how to make molds in which the symbols could be cast. He did not have equipment to cut metal characters directly. Finally he turned to traditional Hmong silverworking and blacksmith technology.

Assisted by Kao Lee, he started with round brass wire one millimeter in diameter, to be transformed into flat ribbon, a task familiar to silver workers. To do this they needed a series of slots through which to draw the wire, each slot narrower than the previous one, until the wire was squeezed down to the required thickness. Such slots were created by heating a steel plate red hot and pounding the cutting edge of a chisel into it several times almost all of the way through, making a series of V-shaped impressions. Steel was then ground off from the reverse side, cutting into the plate just far enough to expose a slot of the right thickness, more for the wider slots, less for the narrower slots.

The resulting steel plate, with its graded slots, was then braced vertically behind two poles. The brass wire was heated and pushed into the widest slot from the wider side, and pulled out the narrower side, where it was attached to a lever, so that a considerable length could be pulled through at a time. Then the length was reheated and pulled through the next narrower slot in the same way, and on down, until the desired thickness was reached. The brass ribbon which Chia Koua made was less than one-half millimeter thick and two millimeters wide. It took three days to finish this process, from making the bellows for the furnace to producing the ribbon.

Chia Koua, whose father had been a blacksmith, then forged three iron tools for forming the letters. Two of these looked like pliers, the third like a double-pointed awl with no handle. He also made other tools out of strips of bamboo with the ends shaved into different forms, around which the brass wire could be shaped.

One of the pliers-like tools had flat jaws to straighten out unwanted bends which developed in the handling of the brass ribbon. The tips of the jaws were also filed down to just the right size and thickness around which to make the larger bends, like the one in ⋂. The other pliers had a tiny transverse groove on one jaw and a corresponding tooth on the other jaw, so as to facilitate making tight crimps in the ribbon, and to start the tiny loops characteristic of letters like ∪.

To form ⋎, for example, the loop was first started on the end of the brass ribbon by pinching it between the groove and tooth. Then the loop was shaped around the awl, perfectly round and the right size. The bend at the foot of the character was formed with the tips of the other pair of pliers. When the resulting shape was acceptable it was cut off the ribbon. Each finished character was a uniform three millimeters high.

Many characters were more difficult than that, of course. ⋒, for example, required three tiny pieces to be soldered together. To make the solder, small chunks of silver and brass were placed in a crucible and melted in the furnace. As they slowly cooled they were stirred constantly until granules formed, about the consistency of coarse sand.

A few granules of the solder would be mixed with saliva, to make them adhere lightly to each other. This small glob would then be placed on the joint to be soldered, and the pieces heated to the right temperature. The result for all the characters was incredibly neat joints and beautifully symmetrical figures.

The type slugs (the heads of the type bars, where the letters are located) were cut out of aluminum. Chia Koua shaped them like the type slugs on the typewriter, except that he left a flat surface to which the brass characters would be soldered. A groove in back fit over the type bar, which was cut from a sheet of brass. The brass was first heated and a shape like the corresponding bar in the Lao typewriter was stamped out roughly with a chisel. Then it was filed smooth, to the exact size.

In all, five type bars were made and installed on the typewriter to test. They worked well. Chia Koua was pleased with the clear, sharp impression they made.

But at this point the project was halted. Chia Koua was sent by the military for training in auto mechanics and electricity from 1969 to 1971. During that time he repeatedly went back to confer with Shong Lue and ask him questions, so that his learning from Shong Lue did not stop, but he had no time to work on the typewriter. Then after he finished his course and Shong Lue was killed, the worsening military situation put ever greater demands on his time, and life in Long Cheng was severely disrupted by the nearby fighting.

When Chia Koua evacuated Long Cheng in 1975, he had to leave the unfinished typewriter behind. He did bring with him the wood block letters and those tiny brass characters which had not yet been mounted on the typewriter. He also brought out the tools he had used in forming the letters, together with samples of the brass wire, brass ribbon and granulated solder. These he shows off with great pride.

The Nam Phong Refugee Camp

Before Shong Lue was sent to prison in 1967 he had told Chia Koua Vang that the Royal Lao Government and the communist Pathet Lao would some day be combined, and that they would kill Hmong people in April and May 1975. After Shong Lue's death in 1971 the military situation continued to deteriorate badly, and in 1973 when a coalition government between the warring sides in Laos was indeed formed, Chia Koua knew the end was near. In 1974 he built a house on land in Vientiane owned by a relative and moved his family there for safety, although he himself was still working at army headquarters in Long Cheng.

In early May 1975, communist forces had virtually taken over the "coalition," and some wealthy Lao people had begun escaping to Thai-

land. Then the government radio began inciting the Lao population
against the Hmong.

On May 14, 1975, Chia Koua, his family and some relatives crossed
the Mekong River by ferry to Thailand, as did many other Hmong in
Vientiane. Thai border officials sent them to a Thai military training
base at Nam Phong, in Khon Kaen Province, which was being turned
hurriedly into a temporary refugee camp for the Hmong fleeing Laos.
That same day General Vang Pao's officers and their families began to
evacuate Long Cheng for Thailand by plane.

A few weeks later, before General Vang Pao left the Nam Phong
camp to settle in the United States, he called a meeting of the camp
population to talk about what had happened. People attending the meeting wept bitterly at the loss of country, homes and loved ones. Among
them was Gnia Yee Yang, who, in his anguish, kept thinking about the
fact that the Hmong people had no books and no education in their language, that this was why they were politically ignorant and had fallen
into their present plight.

Gnia Yee, twenty-one years old at the time, had been educated in the
Lao language, and had graduated from a technical school in Vientiane.
He had also worked for the U.S. military mission from 1972 to 1975. He
had learned to read and write the Romanized Hmong on his own.

Gnia Yee happened to talk about his frustration to a cousin of Chia
Koua Vang, who introduced the two men. As Gnia Yee learned the
Pahawh Hmong from Chia Koua, the two of them prepared to teach it
to others in Nam Phong camp, with Gnia Yee assuming the primary
teaching responsibilities. He was the first person with any education to
become deeply involved with the Pahawh Hmong.

Eighty-four students, mainly young people with little or no education, but a few who were high school graduates, constituted the first
group Gnia Yee taught at Nam Phong in 1975. They learned primarily
the Third Stage Reduced Version, which Shong Lue Yang had produced in prison, the first such group to have ever studied it. Those who
learned it well went on to study the other stages also. Among them the
most notable was Chai Lee (Txais Lis ꘁ꘬ ꗁꗇ), later to be a leader in the
use of the Pahawh Hmong at the Hmong temple in the Ban Vinai refugee camp.

Chia Koua and Gnia Yee had taken the precaution of checking with
two of the ranking Hmong military officers in charge of operating the
camp under Thai authority before beginning lessons. They knew Colonels Shoua Yang (Suav Yaj ꘫꘈ ꗁꘈ) and Wang Seng Vang (Vam Xeeb Vaj
ꗛꙡ Ꙡꗛ ꗛꙡ) to be sympathetic to Shong Lue Yang and the Pahawh

Hmong. These officers assured them that they would take care of any trouble that might arise, now that General Vang Pao was gone.

But the class became a spectacle, with curious people gathered around to watch through the open sides of the training camp classroom, built for free air circulation in the tropical heat. And the class raised ghosts of the past for some of the Hmong leadership in the camp. Dr. Yang Dao (Yaj Dos **ᖁ ᖟᖠᖫ**) came and questioned Gnia Yee about the writing system, but he said the teaching could continue.

However, the colonel who had been Chief of Intelligence under General Vang Pao in Long Cheng informed the Thai authorities that there were "communists" in Nam Phong, and Thai soldiers came to arrest Chia Koua and Gnia Yee. The two men were tipped off in time, and neither of them was at the blacksmith shop (where they normally worked in the camp) when the arrests were made, and so they escaped. The sympathetic colonels arranged for them to keep on teaching without further harassment, providing a classroom with walls, where they would not be seen by the general camp public.

Chia Koua selected a few of the most promising students and gave them separate tasks in the promotion and development of the Pahawh Hmong and of Hmong language and culture. For example, Chao Yang (Txos Yaj **ᖟᖠᖫ ᖁ**) made careful anatomical drawings of the human body, which must have been copied from an anatomy textbook, and Chia Koua dictated to him the names of the different body parts. Most of these were traditional Hmong terms, while others had been coined by Shong Lue.[3]

Shong Lue had also taught Chia Koua about traditional Hmong medicine, and had told him how to find out more from elderly Hmong medical practitioners, and from other healers who knew things the Hmong did not know. Chia Koua enlisted Cher Lee (Ntsawb Lis **ᖟᖫ ᖠᖫ**) to do some of this investigation, and they together wrote out a notebook full of traditional Hmong medicines, the ways in which they were to be administered, and the kinds of sicknesses for which they suitable, arranged in tabular form.[4]

Shua Vang (Suav Vaj **ᖟᖫ ᖁᖫ**) wrote out extensive comments on plants and other matters.[5] Yer Vang (Ntxawg Vaj **ᖟᖫ ᖁᖫ**) wrote a poem about Hmong history. He began with the split in the Nong Het area between those families that had supported first the French and then the Vietnamese and those that had supported the Royal Lao Government.[6] All of these texts, written in notebooks in the Pahawh Hmong Third Stage Reduced Version, reflected a strong desire to preserve Hmong cultural traditions in the deteriorating situation.

But from the standpoint of the Pahawh Hmong itself, the most important assignments went to Gnia Yee Yang and to Chai Lee. Chia Koua charged them with the responsibility for making books in the Pahawh Hmong, and of searching for a way to make typewriters. Both of them have been fulfilling this responsibility in different ways ever since. At Nam Phong, Gnia Yee began by preparing a booklet to help teach the Pahawh Hmong, composing it by hand, with detailed line drawings.[7] Chia Koua himself also wrote a little "grammar" book, consisting of rules for the Pahawh Hmong and other information, composed partly by hand and partly with the use of the wood block letters he had made in Long Cheng.[8]

The Ban Vinai Refugee Camp

On April 15, 1976, Chia Koua Vang, Gnia Yee Yang and their families were relocated to Ban Vinai refugee camp in Loei Province, Thailand, a camp which had been especially constructed for holding Hmong refugees. Before they left Nam Phong, Colonel Soua Yang announced that he was to be the leader of Center 3 (one of the administrative divisions of the camp), and that anyone who knew the Pahawh Hmong, or was sympathetic to it and to Shong Lue Yang, should settle there.

So Center 3 became the primary (but not the exclusive) Pahawh Hmong area of the Ban Vinai camp, and it remains so today. It is where Chia Koua and Gnia Yee began to teach the Pahawh Hmong in 1976; it is where Chai Lee and others continue teaching it at the Hmong temple thirteen years later.

In Ban Vinai the number of people who were interested in learning the Pahawh Hmong increased, a reassertment of the enthusiasm which Shong Lue had sparked when he was alive, a desire which had been suppressed by the brutal killings of the prophet and his followers. Gnia Yee taught different classes morning and afternoon for a time. But there were no supplies or materials for adequate teaching and learning, or for the production of books, so Colonel Shoua Yang called a meeting on June 1, 1976, inviting former teachers, school administrators, government representatives, military officers and other members of the Hmong elite. Eighty-seven such people attended, none of whom had ever learned the Pahawh Hmong, but all of whom had known Shong Lue, or believed in him, or were interested for some other reason.

They made plans and set priorities, placing the development of a typewriter and books for teaching the Pahawh Hmong at the top, and promising to help financially in accomplishing these goals. They agree that the Third Stage Reduced Version should be the system standard.

The American Period

It was clear to Chia Koua and Gnia Yee, however, that they could not accomplish all they wanted at Ban Vinai, especially the making of a typewriter. They thus felt it necessary to move to the United States with their families, arriving in June 1978. Chia Koua settled in Honolulu, Hawaii, and Gnia Yee in St. Paul, Minnesota, where their respective sponsors lived.

Both men sought ways to make a typewriter for the Pahawh Hmong in the United States, but they did not know where to turn. For a long time they were not sure that what they wanted to do was legal. Because of the persecution they had experienced in Laos, and the Lao policy of discouraging the writing of minority languages, they were afraid at first to show the Pahawh Hmong to anyone in America. Their lack of English reinforced their isolation.

As they did make contacts and gain confidence, they asked Americans whom they came to know about the legality of what they wanted to do. They also wrote to boards of education and tried to find out what American government office was in charge of writing systems. As late as 1983, when Smalley first met him, Chia Koua was still concerned about the legality of the use of the script. But as they consistently received the same answer, that the U.S. government did not care what language or what writing system anybody used, and that publications in many writing systems were produced in the United States, they gained the courage to push ahead with their search for ways of making a Pahawh Hmong typewriter and other means of reproducing the script.

In Hawaii Chia Koua met Bruce Bliatout (Pov Thoj ꓖꓲꓼ ꓖꓲꓯ), a Hmong who had been studying in the United States when Laos fell in 1975. With Bliatout's knowledge of English and of how to get around in America, Chia Koua made contact in 1978 with a manufacturer of rubber stamps.[9] Chia Koua stamped out each of the Pahawh Hmong letters with his wood blocks, and a corresponding individual rubber stamp was made for each, at a total cost of $100. But the rubber stamps did not work as well as the original wood blocks.

In St. Paul, Gnia Yee enrolled in a technical school to learn to be a machinist, and he experimented after hours on school machinery, trying to make type slugs with Pahawh Hmong characters. The technique which worked best was to cut the shapes of individual characters in metal slugs with an engraver. He learned to produce good individual slugs, but he was often frustrated when he would go back to continue the following night, because the settings on the machine would have been changed by other users, and he could not fully control variation in the vertical placement of the letters from one slug to another. At one point he inquired in a typewriter store and was told that to have a typewriter made the way he wanted would cost $200,000.

Chia Koua joined Gnia Yee in St. Paul in June 1979 to coordinate these efforts. St. Paul was becoming a major Hmong center in which many scattered refugees were gathering. On March 3, 1980, they met with three other supporters of the Pahawh Hmong to discuss ways of developing the use of the writing system. Three months later nine people attended a second meeting and decided to form an association.

But with some of them still uneasy about how the Pahawh Hmong would be seen by Americans, the group decided to broaden their association to promote all the emphases of Shong Lue Yang, such as Hmong unity and the preservation and teaching of Hmong culture. Promotion of the Pahawh Hmong would of course be included as central to ideal Hmong culture.

They called their association Motthem Family 59 (Mojthem ᨮᨩ ᨤᨲ) *Motthem* means 'cooperation, collaboration'; *1959* was the year that Shong Lue Yang began his teaching, when the Hmong were "awakened to unity." The Motthem Family was incorporated as a non-profit organization in Minnesota on July 27, 1982; and as of 1987 it had 225 members, living largely in California and Minnesota.

The first president of the Motthem Family was Gnia Gao Yang (Nyiaj Nkaus Yaj ᨬᨮ ᨯᨶ ᨲᨯ). Like some of the other members he could not read the Pahawh Hmong, but was drawn by Shong Lue's teaching about harmony and the importance of Hmong culture. The published 1982 bylaws produced under his leadership were written in English and Lao. Pahawh Hmong was not included because some board members were still uneasy about how it would be viewed, aside from the fact that the script could not yet be typed. However, each page of the bylaws has on it the Pahawh Hmong logo for 'Hmong', which identifies the book for anyone who knows the Pahawh Hmong.[10]

In 1980 Gnia Yee also made friends with an American who put him in touch with a machine tool company, which agreed to make type slugs with Pahawh Hmong characters, individually engraved, and put them on an electric portable typewriter.[11] Gnia Yee designed the keyboard placement of the Pahawh Hmong characters, which was approved by the board of the Motthem Family.

This first Pahawh Hmong typewriter was finally delivered May 11, 1982, fifteen years after Chia Koua started making his brass letters for typewriter keys in Long Cheng, and six years after the two men started their search in the United States. The completed typewriter cost $6,000, which was raised by subscription from fifty-six people who wanted to promote the use of the Pahawh Hmong. Contributions ranged from $10 to $176.62 each, with thirteen people contributing the maximum amount, set by dividing equally among themselves the balance remaining after others had given.

No money came from the Motthem Family as such, although members contributed as individuals. Contributions were also received from people not connected with the Motthem Family. Together these contributors constitute an informal network which has no name or organization, but which functions as "Financial Friends of the Pahawh Hmong."

But two problems marred this success in finding a way to have a Pahawh Hmong typewriter made. The electric typewriter had only forty-four keys, which meant that only eighty-eight Pahawh characters could be included. About one hundred characters were needed for the Third Stage Reduced Version, excluding the clan logos, but including numbers, punctuation marks, arithmetic signs, periods of time, etc. So for this electric typewriter the Final Version was used reluctantly instead of the Third Stage, eliminating the need for thirteen of the characters.

With the finished typewriter, furthermore, some keys made very dark impressions, even cutting through the paper, while other impressions were too light. Neither the Hmong who bought the typewriter nor the people in the machine shop who made the slugs knew why, as they were not typewriter technicians. The search for a fully satisfactory typewriter therefore continued.

But in spite of these difficulties, the group in St. Paul ordered a second typewriter, with keys made the same way, this time at a price of $2,500, subscribed by twenty-eight people. The first typewriter had been assigned to Gnia Yee (then in California), and the second was sent to Pa Kao Her, one of Shong Lue's earliest students and teachers of the Pahawh Hmong, for use in his headquarters near Chiang Kham, Phayao, Thailand.

Pa Kao responded by sending an order for one hundred more of these typewriters, expecting them to be paid for by subscribers in the States. The group in St. Paul replied that this was impossible. Pa Kao would have to pay for any more typewriters that he wanted. But then the company which had made the slugs for the two typewriters also declined to take any more orders. This was not their line, and they had too much other work to do.

Beyond the First Typewriter

In early September 1981, after having located the company which would make the key slugs for the first typewriters, and after having designed the keyboard layout, Gnia Yee moved to North Carolina to work as a machinist. While there he worked on another way of producing printable Pahawh Hmong texts.

In St. Paul, Gnia Yee had been trying to find out how to get press-apply letters made. These are letters which transfer to paper one at a time from a transparent plastic sheet when the back of the plastic surface is rubbed. In North Carolina an American friend put him in contact with a manufacturer.[12] He paid $25 for each original film of press-apply characters, and had to place a minimum order of fifty sheets at $3 per sheet. He ultimately produced four different sizes of the characters, and had sheets made with Source Version characters as well. He has sometimes ordered one hundred press-apply sheets at a time, helped by financial donations from other interested people.

The first press-apply order was completed before the typewriter, and Gnia Yee used it to produce an eighty-five-page primer to help teach the Final Version, which would now be the version promoted because it would be available on the typewriter.[13] Two hundred copies were printed at a cost of $300.

In September 1983 Gnia Yee moved to California, after being laid off from his work in North Carolina. He believed he could do more there in his search for a satisfactory typewriter, as more people were interested in the Pahawh Hmong and willing to help. Soon after moving he produced a twenty-nine-page grammar, which consisted of explanations of some of the mechanics of the Pahawh Hmong and other information.[14] The text was produced on the new typewriter, with headings and other large characters produced by press-apply. Fifty copies were printed for $200, and they were used in classes as well as distributed to interested people.

In 1984 an American friend introduced Gnia Yee to a very helpful typewriter dealer,[15] who told him for the first time why the electric typewriters had produced uneven impressions with the Pahawh Hmong. The various keys of electric typewriters strike with different force according to the size of the letters in English. Thus a period strikes more lightly than an m, for example.

The dealer put Gnia Yee in touch with IBM, with whom he corresponded about the possibility of making a type element for the Selectric typewriter. IBM checked over the Pahawh Hmong requirements and found that they could not be accommodated on the Selectric ball.

An electronic typewriter, on the other hand, would work, and had the additional advantage of coming with forty-eight keys, allowing ninety-six characters (with additional ones through use of the "code" key). This made room for the Third Stage symbols, which could not be included on the earlier typewriter, as well as the extra Final Stage diacritics, so that texts could be typed in either Third or Final Stage Versions. And, of course, by changing the printwheel, English or Romanized Hmong could be typed, too. To top it off, the typewriter included a state-of-the-art memory unit.[16] At last the Pahawh Hmong could be written on a typewriter worthy of it.

Gnia Yee laid out a new keyboard accordingly, using the most suitable of several options for combinations of dead keys[17] and character impressions available for this typewriter. The new printwheels were completed by April 25, 1986, and everything worked perfectly! At last the Pahawh Hmong could be typed in fully satisfactory fashion, second to no other writing system in the world.

The development of the printwheel cost $9,400, subscribed by twenty-nine people, members of the financial support group, but each typewriter purchased was paid for by the user at a cost of $1,100. Additional printwheels cost $75–$85, depending on the number ordered at a time. By the end of 1987, the Motthem Family had bought a typewriter for itself; three were owned by individuals (one in California, two in St. Paul); and two were subscribed by friends and supporters of Pa Kao Her and his movement. These last two were sent to Thailand, one to Pa Kao's headquarters and one to Chai Lee at the temple in Ban Vinai.

The new typewriters were all bought with standard English keytops because the cost of keytops with Pahawh Hmong lettering on them would have been exorbitant. Gnia Yee devised ways of marking the keytops himself instead. For each of the first typewriters he used press-apply letters overlaid with transparent "crazy glue" to keep them from wearing off. But later he learned to use a silkscreen process, with an ink which would adhere to the hard plastic of the keytops. This system was simpler to apply and gave more durable results.

In 1985, with the new typewriter capable of typing the Third Stage Reduced Version soon to be available, some people who had helped defray the cost of the typewriters met with Pa Kao Her, who was in the States at the time, and decided to reinstate the Third Stage as the preferred standard. And in 1986, even before the typewriter was available, two booklets were published in the Third Stage Version.

The first of these was a "history" of the development of the Pahawh Hmong, giving the inventory of characters for each of the stages of the writing system, with a little explanation of each.[18] Press-apply characters were used to compose most of it, with one partial page typed on the electric typewriter to illustrate the Final Stage. Fifty copies were made at a total cost of $200. Then a glossy, color Third Stage Version primer was printed. It was entirely composed with press-apply letters. A run of five hundred copies cost $2,000.[19]

But in the meantime another resource had been developing. On December 11, 1983, William Smalley began making contact with the group at St. Paul, and over several months he negotiated with them a joint research project which eventually culminated in this book. Funding granted for the project[20] included the cost of a personal computer and printer, as well as software by which the Pahawh characters could be designed and incorporated in a wordprocessing program which could compose Pahawh Hmong text on the same line as both English and Romanized Hmong.[21] Such equipment would be needed in order to document the various stages of the writing system, and at the end of the project the equipment would belong to the Motthem Family.

The project began September 1, 1986, and Gnia Yee Yang moved back to St. Paul to be a part of it. He learned to design the Pahawh Hmong characters for the computer screen and printer, producing several fonts for the Third Stage Version, extra diacritics for the Final Version, plus all the logographs, punctuation, etc. Source Version fonts were created as well. He followed the keyboard layout of the electronic typewriter, marking the computer keytops with the Pahawh characters in the same way. He also produced larger custom-made letters and pictures for display and for primers, etc., using a separate graphics program.[22]

Within the program for creating Pahawh Hmong characters and wordprocessing Pahawh Hmong texts, Smalley and Gnia Yee have also created computer tables of correspondences between Romanized and Pahawh Hmong symbols, so that texts in Romanized Hmong can be transliterated by computer into corresponding texts in Pahawh Hmong, and vice versa. The source text in either case has to be in a form that is readable by the wordprocessing program.

The computer greatly increased the flexibility and versatility of what Gnia Yee and Chia Koua could now do in the Pahawh Hmong, but for the first time in their search, Gnia Yee had to distort the characters a little sometimes to make them fit the limitations of a new medium. Dot

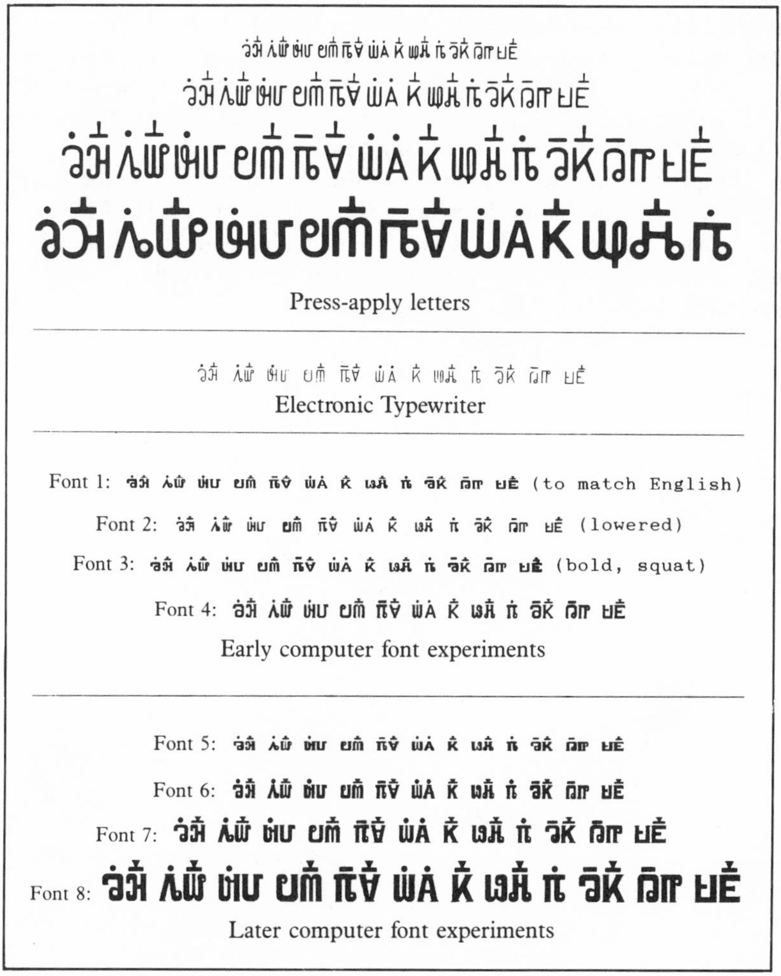

ᦞᦡᦟᦞᦀᦞᦡᦞᦟᦞᦡᦞᦟ

ᦞᦡᦟᦞᦀᦞᦡᦞᦟᦞᦡᦞᦟᦞᦡᦞᦟ

ᦞᦡᦟᦞᦀᦞᦡᦞᦟᦞᦡᦞᦟᦞᦡᦞᦟ

ᦞᦡᦟᦞᦀᦞᦡᦞᦟᦞᦡᦞᦟ

Press-apply letters

ᦞᦡᦟᦞᦀᦞᦡᦞᦟᦞᦡᦞᦟᦞᦡᦞᦟ

Electronic Typewriter

Font 1: ᦞᦡᦟᦞᦀᦞᦡᦞᦟᦞᦡᦞᦟᦞᦡᦞᦟ (to match English)

Font 2: ᦞᦡᦟᦞᦀᦞᦡᦞᦟᦞᦡᦞᦟᦞᦡᦞᦟ (lowered)

Font 3: ᦞᦡᦟᦞᦀᦞᦡᦞᦟᦞᦡᦞᦟᦞᦡᦞᦟ (bold, squat)

Font 4: ᦞᦡᦟᦞᦀᦞᦡᦞᦟᦞᦡᦞᦟᦞᦡᦞᦟ

Early computer font experiments

Font 5: ᦞᦡᦟᦞᦀᦞᦡᦞᦟᦞᦡᦞᦟᦞᦡᦞᦟ

Font 6: ᦞᦡᦟᦞᦀᦞᦡᦞᦟᦞᦡᦞᦟᦞᦡᦞᦟ

Font 7: ᦞᦡᦟᦞᦀᦞᦡᦞᦟᦞᦡᦞᦟᦞᦡᦞᦟ

Font 8: ᦞᦡᦟᦞᦀᦞᦡᦞᦟᦞᦡᦞᦟᦞᦡᦞᦟ

Later computer font experiments

Fig. 4. Pahawh Hmong produced by equipment currently in use (i.e., not including the electric typewriter), reproduced at 64% of actual size.

matrix format was a problem, especially in creating a font for text which was to appear on the same line with Romanized Hmong or English, as in this book. The letters had to be made squat and square to harmonize with the Roman configuration of lower-case letters (Fig. 4, Fonts 1–3, 5). The letters had to be lowered below the English letters to make room for clear diacritics (Fonts 2, 3, 5 as against Font 1). Larger fonts were more satisfactory (Fonts 4, 6–8), but they required two or three passes of the printer head to produce each line of Pahawh Hmong, and were therefore slower.

In 1987 a new, simpler alphabet book for the Third Stage Reduced Version was produced using the computer plus press-apply letters. Five hundred copies were printed, costing $385.[23]

With the electronic typewriter and the computer/printer, the hardware problems in the mechanical production of Pahawh Hmong texts have finally been solved. The Pahawh Hmong has gone from handwriting and movable type (the wood blocks) to wordprocessing in twenty years, 1967–1987.

Shong Lue Yang and Bau Moua, his second wife, outside the home of a Long Cheng photographer, 1967. Photograph by Shua Lue Thao (Suav Lwm Thoj).

Research Team. (*Left to right*) Mitt Moua, Chia Koua Vang, Gnia Yee Yang, William A. Smalley. Photograph by Ted Crouch.

A letter from the imprisoned Shong Lue Yang to Chia Koua Vang, in 1968 or 1969, concerning Chia Koua's attempts to make a book in the Pahawh Hmong. Photograph by William A. Smalley.

A page from Chia Koua Vang's notebook. The discussion concerns the buildings associated with Shong Lue's movement. The drawings depict (1) an ideal round house, used for worship, with twelve doors around the perimeter; (2) an example of the monument associated with the round house; (3) a school for the teaching of Pahawh Hmong. Photograph by William A. Smalley.

Pages from Chia Koua Vang's notebook recounting the story of the twins who taught the Pahawh Hmong to Shong Lue Yang. The left page includes a paraphrase of the letter to Shong Lue from infant Xa Yang, with a depiction of the baby's footprint at the bottom of the page. Photograph by William A. Smalley.

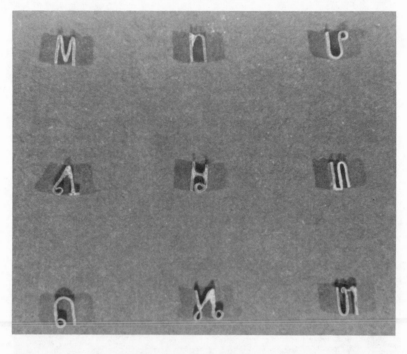

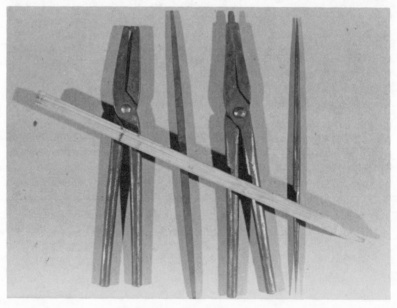

(*Facing page, top*) Brass letters from the Pahawh Hmong alphabet, formed to be mounted on a typewriter. Letters are enlarged from their actual 3mm height. (*Bottom*) Tools made by Chia Koua Vang with which to shape the brass letters for a Pahawh Hmong typewriter. Photographs by William A. Smalley.

Gnia Yee Yang working in Pahawh Hmong at the computer. Photograph by William A. Smalley.

Typical small Hmong village, Xieng Khouang Province, Laos, circa 1952. Photograph by
William A. Smalley.

9

Contemporary Use of the Alphabet

We have seen the initial attraction of the Pahawh Hmong, and then its eclipse in Laos as a result of the events recorded at the end of Chapter 2; we have also seen it re-emerge in Thailand and the United States, kept alive by a small number of devoted people convinced of its importance. It is much more difficult, however, to get a full and accurate picture of how strong its present hold is on the widely scattered Hmong population.

People who currently use the Pahawh Hmong are now clustered in five locations we know of: the Phou Bia Mountain (Phu Npiab ꘖ꘤ ꘪꘫ) area of Laos, the Ban Vinai refugee camp, the military camp of the Ethnics Liberation Organization of Laos, part of the state of California, and parts of the states of Minnesota and Wisconsin. There are individuals and smaller groups who use the writing outside these areas.

New information from the Phou Bia Mountain area comes only in an occasional letter or through a trickle of new refugees from there. Ban Vinai and the Ethnics Liberation Organization camp are more accessible, but we have not had the opportunity to study the present use of the writing in either location for ourselves. In the United States the Pahawh Hmong is used by widely scattered networks of individuals, so that there is no local community to observe directly, and even the term "cluster" implies more concentration than there is.

However, in this chapter we describe what we can of how the Pahawh Hmong is currently being used, and how its use is different from location to location. Part of our information comes from a survey questionnaire sent to every person we could locate in the United States who had ever had any significant contact with the Pahawh Hmong. Fifty-four copies of the survey were also sent to each of the two centers in Thailand, in care of the respective leaders there. The number of replies may be seen in Table 32.

About 30 percent of the survey forms distributed in the United States were completed and returned, as were all of those sent to Thailand. The

Table 32. Location of survey respondents. Respondents without prior contact with the Pahawh Hmong are not included in most of the survey calculations.

Respondents with previous Pahawh Hmong contact		196 (87.5%)
Ban Vinai	54	
Ethnics Liberation camp	54	
California	49	
Minnesota/Wisconsin	31	
Other U.S. locations	8	
Respondents with no previous Pahawh Hmong contact		28 (12.5%)
Total responses		224

ones from Thailand, where many more people use the Pahawh Hmong than received forms, seem generally to have been filled out only by people who know the Pahawh Hmong well, and mostly by ones with a little education. In the United States some respondents were pleased that research was being done on the Pahawh Hmong, but others were uneasy, and thirty people in one Pahawh Hmong class declined to participate in the survey because they did not want their interest in the writing system to be misinterpreted as a political or religious statement. Lack of education and lack of familiarity with the survey medium also probably inhibited some people from responding.[1] So our survey does not give a representative sampling either of the population which uses the Pahawh Hmong or of the general Hmong population, and its results should be generalized only with caution.

Inside Laos

In May 1975, when Chia Koua Vang, Gnia Yee Yang and many thousands of other Hmong began to evacuate Laos, they were not in the majority. Most of the Hmong people stayed behind, some settling permanently into life under the new government, others fleeing the country later. Some who stayed hid themselves in the rugged Phou Bia Mountain area, where Shong Lue Yang had spent his last days, and were joined from time to time by people who had escaped from communist forced-labor "re-education" camps.

These Hmong in Phou Bia continued to resist when the Vietnamese and the new Lao communist government attacked them savagely, saying that they were harboring Americans.[2] Such attacks sent tens of thousands more Hmong fleeing to Thailand in 1977–1979, both from Phou Bia and elsewhere in Laos. Perhaps 50 percent or more of those who tried to flee never made it to Thailand, some being massacred along the way, others dying during the weeks of walking and hiding out in the jungle, or drowning in the Mekong River as they tried to cross.

Those who are left at Phou Bia today hide in the jungle-covered mountains, eking out an existence and defending themselves as best they can. They are not able to grow rice, but they do grow small plots of corn and vegetables in places which cannot be spotted from the air. They also collect wild plants from the jungle for food. Able-bodied men sometimes slip in and out of the area, the perimeter of which is closely watched by the government, but families are trapped. So many people have died trying to escape that few others dare to leave.

Not all the people in the Phou Bia area were believers in Shong Lue. The different groups followed different leaders and lived in different parts of the mountain region, but they cooperated in their mutual defense. In time the non-believers fled to Thailand, as did many of the believers, but those who remain are almost all followers of Shong Lue Yang.

One of the major early leaders of that resistance at Phou Bia was Pa Kao Her, who as we have seen was one of the first students of Shong Lue and one of the first teachers of the Pahawh Hmong. In 1975 he was in the Hmong army, and he stayed behind to continue the fight against the communists. The other primary military leader there with him was Yong Youa Her (Ntxoov Zuag Hawj ꘎꘡ ꘓꘔ ꘟꘘ). Yong Youa still continues to lead the resistance at Phou Bia, but the two leaders decided in 1978 that Pa Kao should leave to enlist support, recruit fighters and train them.

Men come and go from the Ethnics Liberation camp and the refugee camps in Thailand, making their precarious way on foot over mountain trails to assist in the defense of Phou Bia. They are sometimes called "Sky Fighters" by Westerners, from the Lao *Chao Fa* (Cob Fab ꘏ꘐ ꘑꘒ) 'Lord of the Sky'. There are Hmong men now in the United States who spent months or years with the resistance at Phou Bia.

There are other leaders in the Phou Bia Mountain area as well. Lor Youa Vue (Lauj Ntxuam Vwj ꘓꘔ ꘕꘖ ꘗꘘ) leads in matters of religion and worship, following Shong Lue's division of labor between worship leaders and teachers. The leading teachers of the Pahawh Hmong are Chong Vang (Txoov Vaj ꘙꘚ ꘛꘜ) and Kao Lee (Kos Lis ꘝꘞ ꘟ꘠), both of whom were former students of Shong Lue.[3] The writing system was resurrected at Phou Bia as soon as the Hmong military leaders who had suppressed it left Laos, just as it emerged also in Nam Phong.

The people hiding out in the Phou Bia area do not live in cleared villages subject to bombing, but in jungle dwellings. They also have round houses for worship, as Shong Lue taught, and little shelters in which to hold their Pahawh Hmong classes. They have no books or supplies for classes, but students memorize the tables of Pahawh Hmong characters.

The version of the Pahawh Hmong used in the Phou Bia area is the Second Stage Reduced Version, the one current in Laos when Shong Lue was killed, as nobody there knows any other. The writing is used to convey messages locally, and people write letters in it, smuggling them through Vientiane to their friends and supporters in the outside world. These friends, however, reply in Lao, even if they know the Pahawh Hmong, sending their letters via intermediaries in Laos so as not to incriminate the recipients. People are shot if it is discovered that they are *Chao Fa*.[4]

The Ban Vinai Temple

In 1977 in the Ban Vinai refugee camp, a man by the name of Sao Yang (Xauv Yaj **ᏋA ᎦᏇ**) became a foreteller (saub **ᏇᏋ**) and announced that God (Ntuj **ᏋᎦᎦ**) was going to give him a new writing system for the Hmong people, one different from the Pahawh Hmong. He was living in Center 3, where many of the people who believed in Shong Lue lived, and he gathered a following which included some of them. He told his followers to build a place of worship, where God would give him three characters of the new writing system each night. So they built a star-shaped structure (unlike Shong Lue Yang's round one) out of bamboo and thatch in the Center 3 area. This was the start of the present "Hmong temple" at Ban Vinai.

The first night of worship Sao Yang came up with three words, *peb sib hlub* 'we love each other', and one character for each word. We do not know what these characters looked like. On succeeding nights the process fizzled, however, and no more characters were forthcoming. Sao Yang finally announced that God told him they should use the Second Stage Reduced Version of the Pahawh Hmong (the one which had been used since 1965 in Laos), declaring that the time was not right yet for the Third Stage (the one which was being taught by Chia Koua and Gnia Yee in Ban Vinai).

Chai Lee, who had learned the Pahawh Hmong at the Nam Phong refugee camp, and who had been one of the two people to whom Chia

Koua Vang had given responsibility for producing books, had joined Sao Yang's movement because he wanted to learn the additional truth that Sao Yang said was being revealed from God. So when Sao Yang switched to the Pahawh Hmong, Chai Lee moved into a place of leadership in teaching the Second Stage Reduced Version in the Ban Vinai temple.

The primary form of the Pahawh Hmong which Chai Lee had learned at Nam Phong from Chia Koua Vang and Gnia Yee Yang had been the Third Stage Reduced Version, but the better students like him had gone on to learn the other stages as well. So Chai Lee was therefore ready with the Second Stage required by Sao Yang's new directive from God, although he had missed a few details like the writing of the d-tone and of punctuation. For those he ultimately devised his own variants.

When interviewed in 1984[5] Chai Lee said that the later versions of the Pahawh Hmong (and the Romanized Hmong as well) were all right for routine purposes like letters, but that the Second Stage was necessary for research and documentation of Hmong religion and custom, on which he and others at the temple have concentrated.

But as the printwheel for the electronic typewriter was being developed in the United States, the people there consulted both with Pa Kao Her at the Ethnics Liberation Organization camp and with Chai Lee at Ban Vinai. With the typewriter assured, in 1985 the two Thailand groups modified their practice and adopted the Third Stage. Letters from Chai Lee are now written in it, although we have not yet seen any books written by him in that version. He was later sent an electronic typewriter with a Pahawh Hmong printwheel, but we have not yet seen evidence of its use, either.

The classes in the Pahawh Hmong which were established at the temple under Chai Lee in 1977 have continued ever since. In 1984 he said that he had about thirty teachers of the Pahawh Hmong working with him, holding classes morning and afternoon, each session lasting about two hours. He said that it takes one to three months for an adult to learn the Pahawh Hmong, and about a year for children. He estimated that there were three hundred members of the temple, but gave no figure on how many people in all had learned to read the Pahawh Hmong at the temple.

Chai Lee takes trips out of Ban Vinai from time to time, visiting in villages of Hmong people who live permanently in Thailand (not as refugees from Laos), and teaching the Pahawh Hmong there. Some Thai Hmong have learned it, but we do not know how many.

Over the years, Chai Lee has written several small books using the Second Stage Pahawh Hmong. These include an alphabet book, primers, reading books and books on Hmong history and culture. Most of these books have never been published, but at least two were reproduced by offset printing from his neat handwritten manuscripts.[6] People at Ban Vinai may go to the temple to copy unpublished manuscripts by hand.

Chai Lee also set his students to collecting Hmong oral history, writing it down in the Pahawh Hmong. He then read, compared and evaluated what was sent to him, selecting what he believed to be "true." Like the Hebrew priests in exile in ancient Babylon, Chai Lee in exile at the Hmong temple in Thailand is establishing his "canon" of Hmong oral history, custom and religion.

Sao Yang remains the worship leader at the Ban Vinai temple, but Chai Lee has emerged as the stronger leader in every other way. Sao Yang is no longer a foreteller, and the cultural features promoted by Chai Lee have eclipsed the worship. In addition to the teaching of the Pahawh Hmong, Chai Lee has an extensive program for the development of Hmong music and poetry on themes of Hmong cultural tradition and ethics.

Under the influence of Sao Yang, who consulted with a Buddhist priest, strong Buddhist visual symbolism has been introduced into the temple area. This includes Buddha-like statues made of concrete, for example, and "monks" wearing saffron robes like Lao and Thai Buddhist monks.

In spite of this syncretism, traditional Hmong perspective is dominant in the temple. The large Buddha-like statue in the middle of the temple compound wears the traditional short jacket of an unmarried Hmong man. The mythology of the temple as represented in almost all of the statues, including one of a large pig, is derived from Hmong sources, not Thai or Indian. Chai Lee explained the Buddhist imagery as an accommodation. He said that the Hmong of Ban Vinai camp are living in Thailand, so they use Thai symbols, but when they have their own country their monks will wear black robes because the Hmong color is black.

From the standpoint of people like Chia Koua Vang, however, who see themselves as linear descendants of Shong Lue Yang, the temple is an aberration. The Buddhist symbolism does not come from Shong Lue. The temple does not have a round house for worship. The people have followed there a foreteller who has not listened to Shong Lue. Even Chai Lee, brilliant and innovative as he is, and important as he has been for the Pahawh Hmong, is considered to make strange interpretations and to have an undisciplined imagination in some of his writings. The temple continues Shong Lue's writing system and adheres to many of his values, but it is not fully orthodox.

On the other hand, some Hmong leaders inside and outside the Pahawh Hmong movement express admiration for the way in which the temple is preserving and teaching Hmong culture, even creating new forms of Hmong music and performance. They find it to have made a valuable contribution, even though they do not agree with it religiously or in their choice of writing system for the Hmong language.

The Camp of the Ethnics Liberation Movement

After Pa Kao Her moved from Phou Bia Mountain in 1978 he sought help for the resistance from various sources and eventually set up the headquarters of the Ethnics Liberation Organization of Laos, which serves as a rallying point for some Hmong people seeking the liberation of Laos. The Pahawh Hmong is used in the camp by people who know it. Pa Kao Her himself writes it on the blackboard when he is teaching. Students, however, take their notes in whatever way they know, writing the Pahawh Hmong or Romanized Hmong, or using the Lao language.

As is clear from Table 33, most respondents from the Ethnics Liberation camp learned the Pahawh Hmong elsewhere, many doubtless at Phou Bia; others had learned it before Shong Lue's death. Until 1987 there was no systematic teaching of the Pahawh Hmong in the Ethnics Liberation camp, but that year Blia Kao Her (Npliaj Kaus Hawj ꬉꬃ ꬀ ꬮꬪ) became the head teacher for the Pahawh Hmong, and ordered books from the States. He not only teaches in the camp, but also in Thai Hmong villages.

Until 1985, when both the Ban Vinai camp and the Ethnics Liberation camp switched over to the Third Stage Reduced Version, the Sec-

Table 33. Where Pahawh Hmong was learned, number of respondents by location

	Laos	Thailand	U.S.A.
Ban Vinai	4	49	0
Ethnics Liberation	43	7	0
California	11	5	24
Minn./Wis.	15	7	4
Other U.S. locations	5	1	0

ond Stage was the one used in the Liberation camp. In fact, Pa Kao Her himself still mixes in some of the Source Version characters by habit when he writes later versions.

California and Minnesota/Wisconsin

From north of Sacramento to south of Los Angeles, over a distance of nearly five hundred miles down the center of the state of California, are scattered a number of people who know and use the Pahawh Hmong. This is the larger of the two "clusters" in the United States, reflecting the fact that California has the largest general Hmong population in the country.

St. Paul, Minnesota, is the heart of the second largest American cluster, in the state with the second largest Hmong population. St. Paul is also important for the Pahawh Hmong because Chia Koua Vang lives there, Gnia Yee Yang has lived there at times, and much of their effort to develop the typewriter and other use of the Pahawh Hmong has been centered there. Stretching out from St. Paul, through southern Minnesota and into Wisconsin for three hundred miles, are scattered other people who use the Pahawh Hmong as well, so that we have grouped them in the same "cluster" for reporting the results of our survey.

People in the United States who make use of the Pahawh Hmong are widely dispersed even within these two clusters, with no Pahawh Hmong–using neighborhoods such as there are at Ban Vinai and the Ethnics Liberation camp. Thus although the American Hmong can give each other mutual support, as do many interest groups in this country, there is not intensive community interaction. Although there was strong feeling about the importance of the Pahawh Hmong expressed in the survey by respondents in the United States, their responses on the whole did not match the intensity of the replies from Thailand, especially from the Ethnics Liberation camp. Use of the Pahawh Hmong would seem to be diluted in the United States, along with so much else from the Hmong past. There are also no round houses for worship in the United States, so far as we know.

Profiles of Survey Respondents

Taking our survey as a whole, the typical respondent who has some knowledge of the Pahawh Hmong is male, between the ages of fifteen and forty-four, follows traditional Hmong religion, speaks the Hmong Daw dialect, came from Xieng Khouang Province in Laos, and reads

Table 34. Typical characteristics of respondents familiar with the Pahawh Hmong, in percentages. The survey sample is probably better educated than the average user of the Pahawh Hmong.

Male		74.7
Age 15–44		87.0
15–29	57.8	
30–44	29.2	
Follow traditional religion		78.0
Speak Hmong Daw		56.7
Come from Xieng Khouang Province		69.9
Able to read Lao		75.9
Excellent/good	61.0	
Fair/poor	14.9	
Able to read English		63.6
Excellent/good	28.7	
Fair/poor	34.9	
Ability to read Romanized Hmong		55.1
Excellent/good	45.9	
Fair/poor	9.2	
Ability to read the Lao script Hmong		17.5
Excellent/good	5.7	
Fair/poor	11.8	

Table 35. Self-estimates of ability to read Pahawh Hmong and Romanized Hmong, number of respondents by location

	Excellent	Good	Fair	Poor
Pahawh Second Stage				
Ban Vinai	54	0	0	0
Ethnics Liberation	54	0	0	0
California	7	10	10	12
Minn./Wis.	1	4	11	5
Other U.S. locations	1	1	0	3
Pahawh Third Stage				
Ban Vinai	54	0	0	0
Ethnics Liberation	44	9	1	0
California	8	10	8	11
Minn./Wis.	4	3	3	7
Other U.S. locations	0	3	0	2
Romanized				
Ban Vinai	35	2	0	0
Ethnics Liberation	0	0	0	0
California	11	11	9	4
Minn./Wis.	18	7	3	2
Other U.S. locations	4	2	0	0

Lao, English and the Romanized Hmong in addition to the Pahawh Hmong (Table 34).

A breakdown of ability to read the Second Stage and Third Stage Versions of the Pahawh Hmong according to location of respondents (Table 35) shows the considerably greater mastery of both in the two

Thailand clusters than in the United States. A comparison of the ability to read the Romanized Hmong is also instructive. On the one hand the respondents from the highly nationalistic Ethnics Liberation camp had no use for the Romanized Hmong (an opinion sharply expressed in open-ended questions as well), but on the other hand it is well known by most respondents in Ban Vinai. That use of the Pahawh Hmong is in some ways most intensely supported at the Ethnics Liberation camp may also be seen in the numbers of relatives of respondents there who know it (Table 36). How far survey respondents in the United States are behind in use of the Pahawh Hmong is obvious from Table 37.

Although 74 percent of respondents who are familiar with the Pahawh

Table 36. Ability of relatives to read Pahawh Hmong, number of respondents by location

	Spouse	Parents	Children
Ban Vinai	23	28	11
Ethnics Liberation	48	42	32
California	19	11	15
Minn./Wis.	7	2	4
Other U.S. locations	1	0	0

Table 37. Frequency of reading Pahawh Hmong, number of respondents by location

	Daily	Weekly	Monthly	Occasion- ally	Never
Ban Vinai	54	0	0	0	0
Ethnics Liberation	53	0	0	0	1
California	12	13	2	15	6
Minn./Wis.	5	0	0	16	10
Other U.S. locations	1	1	1	2	3

Table 38. Sex differences in self-estimates of ability to read Pahawh Hmong (Second and Third Stage Reduced Versions) and Romanized Hmong, in percentages

	Excellent	Good	Fair	Poor
Second Stage				
Male	58.5	8.5	9.9	9.9
Female	64.6	4.2	12.5	12.5
Third Stage				
Male	56.3	12	4.9	10.6
Female	56.3	14.6	8.3	10.4
Romanized				
Male	40.8	10.6	4.9	2.8
Female	20.8	12.5	8.3	4.2

Hmong are male, Table 38 shows that a slightly higher percentage of the women who responded claim to know the Pahawh Hmong, and that these women judge their knowledge of it to be slightly better than the men judge theirs. A higher percentage of men than women claim to know the Romanized Hmong, however.

As far as dialect is concerned, Shong Lue Yang himself spoke Hmong Daw, and so do most of the leaders in the promotion and use of the Pahawh Hmong. There are five Hmong Leng men out of eleven on the board of the Motthem Family, but Motthem board meetings are conducted in Hmong Daw, and the Hmong Leng men speak it when meeting with the others. Both teachers of the classes to be described in the next section are speakers of Hmong Leng, but one is married to a Hmong Daw and speaks more Hmong Daw now than Hmong Leng.

Of survey respondents who are familiar with the Pahawh Hmong, 56.7 percent speak Hmong Daw, not a large majority; but when we break the figures down by the clusters in which the speakers are located, some fairly large differences emerge (Table 39). Respondents from Ban Vinai are all Hmong Leng (although Chai Lee and Sao Yang both speak Hmong Daw), whereas in the other clusters Hmong Daw is strongly predominant. The acceptance of the Pahawh Hmong by Hmong Leng and Hmong Daw people alike is significant in light of the dissatisfaction which some Hmong Leng have with the Romanized system (Chapter 11).

It is not surprising that adherents of traditional Hmong religion considerably outnumber either Catholics or Protestants among survey respondents. However, Table 40 masks the fact that there were a number

Table 39. Dialect of respondents, by location, in percentages

	Hmong Daw	Hmong Leng
Ban Vinai	0	100
Ethnics Liberation	80.4	19.6
California	89.1	10.9
Minn./Wis.	64.5	35.5
Other U.S. locations	57.1	14.3

Table 40. Religion of respondents, by location, in percentages

	Traditional	Catholic	Protestant
Ban Vinai	92.6	0	7.4
Ethnics Liberation	98.6	0	2
California	53.3	4.4	15.6
Minn./Wis.	53.3	5.7	13.3
Other U.S. locations	83.3	0	16.7

Table 41. Average years of education of respondents (exclusive of classes in English as a foreign language in the United States), by location of respondents

	Laos	Thailand	U.S.A.
Ban Vinai	4.23	5.56	0
Ethnics Liberation	3.74	1.6	0
California	3.23	0.73	4
Minn./Wis.	4.13	0.8	4.19
Other U.S. locations	4.5	0.75	3

of people in the United States (not included in the figure) who marked both "Traditional" and either "Catholic" or "Protestant" as their religious preference. Chia Koua Vang, for example, identifies himself as a Protestant Christian as well as a believer in the teachings of Shong Lue Yang.

In Table 41, the figure for years of education in Thailand probably results primarily from time spent as children or young people in refugee camps. Some people have been living in Ban Vinai for ten years, their children going to school there. There are classes for adults (especially English classes) in the camps, also. The figure may also include a few individuals who had some training in Thailand during the war. The average years of education in Laos is higher in this sample than was the education of the generally non-literate group which came to Shong Lue to learn, partly reflecting changes in the Hmong situation since 1975, but probably also one of the ways in which the sample is not fully representative. Education in the United States would generally be in addition to whatever the individuals had when they came from Thailand.

Twenty-four percent of respondents who are familiar with the Pahawh Hmong are of the Yang clan. The next largest percentage is the Her clan (18.9%). Others taper down from there (Xiong 14.3%, Lee 13.8%, Vang 9.2%, Moua 6%, other 14.3%). Note that Shong Lue is a Yang and Pa Kao a Her.

Learning the Pahawh Hmong

For a period in 1987 two Pahawh Hmong classes for adults were held regularly in Minnesota, each meeting once a week for about two hours at a time. One class was taught in a classroom of a Hmong Christian church in St. Paul and was attended primarily by members of that church, including the pastor. The other was held in an apartment in the city of Winona, about 120 miles southeast of St. Paul. Almost all of those studying the Pahawh Hmong in Winona were from St. Paul or Minneapolis, enrolled at Winona State University.

The class in the church was taught by Sai Long Yang (Xaiv Looj Yaaj ꗃꕮ ꕮꕊ ꕔ), a strong proponent of the Pahawh Hmong, who learned the writing system in the Ban Vinai camp from Chia Koua and Gnia Yee. The class in Winona was taught by Wa Cha Xiong (Vam Tsab Xyooj ꗏꕉ ꕎꕮ ꕮ), who had learned the Pahawh Hmong as a teenager in Laos, and had fought in the resistance under Pa Kao Her in the Phou Bia Mountain area from 1975 to 1977. Both teachers were university students.

More than thirty students were registered in the church class and fourteen in the other when we observed them. Learning was largely by rote recitation, and by writing syllables at the board from dictation. When a mistake was made at the board, another student would go to the board and correct it. Learning materials produced by Gnia Yee and Chia Koua were used, including sheets with large characters produced on the computer. Almost all students jotted down the Romanized Hmong alongside the Pahawh Hmong characters to remind them of the character values.

Neither of these classes lasted long, however. Sai Long became too busy with his own university studies, and Cha Xiong moved from Winona. It seems clear that there has been little or no sustained group teaching of the Pahawh Hmong in the United States, but only sporadic efforts.

Our survey included open-ended questions asking why respondents had learned the Pahawh Hmong and the Romanized Hmong. The multiple responses to these questions have been grouped under six themes: symbolization of Hmong identity, preservation and development of the Hmong language and culture, desire to establish the comparative worth of Hmong in relation to other languages, pragmatic reasons, affective reasons, and religious ones (Table 42).

Several individual respondents who listed reasons for learning the Pahawh Hmong in the identity, cultural preservation and worth categories correspondingly listed letter writing as a reason for learning the Romanized alphabet. This was especially noticeable in Ban Vinai, and is consistent also with the view expressed by Chai Lee, as described above. Almost all the respondents who mentioned learning the Romanized "for fun" (i.e., for non-serious purposes, in contrast to purposes of cultural preservation and religion) were also in Ban Vinai. The most commonly mentioned reasons for learning Pahawh Hmong are not listed as reasons for learning the Romanized Hmong at all.

Similarly, when people were asked why they did *not* learn the Ro-

Table 42. Reported reasons for learning Pahawh Hmong and Romanized Hmong (in percentages). The total number of reasons given in these open-ended questions was 259 for the Pahawh Hmong and 120 for the Romanized Hmong. See also Table 43.

		Pahawh Hmong	Romanized Hmong
Hmong identity		37.8	0.0
Belongs to the Hmong	15.4		
I am Hmong	12.0		
The only authentic Hmong	5.4		
Unique to the Hmong	2.7		
Created by a Hmong	2.3		
Preservation and development		28.6	3.3
Of Hmong culture	15.8		
Of Hmong language	12.7		
Comparative worth		9.7	0.0
Makes Hmong like other languages	8.9		
Important for the Hmong	.8		
Pragmatic		14.7	55.8
Needed/useful	8.9		5.8
Most efficient system	3.5		
Easy	2.3		3.3
Letters, communication			55.8
Pahawh not yet available			15.0
Majority know it			8.3
Because live in U.S.A.			.8
Affective		6.9	37.5
Like it/proud of it	3.9		
Curiosity	3.1		12.5
Fun			25.0
Religious		2.3	3.3
Given by God	1.2		
Taught by Shong Lue	.8		
For Hmong worship	.4		
Used in Church/Bible			3.3

manized and Lao script Hmong, they rejected those alphabets as not authentically Hmong. Many also checked off "Not useful" as well as "No opportunity" and "Too busy."

Pahawh Hmong Population Size and Mystique

Of the 196 people in our survey who reported acquaintance with the Pahawh Hmong, 94.9 percent believed that all Hmong should have the same writing system, and 94.4 percent believed that the Hmong writing system should be the Pahawh Hmong. But the actual number of people in the world who use it is clearly small, although we can only guess at how many. Even some people who believe in the Pahawh Hmong do not know it, and some of them use the Romanized Hmong.

Perhaps two thousand five hundred people studied the Pahawh Hmong in Laos when Shong Lue was still alive (Table 44). We do not know how well the majority of them learned it, or how much they used it until they were afraid to use it any more. Perhaps between four and five thousand more people have learned it since then. That depends on how many learned in Phou Bia and in Ban Vinai (and in Thailand out-side the camps), the main areas where the Pahawh Hmong has been taught since 1975. Three hundred a year does not seem an exorbitant guess for Chai Lee's active program, if he has the thirty teachers he

Table 43. Frequency of reasons reported for learning Pahawh Hmong and Romanized Hmong, in percentages

	Pahawh Hmong	Romanized Hmong
Identity	37.8	0
Comparative worth	9.7	0
Preservation/development	28.6	3.3
Pragmatic	14.7	55.8
Personal	7	37.5
Religious	2.3	3.3

Table 44. Estimates of number of people who have learned Pahawh Hmong. The top group reflects the events up to the time of the repression of Pahawh Hmong in Laos, the lower group the period since 1975.

Dates	Elapsed Time	Place	Students
Sept. 1959–end 1963	4 yrs.	Tham Ha	500
end 1963–early 1964	3 mos.	Fi Kha	250
early 1964–Feb. 1964	1 mo.	Pha Bong	
Feb. 1964–early 1966	2 yrs.	Kiaw Boua	1,000
early 1966–Sept. 1967	1.5 yrs.	Long Cheng	500
Sept. 1967–Nov. 1970	3 yrs.	Pha Khao jail	
Nov. 1970–Feb. 1971	3 mos.	Nam Chia	
Feb. 1971–Nov. 1971	9 mos.	Houi Kinin	500
1971		Nam Theng	300
			3,050
July 1975–April 1976	9 mos.	Nam Phong	84
June 1976–June 1978	2 yrs.	Ban Vinai	76
1978–1987	10 yrs.	Ban Vinai	3,000
1975–1987	12 yrs.	Phou Bia	1,000
1978 (?)–1987	10 yrs.	Ethnics Liberation	100
1978–1987	10 yrs.	California	250
1978–1987	10 yrs.	Minnesota	50
1978–1987	10 yrs.	Other U.S. locations	25
			4,585
Combined total			7,635

claimed in 1984. Our estimate, then, is a total of over seven thousand people who have ever studied the Pahawh Hmong.

Of these, many who learned the Pahawh Hmong died in the war, in the brutal communist attempt to wipe out pockets of Hmong after the larger war stopped, and in the consequent exodus from Laos. Others have since been persecuted for using the alphabet in Laos and elsewhere. We know that people who live in Vietnam and in areas of Laos under government control do not use it for fear of death.

Many people probably did not learn it very well. Some perhaps never got beyond memorizing the tables of characters and may never have used them. Some have forgotten how to use the system or can only recall parts of it. The two cases known to us where the Pahawh Hmong was recorded by Westerners were incomplete and contained errors, possibly in part because the people from whom they got the data were not fully at home in the system.[7]

As a guess, we suggest that about two thousand people may regularly use the Pahawh Hmong as a functional writing system at the present time. In addition, there are supporters, people who believe in the Pahawh Hmong, but who have not learned it, like some of those who helped pay for the typewriters.

Although there is extensive use of the Pahawh Hmong by some people for correspondence, recording traditions, note taking, etc., there is nothing in print for them to read. Chai Lee's books are not available. Chia Koua Vang and Gnia Yee Yang's books do not go beyond introductory primers and grammars. Chia Koua and Gnia Yee have now written about the life and teaching of Shong Lue Yang in connection with our research, however, and when published that may provide a start toward some reading material.[8]

But what has kept the Pahawh Hmong alive is not its usefulness for recording things Hmong and for correspondence. The greatest importance of the Pahawh Hmong to many of those who use it is its symbolism. In the minds of people sympathetic to it, the Pahawh Hmong represents a unique Hmong identity and equality with the other languages around them in Asia, most of which possess their own individual scripts. For users of the Pahawh Hmong, it also represents their doing something for themselves instead of foreigners' adapting other peoples' writing systems to their language. It represents the preservation of the language against the encroachment of Lao, English and even Thai.

Some of the supporters of the Pahawh Hmong also see it as a gift from God, to be treasured, even if they do not use it. Like the writing systems of many peoples in antiquity and some in the present world,

Pahawh Hmong writing is sacred for many believers. Some of the respondents in our survey learned the Romanized Hmong "for fun" and for writing letters, but the Pahawh Hmong is serious. It is for religion, and for the recording and preservation of a Hmong culture threatened by dispersal, political powerlessness, persecution (in Laos and Vietnam), struggle for survival (at Phou Bia), confinement (in refugee camps) and the demands of day to day life at the bottom of the American economic scale. All these factors, as well as poor education, severely limit what can be done with the Pahawh Hmong.

This is the sad truth in spite of phenomenal ingenuity and perseverance shown in the quest for a typewriter, and in the dogged resistance at Phou Bia. If it were not for Chia Koua Vang, Gnia Yee Yang, Chai Lee, Pa Kao Her and a very few others, the Pahawh Hmong would be little more than a memory now. They have carried on and kept alive the writing because they believe in Shong Lue's vision, and because it symbolizes their values so strongly.

Lemoine, an anthropologist and authority on the Hmong, has suggested that "the Hmong did not come to our countries only to save their lives, [but] rather came to save their selves, that is, their Hmong ethnicity."[9] The irony is that such a radical move makes the preservation of some symbols of ethnicity very difficult, and children grow up with other models to follow. In America it will probably be difficult to keep the intensity of vision for the Pahawh Hmong alive across the generations.

The young people growing up as Americans do not remember the conditions which created a need for Shong Lue Yang and his writing, conditions seared so deeply into the minds and emotions of their parents. Most Hmong in America do not know much about the Pahawh Hmong. Many have only heard rumors, or remember the controversy in Long Cheng and believe the writing is a communist system. We do not know how much such attitudes are now to be found among Hmong in Laos, outside the Phou Bia area, as well.

If the Pahawh Hmong is to become permanently viable, it will not do so in the United States, but in Laos (perhaps also in Thailand), where some of the conditions which gave rise to Shong Lue's messianic message still exist. Otherwise the enormous creativity and ingenuity of Shong Lue Yang and of his followers could fade away like writing systems developed for different languages in the past, those not maintained and supported by people in power.

10

The Alphabet in History

Many different forms of communication, ranging from picture messages to what computers do when recording a file, are frequently called "writing." In this book, however, the term has a more narrow meaning, restricted to a particular kind of representation of natural human languages. That means that it represents languages like English or Hmong or Vietnamese, not "body languages," "computer languages" or mathematics, etc. It also means that it directly represents the elements of the languages themselves, not directly the ideas people may want to convey.

A writing system, in our terms, therefore, is a consistent system for representing a natural language in visible symbols on a physical surface, with sufficient flexibility and scope such that people can use it to record substantially everything they can say. It includes the symbols themselves, the level of language units represented by the symbols (e.g., sound, syllable, word) and the ways in which the symbols are organized.[1]

Although many different writing systems[2] have been developed in the world, the concept of communicating language messages through systematic visible symbols on a physical surface was invented possibly no more than once, certainly no more than three times, in the ancient past. It has traditionally been credited first to the Sumerians between five and six thousand years ago, when the civilization of Sumer was located at the head of the Persian Gulf in what is now Iraq and Iran, but they may have learned it from others who created it not long before (Driver 1976: 1–2). It may possibly have also been invented by the Chinese, perhaps four thousand years ago, but only if the people who developed the earliest stages of Chinese writing had never heard of other people reading or writing any language. Probably it was invented as well in Central America, perhaps by people of the Olnec civilization, nearly three thousand years ago (Justeson et al. 1985: 32–37). No descendant of this last system is still in use.

The evolution of present writing systems, furthermore, is to be found primarily in two main historical lines, descended from the first two of these early sources. The Tricontinental line (developed in Asia, Africa and Europe) leads from Sumerian to scripts as varied as Roman, Arabic and Indic, and adaptations from them (Cross 1967; Driver 1976: 128–197; Naveh 1982: 8–42). The East Asian line leads from ancient Chinese writing to that of modern Chinese, Japanese and a few other writing systems. The number of people using systems within each of the lines is enormous.

But if inventing the idea of writing has happened only very seldom in the history of the world, adapting a writing system from one language to another has been done hundreds of times.[3] Greek writing was adapted from one of the forms of Semitic writing, Latin writing by stages from Greek, the writing of Western European languages from Latin, and Vietnamese, Navajo, Swahili and Romanized Hmong writing from Western European languages.

Arabic writing, likewise, was ultimately developed by adaptation through intermediary language writing systems from earlier Semitic writing, and systems for Farsi (Persian, Iranian), Urdu, Turkish, Indonesian and other languages were adapted from the Arabic system. Some of these languages are also written alternatively in Roman systems.

Another division within the Tricontinental line led from one of the early Semitic systems to the Indic writing systems. Then, from some of these writing systems of India, through the intermediary of the Khmer (Cambodian) system of writing, were ultimately adapted the type of Tai-language systems of Southeast Asia described in Chapter 7.

In the East Asian line, Japanese writing was adapted from Chinese. Chinese characters were used at times to write Korean and Vietnamese as well, but in both of these cases alphabetic writing systems eventually supplanted, or partially supplanted, the Chinese-based system. Some minority languages in China (including Hmong) have been written in Chinese characters at various times.

Adapting a writing system from one language to another means that not only is the idea of writing taken over, but so also are the basic system and symbols in which the writing is done, although these may be modified in the transition to fit the needs of the new language. The newly written language, for example, may need more consonant or vowel symbols than did the source language because there are more spoken sounds. Or sometimes features like tone may not occur in one of the languages, but must be represented in the writing system of the other.

When we say that a particular writing system is a Roman system, therefore, we are saying that its organization and the forms and values of its letters are adapted from writing systems historically descended from the Latin system. Likewise, a Tai-language system has the structural characteristics described in Chapter 7, and has many characters which look similar to and have values the same as or similar to corresponding characters in other Tai-language systems.

But between the unique or nearly unique invention of the idea of writing and the extensive adaptation of a writing system to another language lie some cases where new writing systems were developed by people who already had the concept of writing, but did not adapt an existing system, inventing their own new system instead. So in addition to the primary East Asian and Tricontinental lines of historical development, some very much smaller lines also exist, many of which include only one language.

Such is the highly sophisticated and almost unique *hankul* writing developed for Korean over five hundred years ago. Many people in Korea could read Chinese when the *hankul* system was invented, but the Korean system is radically different from the Chinese system and, although alphabetic, not closely similar to any other system. Such also was the Pollard script created for Hmong in China, as we will see in the next chapter, and such is the Pahawh Hmong.

Types of Writing Systems

Not only are the East Asian and Tricontinental lines of development historically different, but they also typically involve radically different types of writing. The Tricontinental systems have for centuries been alphabetic. But in the East Asian line alphabetic systems are not as prevalent as logo-syllabic, logographic and syllabic ones.

The Tricontinental line was not originally alphabetic, however. The first alphabetic writing was developed between three and four thousand years ago for Semitic languages of the Middle East and North Africa. These first alphabetic systems provided only for writing consonants, ignoring vowels. Later, the Greeks finally developed the type of alphabetic system we now know in the West, with consonants and vowels of equal status.

In both the major lines, writing developed originally out of the representation of messages in pictures. The significant difference between picture communication and writing as defined above is not in the pictures, however, but in the fact that the pictures do not represent language.

Imagine, for example, a picture (or a sequence of pictures) showing a person lying on a bier, with symbols of royal status, and some people wailing. This could well convey a message expressed in various ways in English, including the following:

"The king is dead and the people are mourning."
"People are mourning because the king has died."
"The king has died and is lying in state; people are coming to mourn."
"We mourn because our king has passed away."

Communication takes place through such pictures, but the pictures represent a general set of concepts, not language. Each of the written interpretations of the picture message listed above, however, represents a different language utterance. Any of these utterances, in turn, expresses at least part of the meaning of the picture.

Picture communication has severe limitations. It would be hard, for example, to picture a message such as that expressed in the last sentence of the previous paragraph, as well as to distinguish between the various linguistic interpretations of the picture communication above. When the ability to do such things was developed, true writing in our sense began.

For true writing, some system of conventional symbols which represent language units like words or sounds must be created, including non-picturable units; and these symbols must be displayed in conventional ways based in part on language. The symbols, for example, are typically arranged in the same order as that in which the language units they represent are spoken. In the Romanized Hmong, for example, h̲ is written before m̲ but after p̲ (as in the words *Hmoob* and *Phajhauj*) because the spoken puff of air it represents precedes /m/ but follows /p/.

However, there are complications to that principle of arrangement in linguistic order. In alphabetic systems, as we saw in Chapter 7, vowel symbols are sometimes written above or below consonants which they follow in speech, or in some other position than their linguistic order. Pahawh Hmong consonant symbols follow vowel symbols although consonants precede vowels in speech. But even in such cases the nuclear symbols follow each other in the order of speech, as do the syllables, words, sentences, etc. The important criterion is that symbols follow a systematic, conventional order, and that the organization is at some level (usually at the level of the word or lower) related to the organization of the language.

On the other hand, writing right to left, left to right, or top to bottom is not related to language. Such arbitrary conventions are inherent in the particular writing system itself. So is the position of the tone symbol, whether at the end of the syllable as in the Romanized Hmong or over the vowel as in the later stages of the Pahawh Hmong. So some aspects of the arrangement of the symbols in written text follow the language, and others do not, but there are conventional requirements in either case.

When picture communication develops directly into writing without other influence, some kind of logographic system usually emerges first. Some of the conventional symbols may continue to show resemblance to the pictures from which they came, although they tend to become more and more stylized and simplified (and so look less like a picture) as time goes on. In Chinese, for example, a round symbol with four short lines radiating out from it and another in the middle represented 'sun'. It became stylized to an oblong with a line across the center. A stick-figure symbol for 'man' was simplified to one with only the legs.

Additional logographic symbols needed for words that cannot be pictured are also developed in a variety of ways. Again in Chinese, the symbol for 'love' consists of a woman and a child. More arbitrarily a symbol for 'village' together with symbol for 'jade' represents both 'cut jade' and 'regulate, reason, principle' (Sampson 1985: 150–158).

But in the Tricontinental line, writing systems did not stop with logographic writing because a logographic system requires thousands of symbols to represent all the different words. Some logographic characters came to symbolize the sound of the word they represented, in addition to or instead of representing the word itself. Thus, to make up an example, the logograph for 'dog' could be used for the syllable /dɔg/ in any word, like *dogged* or *dogmatic* or *doggerel*. This produced a major shift in the system, because symbols no longer represented meaningful units (words), but sound units, in this case syllables. There was a transitional logo-syllabic period where both systems were combined. Then the move to alphabetic systems followed, in which a symbol was used to represent just the initial sound of a syllable rather than the whole syllable. The logograph for 'dog', which had become the representation of the syllable /dɔg/ might now symbolize the consonant sound /d/.

In this sequence of development, the number of symbols needed changed from thousands of logographs to hundreds (or fewer) syllable symbols, to normally less than one hundred alphabetic characters. But logical as the process of development seems to Westerners now, it took centuries to evolve from the early stages of the Tricontinental line of writing.

Alphabets have never fully replaced the logo-syllabic and syllabic systems of the East Asian line, although they sometimes supplemented them. The Chinese writing system is the most extreme example of a system used by millions of people, and lasting over centuries, that continues to have a strong logographic element. The nucleus of most Chinese characters is related to pronunciation of the syllable, but along with that nucleus there usually are other elements which indicate what word it is, to distinguish the particular syllable from others. The syllabic representation is inexact and inconsistent, and the logographic element sometimes indicates that the pronunciation is not exactly what the syllabic nucleus would indicate.[4] That is why Chinese is called logo-syllabic.

But alphabetic systems are not all the same, either. We have seen that there were changes within the alphabetic Pahawh Hmong and that there are differences between it and the Romanized Hmong, for they symbolized different levels of pronunciation and had different structures. In Table 45, we compare various types of alphabets to other writing systems.

The type of alphabetic system most familiar to users of the Roman alphabet is the "phonemic,"[5] where most of the letters represent what Westerners and many others perceive as individual sounds, what some linguists call phonemes. Thus, in the Romanized Hmong m̲ represents /m/, u̲ represents /u/, b̲ represents /ɾ/, etc.

The "demi-syllabic" type (sometimes grouped with syllabic because such systems symbolize a unit of sound larger than the typical phoneme) represents each of two halves of the syllable, initial and final.[6] This is what Shong Lue Yang created in the Source Version. But whereas

---

Table 45. Types of writing systems. Most actual writing systems are predominantly one or another of these types, but most have elements of some of the other types as well.

Writing (symbolizing language)
   Logographic (symbolizing words)
   Logo-syllabic (combined syllabic and logographic)
   Phonographic (symbolizing sounds)
     Syllabic (symbolizing syllables)
     Alphabetic (symbolizing sub-syllabic sound units)
       Types
         Demi-syllabic (symbolizing initial and final halves of a syllable)
         Phonemic (symbolizing individual sounds such as consonants, vowels, and tones [where present])
         Featural (symbolizing features of consonants, vowels and tones [where present])
       Structures
         Consonantal (symbolizing only individual consonants, omitting vowels)
         Nuclear (symbolizing either consonants or vowels as nuclear, the other as satellite)
         Equivalent (symbolizing both consonants and vowels on equal basis)

the Source Version was completely demi-syllabic and the consonants in later versions remained so, the vowels and tones in the Third Stage Reduced and Final Versions became phonemically written.

"Featural" writing symbolizes features or sound components of phonemes. It may be seen in some parts of the Romanized Hmong, where, for example, the feature of nasalization on a vowel is represented as a doubled letter (e.g., e represents non-nasalized /e/, but doubling to ee represents an additional nasalization feature). Also, the feature of aspiration is represented by h, that of the pre-nasalization by n, etc. The Romanized Hmong system is thus partially phonemic and partially featural.

It takes more analytical sophistication to detect features than phonemes, more to detect phonemes than demi-syllables, etc. However, a featural system requires fewer symbols than a phonemic system, which needs fewer than a demi-syllabic system.

In addition to these three types of alphabets, Table 45 lists three structures for alphabetic systems. The one most familiar to Westerners treats consonants and vowels in equivalent manner, placing them on the same line, using characters of equivalent size and prominence, and arranging them in the order in which they are spoken. Other alphabet systems are strictly consonantal, ignoring the vowels, as in the earliest alphabets of the Tricontinental line. Still other systems may be structured so that either the consonant element or the vowel element is nuclear, with the other related to it in some subordinate or satellite fashion, as in modern Arabic and Hebrew, the Tai-language systems and the Pahawh Hmong. So far as we know, all nuclear alphabets except the Pahawh Hmong have the consonant as the nuclear element. In the Pahawh Hmong it is, of course, the vowel.

Writing Systems Developed by Non-literates

In order to understand more fully the implications of the claim that Shong Lue Yang developed an alphabetical writing system although he could not read or write any language, we now describe briefly some other documented cases where that happened, or probably happened. It is impossible to know how many undocumented cases there may have been, or may yet exist.

The Cherokee Syllabary. The best-known case of the formation of a new writing system purely through stimulus diffusion is a syllabary developed for the Cherokee Nation of Native Americans by the famous

Sequoya,[7] also named George Guess (or Gist), who is memorialized in the name of the giant Sequoya redwood trees. Sequoya lived from about 1770 to 1843 in Tennessee. He was uneducated, unable to read or write, but he observed people around him using those skills. He visited a class once to find out how reading and writing were done, but could not figure out the process from that brief exposure. He once observed that "white men make what they know fast on paper like catching a wild animal, and taming it."[8]

About 1809 Sequoya began experimenting with a writing system for Cherokee. He started by trying to modify traditional Native American picture communication to logographic writing, but soon realized how difficult that would be for anyone to learn because of the enormous number of symbols which would be required. His attempts at simplification led him to develop a syllabary.

To do this, he gave up the pictures and began to use English letters as models from which symbols for the syllables were evolved. Some letters were taken unaltered, others were modified to produce additional symbols, for the Cherokee syllabary needs far more symbols than are available in the English alphabet. None of these symbols in the Cherokee syllabary, however, have the same values as in English. At first Sequoya created two hundred symbols, but over the years he simplified the system and refined it down to eighty-five.

Sequoya faced ridicule by his fellow Cherokee, and even persecution, including the burning down of his house. But by 1821, after twelve years of work, he had refined his system, and it was approved by the Council of the Cherokee Nation. In time thousands of people learned to read it and write it. Books and newspapers were published in it, including the New Testament in 1860, revised in 1951.

Although the Cherokee syllabary is no longer widely used, many Cherokee people still remember it with pride. English has taken over instead as the primary written medium of the Cherokee people. But Sequoya remains one of the world's unlettered geniuses, driven by some of the same motivation to preserve and enhance his people's culture and stature that we see in Shong Lue Yang.

The Vai Script and Its Imitators. Over a period of about a century beginning in the 1830's, four new writing systems were developed in Liberia and Sierra Leone, West Africa.[9] One of the systems preceded the others by most of a century, and is presumed to have been a stimulus for the rest. This was the Vai syllabary, a writing system whose origin is disputed, but which has been and still is extensively used by a significant part of the Vai people, though the number who know it may have decreased in the present generation.

The Vai syllabary was first reported in detail in the West in 1849, and the originator was named as Momolu Duwalu Bukele, who was about forty years old at the time and not literate in any other language. Bukele said that he had learned about the importance of books in a dream vision fifteen years earlier. When he awoke, however, he did not remember any of the symbols he had been taught in his dream, so he and some friends put their heads together to form new ones. Some scholars have speculated that Bukele probably developed the syllabary from earlier logograms, perhaps very old. It is hard, however, to know how much of such conjecture is based on elitist assumptions that an uneducated African would not be capable of doing something as original as he claimed.

Bukele had had some contact with the Roman script, first as a boy, when he started to learn it while employed by missionaries for three months, and later when he worked for various traders, observing them as they communicated magically over long distances with pieces of paper. Apparently Bukele did not learn enough to use these systems, and certainly the syllabary he and his friends created was not adapted in any way from Roman or Arabic models.

There are also other, sometimes conflicting accounts of the origin of the Vai script, told by Vai people in different parts of Vai territory at various times up to the present. Just as in the case of the Pahawh Hmong, rumors and stories have multiplied. The Bukele account may not be true, but it dates from around the time that the writing system began to be used, and the other accounts are much later explanations.

The Vai syllabary is maintained in spite of competition from Roman and Arabic writing systems (used primarily for English and Arabic languages rather than for Vai) and in spite of the fact that it requires learning as many as 212 symbols. Usage varies, as some of the characters have changed over time, but changes have not usually been made systematically and have spread unevenly through the community. With some Vai getting more advanced education there have been attempts at standardization.

Spoken syllables in Vai are of a simple structure, consisting of a consonant followed by a vowel and carrying a tone or sequence of tones. Spoken consonants are not nearly so numerous as they are in Hmong. The system lacks a way to represent the Vai tones, but to have included them in the Vai syllabary would have multiplied the number of symbols several times.

There are some other omissions as well. Vowels which occur without a preceding consonant are not distinctively symbolized. Nor is a syllable consisting of an /n/ without a following vowel. So the system does not fit the Vai language as perfectly as the Pahawh Hmong fits the Hmong language, but it is close enough for its general use.

The other systems probably stimulated by the Vai have not been as widely used, and in some cases have possibly been developed by people who were literature in other languages, including the Vai script. However, in none of these cases were the Vai symbols taken over wholesale to represent similar sounds in the other languages. There was almost no adaptation of characters involved.

The system for the Mende language, for example, invented in 1921 by Kisimi Kamara, a tailor, is written from right to left, like Arabic, rather than from left to right, like Vai. Kamara was a Muslim, and it is not clear whether or not he had ever studied in a Koranic school or learned elsewhere to write Arabic. He had visited Vai country, but it is not known whether or not he had actually learned the Vai syllabary. So he could have been literate before doing the Mende syllabary, or he might simply have been stimulated by the observation of the Vai and of Arabic. The Mende system is not now in widespread use.

Syllabaries were likewise developed for the Loma and Kpelle languages of the same area in the 1930's. Originators of both were apparently unable to read or write any language when they made the syllabaries, but that is not certain. They claimed to have been inspired by visions, as did Bukele of the Vai syllabary. Both systems are written from left to right, but neither is a direct adaptation from Vai. There is even some partial indication of tone in the Kpelle syllabary, unlike the others. Neither system became established as did the Vai, and use of both has virtually disappeared.

The Bamoun Writing Sytems. The Sultan Njoya, ruler of the Bamoun people of the Cameroon, Central Africa, began developing a writing system about 1895. He dreamed a logographic symbol for 'hand', and when he awoke he wrote the symbol on a slate, washed it off, and drank the water. He went on then, as a first stage, to design about a thousand logographic symbols. Then he moved on in several stages to a syllabic system, and finally arrived at an almost full alphabet in 1918.

At that time some Bamoun people could already read and write Arabic, and there is indication that the Sultan had had at least some exposure to Arabic and to Roman script in German and English form. It is not clear how much he knew of these systems. He seems, however, to have worked also with Muslim religious leaders, who would have known Arabic. This probably puts the Sultan's work outside that of the small group who invented a writing system without knowing how to read or write any language, but we mention it because he did not adapt any existing writing system, and because he made a series of documented revisions, as did Shong Lue Yang.

Njoya's series of writing systems was taught in schools and was used for official purposes. The status of the Sultan of course eliminated the problems that Shong Lue Yang had as a poor and politically powerless man. Njoya had the power to implement the use of his creation. Copies of reminiscences of the king and of Bamoun folklore were sent to European libraries. The writing system continued to be used after the ruler died in 1932, but since then its use has gradually diminished.

The Ndjuka Script. In 1910 a man by the name of Afaka had a dream in which a person carrying a sheet of paper told him to devise a script for his people. Afaka lived in Suriname, on the northeast coast of South America. His language was Ndjuka, a creole language spoken by people of African descent. He could not read or write any language.

Over the next weeks he devised 56 characters in a syllabic system with which he was able to write down what he wanted to communicate. These characters, however, had to symbolize 336 different syllables, or 168 if tone is not represented. Many features were also represented inconsistently.[10] A small number of people learned and used the writing, including at least two Dutch men interested in the Ndjuka people. It was used primarily for letter writing, but Afaka, a Catholic, also wrote some brief religious materials. Afaka died in 1918, but his writing was still in use by a very few people in 1958. There may not have been more than one left in 1987.

In summary, then, before Shong Lue Yang we have been able to find record of only two cases where the sources state unequivocally that the originator of a writing system was not previously literate (Cherokee and Ndjuka), and one where he was probably not literate (Vai). There are, in addition, four cases where the originator was possibly not literate (Mende, Loma, Kpelle, Bamoun). There are other cases of logographic systems where nothing is known about their origin. Unlike the Pahawh Hmong, all of these other documented writing systems were syllabaries, although the Bamoun was initially logographic and ultimately alphabetic.

The Place of the Pahawh Hmong

The Pahawh Hmong, together with the Pahawh Khmu', constitutes a separate line in the history of writing. That is so even if Shong Lue Yang could read another language before he devised the Source Version. We find no reasonable basis for thinking his work was adapted from anything else.

Shong Lue's new line had several features which are rare in writing systems, and others apparently unique. In addition to the new shapes of most of its characters, his was a vowel-nuclear system, of which we know of no other example; few writing systems represent tone as completely and accurately as his does; the Pahawh Hmong was explicitly designed to accommodate two significantly different dialects (Hmong Daw and Hmong Leng); and Shong Lue Yang created parallel writing systems for two radically different languages (Hmong and Khmu').

Furthermore, we have no other documented case of a person who could not read or write any language devising such a perfect alphabetical system. Syllabaries were developed by Sequoya, Afaka and some of the West African people. Logographic systems developed under these conditions may have been more common, but we have no idea who originated some of those which are known. The Pahawh Hmong, however, is the only full alphabet we know developed under such conditions.

A scholar who has looked extensively into the history of writing argues that

all the writings which have gone through an extended process of evolution, like the Cherokee and Alaska systems in North America or Vai and Bamum [Bamoun] systems in Africa, have evolved from primitive semasiography and have passed successively through the stages of logography and syllabography, showing at times in the final stages certain tendencies toward alphabetization. Thus, the sequence of stages in writings introduced among primitives fully parallels the history of writing in its natural evolution. (Gelb 1963: 210).

Of course the number of known cases on which Gelb bases his generalization is very small, and the Ndjuka script (which he does not cite) may be another exception. Much else of which we know nothing may have also happened in the history of writing.[11] But the Source Version of Pahawh Hmong which appeared in 1959 does not fit the pattern Gelb describes at all. It is a perfect demi-syllabic alphabet. Gelb may consider such demi-syllabic systems to be "syllabic," as some authors do, but that terminological difference would not supply the missing (from his point of view) logographic stage.

There is psychological evidence that people who have not learned to read an alphabet have trouble isolating speech sounds smaller than the syllable, whereas typical first graders who are learning to read in an alphabetic system can readily do so. This phenomenon has been demonstrated in tests of adult literates (who know an alphabetic system) as against non-literates, as well as with people who are literate in a syllabic or logographic system as against those who are literate in an alphabet. It would seem clear that the capacity to abstract individual sounds needs some additional stimulation beyond normal maturation of human intellectual faculties.[12]

Shong Lue's Source Version differentiated vowel-tones from consonants, a more difficult task than isolating syllables, but less difficult than abstracting the tones from the vowels (which came in the Third Stage Reduced Version). What stimulated him? Our information on how Shong Lue Yang worked before the emergence of the Source Version is a complete blank. Perhaps he did experiment with picture communication and logographic and syllabic forms of writing before producing the Source Version and found that syllabic writing would have required several thousand symbols. We know he experimented and changed the writing system he did produce several times even though he considered the Source Version to be divinely revealed. As we suggested in Chapter 7, the fact that he was working on writing systems for two different languages at the same time may have given him greater insight into their operations.

But to insist that Shong Lue must have gone through a logographic or syllabic stage is to impose a theory without empirical evidence behind it on the evidence we do have. It would also impose theory on the evidence to insist that his alphabetic writing system must have come from some other source because he did not go through the logographic to syllabic to alphabetical sequence. At the same time, the lack of evidence about how Shong Lue arrived at the Source Version constitutes the most significant gap in our knowledge of the evolution of his writing system, and in our ability to assess its significance. It seems to Smalley that he must have done some experimental trial and error, the nature of which we can probably never recover.

11

Other Hmong Writing Systems

There have been at least fourteen major attempts to develop writing systems for the Hmong language over the past one hundred years, some with several variations. Each has been accessible to only part of the population scattered over South China, North Vietnam, North Laos and North Thailand, some never spreading very far even in the local area where they were attempted.

Six of these fourteen writing systems we know to be in current use: the Romanized system used in this book, the Pahawh Hmong, the Chinese Romanized, the Whitelock Lao-based system, a variety of the Whitelock Thai-based system and the Sayaboury system. Two other systems are likely still in use, namely, the Vietnamese system and the Pathet Lao system, but we have no up-to-date information on them.

In this chapter we will characterize briefly all these known systems for writing the Hmong language,[1] and then outline the issues on which the Pahawh Hmong was or is directly in rivalry with them. The controversies themselves sometimes shed light on the Pahawh Hmong story.

Documented Writing Systems for Hmong

Chinese Characters. Chinese-character logographic writing for a dialect of Hmong was documented in 1912 in Sichuan Province, China, by a French officer named d'Ollone.[2] The characters had been adapted from Chinese symbols,[3] with some additions. The Hmong person who wrote out the extensive examples for d'Ollone was secretive about the system, and d'Ollone could not find anyone else who would admit to knowing anything about it.

The Pollard Script. An alphabet designed by missionary Samuel Pollard was used for Hmong Bo, also in Sichuan Province, China. Hmong Bo is probably mutually intelligible with the Hmong dialects of Laos. The

Gospel of Mark in this dialect was published in the Pollard script in 1922 with a revision in 1938.

The Pollard script had first been created at the beginning of the century for the A-Hmao language (Hwa Miao, Flowery Miao) in Guizhou (Kweichow) Province. A-Hmao is a different language from Hmong Daw and Hmong Leng, though it is closely related. The script was enthusiastically received by speakers of A-Hmao, as the Pahawh Hmong had been in Laos, perhaps for some of the same reasons, including messianism and the Hmong cultural traditions about the importance of writing.[4] The Pollard script may not have been as extensively used among the Hmong Bo, however.

Pollard did not follow the Tricontinental line of writing development characteristic of his British background, or the East Asian line of China, where he was working. Like the Pahawh Hmong, his script was demi-syllabic. Unlike the Pahawh Hmong, the consonantal part of the syllable was the nucleus, with the vowel written in smaller letters around the consonant, placed according to the tone.

We do not know whether the Pollard script is still used by speakers of Hmong Bo, but it is still used by many speakers of A-Hmao, even though there have been attempts by the government to replace it with a form of Chinese Romanized (see below). An A-Hmao primer published in 1983 has interlinear text in Chinese Romanized and Pollard scripts throughout.[5]

The Savina Romanized Alphabet. F. M. Savina was a missionary who worked with Hmong people for many years in China, Vietnam and Laos, and he wrote a major history of the Hmong.[6] He also prepared what is probably the first in a number of different Romanized alphabets for Hmong, perhaps a dialect different from either Hmong Leng or Hmong Daw.[7] The writing was based in part on Vietnamese writing conventions, notably in x for /s/, some of the Vietnamese vowel symbols like ư for /w/, and the Vietnamese tone diacritic marks. Unless the dialect recorded was considerably different in major respects from the Hmong dialects of Laos, the transcription was linguistically defective, lacking the /q/, /qh/, /nq/, /nqh/ series, some other consonants, and two of the tones. The first Hmong dictionary[8] was published in this writing system, but not a great deal more than that was ever produced, and it never caught on widely among Hmong people.

The Trung Alphabet with Thai Characters. In 1932 the Gospel of Mark in Hmong Leng was published in Thailand using Thai characters. It was the work of a Vietnamese missionary, C. K. Trung. Although Trung used Thai symbols he did not follow the Thai system of writing in any way. The order of the vowels in relation to the consonants, for example, follows the spoken order, not the conventional Thai order. Thus, all vowels which are written before consonants in Thai are written after the consonants in this system. So far as we know, the effort was entirely abortive, and never had any following among Hmong people.[9]

The Homer-Dixon Romanized Alphabet. About 1939 the missionary Homera Homer-Dixon devised a writing system for a dialect in Vietnam which seems close to Hmong Leng. In some ways it was adapted even more closely to Vietnamese than was the Savina system, using c̠ for /k/, g̠i̠ for /z/, b̠ for /np/, and other Vietnamese values which Savina does not use. Like the Savina alphabet, it symbolized only six tones, and the small sample we have of it seems otherwise incomplete as well. A primer, a booklet on Christianity, and one on music were published in the system about 1941. The writing system was not ever extensively used.[10]

Romanized Popular Alphabet (RPA). The RPA, the Romanized system used in this book, has become the most prevalent Hmong writing system, the medium for a number of publications, and an instrument for widespread general use by Hmong. It is also the vehicle for much Western and Hmong scholarship, including several dictionaries, Hmong text in works by linguists (including doctoral dissertations), collections of Hmong folktales, verbal art, religious culture, etc.

The RPA was devised in 1951–1953 in Laos by three missionaries working with various Hmong assistants. G. Lindwood Barney was a Protestant missionary learning and analyzing the Hmong language in Xieng Khouang. He was working at that time primarily with Geu Yang (Tooj Ntxawg Yaj [illegible]) and Tua Xiong (Tuam Xyooj [illegible]), speakers of Hmong Leng.

William A. Smalley was a Protestant missionary linguist analyzing the Khmu' language in Luang Prabang. His contribution to the writing system was linguistic, including a knowledge of how writing systems are effectively adapted to new languages.

Yves Bertrais was a Catholic missionary more advanced in the study of Hmong than Barney, living in Kiu Katiam, Luang Prabang Province. He was working with Chong Yeng Yang (Txoov Yeeb Yab [illegible]) and Chue Her Thao (Tswv Hawj Thoj [illegible]) at the time. He has since gone on to become a major scholar in Hmong studies, contributing numerous works which interpret Hmong language and culture to outsiders, keeping a record for Hmong posterity in a changing world.[11] All the while he has continued his spiritual, educational and developmental ministries among Hmong people in Laos, Thailand, French Guiana and China.

In the course of his work Barney encountered difficulties with the Hmong sound system and invited Smalley to consult with him in Xieng Khouang in October 1951 and April 1952. They also worked together from May through July 1953 in Dalat, Vietnam. On the first two of these visits Smalley checked and helped clarify Barney's work, so that they arrived at an understanding of how the Hmong sounds work and made some tentative proposals as to how the language might be efficiently written.[12]

Sometime in the latter part of 1952, at the suggestion of Bertrais, the three met and agreed that Catholics and Protestants should not have different writing systems for Hmong. Bertrais had himself arrived at conclusions concerning the Hmong sound system which were almost identical to those of Barney and Smalley, and he had some tentative ideas about how to write the language. These were somewhat more inclined toward Vietnamese usage than were the Barney-Smalley suggestions.

However, the differences between their proposals were relatively small. Where there was a rational basis for selecting a detail of one proposal over the other, it was adopted. Where there seemed not to be any such preference, they arbitrarily picked solutions from one proposal or the other. Agreement was reached in 1953.

The resulting system survived its initial years only because Bertrais and other Catholic missionaries used it and taught it, whereas the Protestant mission never followed through after Lao government officials objected to it on the grounds that languages in Laos should be written in Lao script, if at all. Barney and Smalley, furthermore, did not return to Laos after 1954.

Bertrais and his Hmong associates put out one hundred copies of their first mimeographed book for teaching people to read the RPA in Kiu Katiam in 1955, and taught the system there. In 1959 small groups began to learn the script in and around Sam Neua, a provincial capital near the Vietnam border.

Then in 1962 a significant spread began to take place, centered in two Catholic student hostels in the Simuong and Nongbon sections of the national capital, Vientiane, and in a school for Catholic religious leaders also in Simuong. Many Hmong students were now attending high school and beyond in the capital, and a significant number of those lived at these hostels. Other people (including Chia Koua Vang) learned the system there as well, as they stayed at the centers when visiting or passing through Vientiane. Five revisions of the reading book were made there between 1962 and 1965, and the first Hmong cultural periodical (Xov Xwm Ntawv Hmoob ບ໋A ໄA ເຈ໊ ບໍ໌) began to appear monthly in 1963, edited by the students, the lay religious leaders and a few Hmong officials in town.[13]

People who learned the writing in Vientiane sometimes taught it back in their villages, and the religious leaders in training taught it to villagers where they served. As the small Hmong educated elite gradually increased, this writing system was adopted by some of them, who frequently learned it on their own or from each other. Then, with families separated under war conditions, less educated people also began to take it up so that relatives and sweethearts could correspond. Beginning in 1975 many thousands more people learned it as they waited in the refugee camps, with time on their hands and facing an uncertain future in a foreign land. The system continues to spread among Hmong in the countries where they have resettled.

The RPA also began to be used in Thailand in the 1960's, as both Catholic and Protestant missionaries introduced it there.[14] It did not catch on as extensively there as in Laos, however, although its use continues, especially by the Catholics. There have been a number of publications in it for the use of the Hmong people in that country.

The RPA is now spreading in China as well, in spite of the fact that there is a different official Romanized system there, as described below. In 1985 the government Institute for Southeast Asian Studies in Kunming, Yunnan Province, even invited Yon Yia Yang (Ntxoov Yias Yaj ຍ໊ A໋ ວ໌), a Hmong who had come to China as a refugee from Laos, to teach the RPA for about three months so that Institute scholars and Hmong people from the surrounding area could learn it; other Chinese Hmong also continue to learn it.[15]

Some Hmong in China are motivated to use the RPA because it provides a means of communication with Hmong in the rest of the world. A leader in its promotion and use there is Chi Chang (Chij Tsab A໋ ວ໊) who earlier prepared a book for teaching the Chinese Romanized in the Wenshan region. He began to publish a cultural bulletin in RPA in August 1986, and at least three books were being published in 1988, edited by Bertrais in French Guinea and printed in Bangkok.

Over the years a number of variants of the RPA have developed, reflecting certain controversies which will be outlined below. Some are simply personal variations, but others are more widely held. Two groups of Hmong Leng have produced a number of publications in their respective modified systems which are typical of the kinds of changes also made by others.

One of these groups is in France, where a system worked out by Yi Vang (Yis Vaj **ЛШ ꓕC**) includes modifications in the direction of French conventions, reduction in the length of some of the complex consonant sequences and the elimination of spellings which seem to reflect Hmong Daw pronunciation. The other group is in the United States, where members of the Mong Volunteer Literacy Group led by Djoua X. Xiong (Xeev Nruag Xyooj **ꓤA ꟽĊ ꓴꓛꓵ**) have likewise made modifications intended to eliminate the spellings which seem to reflect Hmong Daw pronunciation.[16] Some or all of the latter changes are quite widespread among the Hmong Leng.

There are many purely individual variations, too. Gnia Pao Lee (Nyiaj Pov Lis **ꓴꓘ ꓴꟼꟿ ꓮㄩꟲ**), a Hmong novelist in Australia, uses his own set of innovations, for example.[17] Some people change the system extensively, others modifying only a letter or two.

The Vietnamese Romanized Alphabet. In 1956–1957 North Vietnamese linguists developed a writing system for Hmong Daw based in part on Vietnamese conventions. As such it has similarities to both the Savina and the Homer-Dixon systems, but differs notably from them and from Vietnamese writing in the fact that it represents tones by final consonant letters, as does the RPA. It is complete in representing all of the phonemic contrasts in the language, but some choices for symbols seem somewhat illogical. For example, corresponding to RPA k̲ and q with their matching aspirated k̲h and qh, the North Vietnamese system has c for /k/ and k̲ for /q/ (not bad choices in themselves), but then uses k̲h for /kh/ and k̲r for /qh/. Thus k̲ represents /q/ by itself and in the combination k̲r, but /k/ in the combination k̲h. A dictionary was published in 1971, but we do not know how much use the system has had.[18]

The Chinese Romanized Alphabet. A writing system was developed officially for Hmong in the People's Republic of China in 1957–1958,[19] and like many other such writing systems for minority languages developed there at about the same time, it follows the Tricontinental line in its Romanized form rather than the East Asian line of writing systems. The symbols in this Chinese Romanization are generally based on Pinyin, the present official Chinese system for transliterating Chinese words into Roman letters. It therefore has notable differences from the other Romanized systems for Hmong. Tones, however, are written with consonant symbols after the vowel, as in the other Romanized systems of the decade.

Although the system is official, the government has neglected teaching it to the Hmong. It has been used more by Chinese researchers. On a visit to the Institute for Chinese Nationalities in Peking in 1975, however, Dr. Yang Dao (Yaj Dos ꯖꯋ ꯀꯤꯘꯤ), a Hmong scholar, found no trace or knowledge of the system. Some Hmong people were first taught the system in 1982, but it is not taken seriously by officials or educators, it is not strongly pushed, and it is taught in only a few schools. The Hmong know this, of course, and the fact sometimes strengthens demand for the RPA.[20]

Dictionaries and other publications have appeared in the Chinese Romanized Alphabet. The Hmong in China number over a million people, far more than those in all the rest of the world combined. Whatever writing system for the Hmong language should catch on among them would be of great importance.

The Pathet Lao Alphabet. During the Indochina War, Hmong people in Laos fought on both sides of the conflict, and Lao-based systems for writing Hmong were correspondingly devised on each side. The first of these was developed apparently in the late 1960's by people in the faction allied to the communist Lao, Vietnamese and Chinese.

Where an existing Lao symbol with similar phonetic value was available it was used with that value in Hmong, and a few existing symbols were shifted from their Lao values to meet Hmong requirements. But beyond that, seventeen new symbols were invented for the remaining Hmong spoken consonants. All the spoken sounds were represented except for the anomalous d-tone.

But although Lao characters were used in this Pathet Lao alphabet for Hmong, the Lao system was only partially used. Lao writing, like other Tai-language systems, involves rather radical differences from Romanized writing in its order and organization (Chapter 7). In the Pathet Lao alphabet the Lao way of writing the vowels in an orbit around the nuclear consonants was followed, but the writing of the tones was not. Instead, each tone was symbolized with a different marker. We have no idea how widely the Pathet Lao alphabet has been used, or even if it is still being used. We are not aware of any major publications in it.[21]

The Whitelock Thai-based and Lao-based Alphabets. After the Protestant mission in Laos stopped using the RPA because of the opposition of government officials, it needed some other way in which to write Hmong. Some Protestant missionaries in Thailand were also conscious of the fact that Hmong children were going to Thai schools in increasing numbers, and they hoped that children who learned to read Thai in school would be able to read Hmong without great additional effort, or that people who learned to read Hmong would be able to transfer that knowledge also to reading Thai, if they spoke it.[22]

Missionaries began a period of trial and experimentation, using first the Thai script and then the Lao. Doris Whitelock worked on the Thai-based version in Thailand in the 1960's, and then on the Lao-based system in Laos in the early 1970's.

Unlike the Pathet Lao system, the Whitelock systems followed the conventions of Thai and Lao as much as possible in writing tones. Also unlike the Pathet Lao system, no new consonant symbols were invented, but existing ones were adapted to new uses, and some of the same kinds of featural writing which characterize the RPA were followed. For example, in a consonant like Hmong /npl/, three Thai or Lao characters would be written in sequence, just as three are written in the Romanized.

In Thailand the original Whitelock system has been replaced by a variant, a simpler system in which tones are written directly (as in the Pathet Lao writing of Hmong but not the Tai-language way). But neither system has been widely accepted by Hmong people.

In Laos the Whitelock system was well accepted and used by several hundred Protestant Christians, generally people who could not already read and write the RPA. On the other hand, it was generally opposed by more educated Hmong who knew the RPA and were committed to it. The most powerful person to advocate use of the Lao-based system was Hang Sao (Ham Choj ຮາ ຕຈ), chief of the Intelligence Division in the Hmong army, who supported it primarily because of Lao government policy.

There has been little motivation among Hmong refugees to continue to learn the Whitelock system since 1975 when they began to flee Laos, but books written in it are still used (along with the RPA) in some Protestant congregations in the United States and in Ban Vinai refugee camp. We do not know whether or not it is still used by any Hmong in Laos.

An Anonymous System. For the sake of completeness we mention that another writing system was developed for Hmong in Laos in the late 1960's or early 1970's. The characters were newly devised by an educated man, who now lives in the United States. He declined both to have his name mentioned (although it is well known to many Hmong people) and to explain the system to us so that we could describe it here. Apparently very few people have learned it.

The Sayaboury Alphabet. In July 1983 a young Hmong man by the name of Ga Va Her (Nkaj Vas Hawj **ɔ̃n ữe ῖΊr**) showed a collection of nine volumes of hand-written and illustrated texts in an unknown script to Nina Wimuttikosol, then a field officer under the United Nations High Commissioner for Refugees. She had befriended him along with the rest of a group of Hmong from Sayaboury Province, Laos, while she was working in the refugee camp at Chiang Kham, Thailand. The group eventually entrusted eight of the manuscripts to her for safekeeping lest the manuscripts fail to survive the difficult refugee conditions.[23]

Ga Va said that the manuscripts had been passed along to him by his father, who had declared them to be 706 years old. They were of a messianic nature, kept secretly and used in religious ritual, to be preserved because they would be of fundamental importance when the Hmong had their own land to govern. Their complete and clear interpretation would take place then. One of the volumes is an alphabet book, to teach the system.[23]

Wimuttikosol showed these manuscripts to Jacques Lemoine, an anthropologist noted for work on the Hmong, who studied them with Ga Va. Lemoine was more interested in the contents than in the script itself, and so he did not attempt to decipher it. When Wimuttikosol learned of our research on the Pahawh Hmong she wrote to Smalley, later sending him the material, together with a transcription of much of it in the RPA, as provided by Ga Va and his associates.

Ga Va calls the system *Ntawv Puaj Txwm*. The dialect represented is Hmong Daw, and the system fits the spoken language well, although neither the rare Hmong phoneme /ŋ/ (represented by g in the RPA, **Ữ** in the Pahawh Hmong) nor the onset of syllable without glottal stop ('**ʊ**) is included. In addition to the alphabet, there are symbols for the sound made by a shaman, for shooing and calling chickens, etc.

We do not know whether the person who designed this system was literate in any language. The system shows more resemblance to Tricontinental line systems than does the Pahawh Hmong, although the character shapes are as different as Pahawh Hmong is from other alphabets. Symbols follow the order in which the consonants and vowels they represent are spoken, for example, and tone is represented by a symbol at the end of the syllable. The system may be adapted from the RPA.

On the other hand, the Sayaboury is certainly more than an adaptation of any other system. Unusual features mark both consonants and vowels. In formal writing of things conceived to be of great value (as in the volumes) each written consonant is double, for example, so that every consonant symbol is written twice in sequence at the beginning of every syllable. This feature does not occur when Ga Va has used the system in his letters to us.

There are just five vowel symbols, none of which represent anything in themselves, but which are always combined in pairs to represent the spoken vowels, simple and complex. For example, if they were characters in the Sayaboury script, @ and % would not ever occur representing a vowel in themselves, but @% would represent /ee/, %@ would represent /au/, @@ would represent /i/ and %% would represent /w/.

The Pahawh Hmong and the Sayaboury script are similar to each other, and different from RPA, in that in both the complex consonants are all represented by unitary symbols. This is significant evidence concerning the perception which Hmong people have of the phonological structure of their language, especially when put alongside the great objection which many other Hmong people have voiced for years to the featural writing of the consonants in the RPA, an objection we discuss further below.

The ingenuity of the indigenous Pahawh Hmong and Sayaboury writing systems is indeed remarkable. We wonder how many other indigenous writing systems for Hmong are out there, or have been developed in the past, ones that have never been reported.

Summary of the Systems

Some of the preceding information can now be summarized as follows (dates show when the writing system was developed unless specified otherwise):

East Asian line of writing systems
1. Chinese character system, discovered between 1906 and 1909
Tricontinental line of writing systems
Romanized
2. Savina Romanized alphabet, before 1917
3. Homer-Dixon Romanized alphabet, 1939
4. Romanized Popular Alphabet (RPA) in numerous variations, 1951–1953
5. Vietnamese Romanized alphabet, 1956–1957

    6. Chinese Romanized alphabet, 1957 – 1958
Thai-based
    7. Trung Thai-based alphabet, before 1932
    8. Whitelock Thai-based alphabet, in two major versions,
       late 1960's
Lao-based
    9. Pathet Lao alphabet, late 1960's
    10. Whitelock Lao-based alphabet, early 1970's
Independent lines of writing systems
    11. Pollard script, applied to Hmong Bo before 1922
    12. Pahawh Hmong, in four versions, 1959
    13. Anonymous system, early 1970's
    14. Sayaboury alphabet, date unknown

Controversies about Hmong Writing Systems

There were three levels of controversy in Laos about Hmong writing systems, some of which have carried over to other parts of the world as Hmong people have been dispersed since 1975. On one level the Royal Lao Government was reluctant to have any minority language written at all, as minority peoples were supposed to be Lao, to be educated in Lao and only read and write Lao. This attitude was never solidified into a strongly enforced policy, but it created tension at times between the people using the various writing systems and Lao officials. The Protestant mission, as we have seen, backed off from the RPA because of this government position. In a weaker form this government attitude restricted writing systems for minority languages to Lao-based systems, in response to which the Whitelock system was produced. This first level of controversy did not particularly affect the Pahawh Hmong, which appeared in remote areas, so that Lao officials knew little or nothing about it.

On a second level the controversies were within the Hmong community over which available writing system to use. The RPA got a head start in Laos because it was the first system produced there and because the Catholic missionaries who used it were the only ones teaching the Hmong to read at all for some time. It became the system which educated people used if they used anything. Then the Pathet Lao alphabet, the Whitelock Lao-based alphabet and the Pahawh Hmong were introduced and gained ground in other constituencies, only beginning to compete with the RPA as they spread. At this point debate began on which system the Hmong people should use.

Meetings were held in Long Cheng and in Vientiane, Laos, when Hmong leaders and intellectuals got together at the instigation of General Vang Pao to try to agree on which writing system to use.[25] In each case the RPA prevailed in the sense that it won the votes which were taken, but such votes did not usually change the minds of those who espoused other systems.

For the RPA the primary arguments were that more people knew it, that it could be produced on readily available typewriters and print fonts and that it represented modernization. Those who espoused the Whitelock Lao-based alphabet argued that this system would make it easier for people who learned to read Hmong or Lao to read the other as well, and the system would be less offensive to the government.[26]

But for those who advocated the Pahawh Hmong the great issue was that it was a Hmong product, and that all Hmong should use their own alphabet. These advocates reflected the common Southeast Asian point of view that each language should have its own unique writing system. And they drew on the nativistic emphasis of the movement of which it was a part, wanting to symbolize in this way the uniqueness of the Hmong culture. This system and this alone, they felt, was Hmong. It was a cultural crime to have to beg your system from somebody else's language.

The Lao-based system is out of the running now, so far as Hmong in the United States are concerned, and the Pahawh Hmong is running far behind the RPA there, too. But proponents of the latter two systems still argue their respective merits. Sixty-three percent of the people in our survey who advocate the Pahawh Hmong give as a reason the fact that it is a Hmong product. This was in answer to an open-ended question, with no choices suggested to the respondents. The Hmong authors of this book, who know and use the RPA as well as the Pahawh Hmong, say, "Japanese can be written in Roman letters, but such writing is not truly Japanese." For them the issue is identity.

The third level of controversy involved disagreement about details within any individual system, as none of these had been standardized by any well-established and universal institution such as a school system. As long as Shong Lue Yang was alive this was not an issue among those using the Pahawh Hmong, who learned whatever he taught, but as we have seen, later some people were reluctant to use the Third Stage Reduced Version, as advocated by the leadership outside of Laos. Many still use the Second Stage.

There has been considerable third-level controversy over the RPA, as well, and an examination of some of the issues there throws light on some of the strengths of the Pahawh Hmong. We will describe the primary objections to features of the RPA without trying to defend the original system here.[27]

The system spells the Hmong Daw pronunciation rather than the Hmong Leng. This objection is felt very strongly by some speakers of the Hmong Leng dialect. We do not need to repeat the description of the dialect differences from Chapter 3, but in the spelling Hmoob, for example, the very name of the people and the language seems to be spelled in a Hmong Daw way because they pronounce the word with an /hm/ while the Hmong Leng say /m/. For such reasons, the two groups of Hmong Leng mentioned above have changed the system in those places which are offensive to them.

The consonant symbols are too long. Written sequences like ntxh for an initial complex consonant are troublesome to many Hmong, and so are some shorter ones like np, which some write as b. Some of these same people become frustrated because they cannot find shorter ways of writing all of the more complex initial consonants within the limitations of the Roman alphabet.

The spelling should be more like French. This argument was made by some French-educated Hmong in Laos, and has prevailed among some Hmong now in France. The changes associated with Yi Vang, for example, are u written as ou, w as u, aw as eu, z [ž] as j, etc., all reflecting French values.

On the other hand, there are Hmong who strongly oppose all or some of these arguments. They stress the need for standardization, for unity. A few see the symmetry in the RPA system, reflecting the symmetry of spoken Hmong pronunciation. The shorter spellings would obscure that symmetry.

But these objections to the way the RPA is written are not all matched by corresponding problems in the Pahawh Hmong. For one thing, the Pahawh Hmong consonants are all single symbols, and no syllable is written with more than three symbols (vowel, consonant, tone). The issue of making the spelling seem more like French never enters the picture for the Pahawh Hmong because none of the Pahawh symbols correspond to qualities in any other language. Nobody questions the choice of ʊ to represent /i/ (RPA w), for example, on the basis of French or English or any other language, because everybody knows it is exclusively Hmong.

The issue of Hmong Leng versus Hmong Daw is not strong in the Pahawh Hmong for much the same reason. It seems wrong to many Hmong Leng who pronounce /a/ to write ia because ia creates expecta-

tions from their knowledge of European languages. In contrast, Ⅱ, pronounced as /ia/ by speakers of Hmong Daw, and /a/ by speakers of
Hmong Leng, creates no such problem because Ⅱ has no independent
value in any other language. It does not seem "wrong" in either dialect
because there is no conflicting usage in English or French. The only
points of potential conflict lie in Hmong Daw words beginning with
/hm/, /hn/, /hñ/ (hm, hn, hny) where Hmong Leng speakers (who pronounce them with /m/, /n/, /ñ/) write them sometimes with Ě, Ӄ, Ė
(/hm/, /hn/, /hñ/ in Hmong Daw), and sometimes with R, U, Ă (/m/,
/n/, /ñ/ in Hmong Daw).

Comparative Merits

Selection among writing systems is usually political and emotional.
From a strictly linguistic point of view there is little difference between
the RPA and the Pahawh Hmong. Both represent spoken Hmong in
equivalent ways. For someone who knows a Western language it is
quicker to learn the RPA than the Pahawh Hmong because the RPA
characters and some of their values are already familiar.

It is difficult to know which would be easier to learn for someone
who does not know how to read and write any language, however. On
the one hand the Pahawh Hmong has more letter shapes to remember,
but on the other hand it does not have the long clusters of the RPA
which are so objectionable to some Hmong. If these clusters were
taught componentially, as they were presented in Chapter 3, the RPA
should probably be easier for the pre-literate. However, they are usually
taught by rote as individual items, the logic of their structure obscured
by a presentation in alphabetical or some other linear order, so in fact
their logical structure may not present an advantage. Only a controlled
experiment could determine if there is any significant difference in ease
of learning between the two.

There is much more literature available in the RPA script than in the
Pahawh Hmong, of course, and many more people already know it. It
still has the edge, also, in ease of reproduction, in spite of the heroic efforts to create a Pahawh Hmong typewriter, because Roman script typewriters and wordprocessing programs are more commonly available.

But those are not always the critical issues on which choices of writing
systems are made, as we heard from proponents of the Pahawh Hmong
in Chapter 9. And because disputes about identity symbols have to be
solved among the Hmong themselves, Smalley does not take sides in
discussion about selecting one system over another. He does regret the

proliferation of RPA variants as technically unnecessary and confusing. Bertrais, however, who has given a lifetime to the development of Hmong culture, and who has fostered much of the printed literature in the language, is more outspoken. He summarizes the case for the RPA in its original form as the exclusive writing system for the Hmong:

I am only interested in the development of a single system, the RPA, and in staying as close as possible to what was decided in 1953. Everything which can advance another system is in fact one more source of division among the Hmong. And unity is what they need most of all for cultural survival. I am happy to see publications in Hmong Daw or Hmong Leng when they are faithful to the RPA as it was at the beginning. I am saddened to see Hmong follow other ways, dissipating their strength in these years when the possibility of survival is yet to be determined.[28]

12

Other Views on "Mother of Writing"

In the first two chapters of this book we presented a believer's account of Shong Lue Yang, his supernatural origin, the revelation of the Pahawh Hmong and the major subsequent events of his life and death. Much of the rest of the book has likewise been based primarily on information from believers. But what we have written so far about the Pahawh Hmong would surprise many Hmong in the United States, some of whom would not be inclined to think that it is true. Their views of Shong Lue and his writing system are often very different.

To give Westerners a sense of how some educated Hmong feel about Shong Lue Yang, imagine our reaction if we were to hear of an illiterate Arkansas faith healer who has attracted a large following of equally uneducated poor people who call him "Savior." Suppose that this person is teaching an outlandish-looking writing system for English, one which he says he brought to earth from God. Hundreds of people, both whites and blacks, are flocking to learn it.

Suppose also that the United States is in a civil war, and the Mexican army, backed by the Russians, is assisting an insurgent group which is well established in the Southwest. The Mexican army, with its Russian advisers, has penetrated deeply into the United States, inflicting enormous casualties and disrupting millions of lives. We do not know Russian, but some of the characters in this man's writing system look to us as if they might be Russian characters, and some of our military commanders, intelligence experts and leading intellectuals are telling us that the writing system and the movement are part of a plot by the insurgents and the Russians to undermine our defenses and help the enemy. The faith healer, incidentally, was born and raised in Mexico. . . .

Or suppose we are educated Hmong in Laos in the late 1960's, concerned about the education and advancement of our people and the development of our culture, which has always been dominated by more powerful peoples. For the first time a writing system (the Romanized) has been gaining a foothold among us, with the possibility of becoming the universal writing system for Hmong in the country.

Some rival systems have been introduced as well, but they do not have a large following. There is one strange one, however, which looks different from anything which we have experienced in our education (including, collectively, Lao, French, English, Thai, Vietnamese, Chinese and Khmer). It is gaining ground among the uneducated (and a few others who have not learned it, but nevertheless support it), who say that it is the one for Hmong people to use because it was produced by a Hmong and came from God.

We have never examined this system, but are sure that even if it should not actually be the product of a communist plot, it must be totally inferior to the Romanized system, and an article by an illustrious anthropologist who has more knowledge of our people than almost any other Westerner supports that view; it says that the new writing system, though ingenious, is defective for representing our language.[1]

The writing has more recently become associated with Hmong religious and military fringe groups in Laos and Thailand, people at the Ban Vinai temple and people still doggedly defending themselves at Phou Bia Mountain. We have varying degrees of admiration for them and sympathy for their cause, but do not believe it has a chance. . . .

Under either of these sets of suppositions we would not likely have positive feelings about the Pahawh Hmong, which we do not even know by that name, but as "Chao Fa writing" (Ntawv Cob Fab ꗃ ꗁꗬ ꗏꗹ). We might consider it anything between dangerous and irrelevant. Our most charitable reaction would probably be to dismiss it in terms similar to those of Jonas V. Vangay:

> The Hmong in the rural area still believed in supernatural spirits. They had their own alphabet created by "Niam Ntawv" (mother letter) . . . who was considered a sage with supernatural powers.[2]

The Pahawh Hmong is an embarrassment to some Hmong, a relic of a superstitious past they are outgrowing. By others it is considered a roadblock to the enlightenment and advancement of the Hmong people, a hindrance to their hope for the future, which they see as coming through education on a Western model. Many believe it to be completely impractical, even if it does work, in comparison with the ease of typing the Romanized Hmong system on any Western typewriter. Some cannot understand why Smalley (known to some for having helped develop the Romanized system) would take an interest in this bizarre phenomenon, giving it exposure, perhaps delaying its disappearance.

Another whole cluster of impressions which affect the thinking of some Hmong people about Shong Lue Yang and his writing system comes from the multitude of rumors and accusations which surrounded the prophet toward the end of his life, the stories of his assassination, the massacre at Houi Kinin (Haib Kees Nees **HIΓ ꞋꞌꞋ ꞋꞌꞋU**) and the bombing of the round house for worship there. For some it is a time best forgotten; others have residual fears. For most who have heard of it at all, the writing reverberates with dangerous political controversy.

In this book we have tried to present as accurate a picture as we could, admittedly through the perspective of believers, but verifying dates, participants and major events as much as possible. Our sources were often people involved in the events, not only Chia Koua Vang with his notebook, but also people like Shong Lue Yang's sister, neighbors in the early years and the pilot who flew the plane that bombed Houi Kinin.

Knowledge of events connected with Shong Lue and his writing is muddled for many Hmong, who have heard only rumor. If we assume that the account in Chapter 2 is approximately accurate, then many of the widely varying stories told about these events[3] appear to be conflations of more than one event, or to contain an intermingling of events associated with earlier messianic movements such as that of Pa Chai. Also, later events at Phou Bia seem sometimes to be projected back on Shong Lue. The term *Chao Fa* carries its own set of images, which are often attributed to Shong Lue because his movement is known to outsiders by the same name. Mutually contradictory stories abound.

The following summaries of interviews with three members of the Hmong elite, leaders in the Hmong community in America, illustrate part of the range of non-believer views. One presents the perspective of a former military officer, the other two of intellectuals. All three people are sincere; all are people whose opinions carry great weight among Hmong.[4]

A Military Officer's Perspective

One of the Hmong people who accepts explicitly a communist origin for the Pahawh Hmong, and who espouses that theory vigorously, is Geu Vang (Ntxawg Vaj **ᑌᶘᡴ ᎐ᑕ**),[5] commander of a regiment in Long Cheng at the time of Shong Lue Yang's assassination in 1971. In Geu Vang's view, the writing system originated with the communists and was used for their purposes. He says that the letters are taken from Russian and Arabic and Polish, pointing out *Txau* **V̌** as an example of a Russian letter. Geu Vang insists that Shong Lue did not create the writing system, and that Chia Koua Vang did not learn it from him, but he does not know where Chia Koua did learn it.

Geu Vang does not know whether it was the Russians or the Chinese who actually created the Pahawh Hmong, but he is sure that the communists used the writing system to get control of people and as a code to get messages from the Long Cheng military base to communist authorities. Shong Lue was "eliminated" because he and the writing served communist purposes.

He lists the following points as evidence in support of this view:

1. All of the people who could write the script were against "us," against the government, against the Romanized writing. They used it for communist propaganda, to attack the government.

2. When the government forces were in retreat these people said that Hua Tai Ndu (Huab/Fuab Tais Ntuj [illegible] 'King/Lord of the Sky') was coming, would soon be here. When government forces were advancing they said that Hua Tai Ndu was not happy.

3. There was a famous healer in Pak Lai, Laos, who was part of Shong Lue's movement and to whom even General Vang Pao sent patients. In 1969 or 1970, when Geu Vang, professing ignorance, asked to see the medicine which the man used, it turned out to be made in smooth, symmetrical tablets which must have been manufactured with special tools only the Chinese would have. That is, the healer must have had connections to the communists.

4. Yong Youa Her (Ntxoov Zuag Hawj [illegible]), a major in the government forces and a member of Shong Lue's movement, did not fight well. He would run away, taking his troops with him, and he deserted the battle in 1972 on "La Plaine des Jarres" (a wide strategic plateau in Xieng Khouang Province).

5. Shong Lue's adherents did not leave Laos in 1975, but started to organize people militarily for resistance and hid in the jungle. However, the communists ceased to support them, and then attacked them. Yong Youa Her is still fighting there, asking for help from Hmong people in the United States.

6. Pa Kao Her went to China in 1979 and 1980 to get military support for his resistance movement, but he was not successful.

7. The Lao-character writing system of the Pathet Lao came out about the same time as the Pahawh Hmong.

According to Geu Vang, Yang Shong Lue was put in prison because of political issues and the alphabet. He tried to escape from prison with the aid of some police over whom he had gained control; two of them were discovered and killed with him as he fled. This was in 1967, before

Geu Vang got to Long Cheng. Not only does his account of the assassination differ from that given in Chapter 2, but he also doubts that
Chia Koua was part of the military party which went to Nong Het to
rescue Shong Lue in 1965.

Finally, in Geu Vang's view, the Pahawh Hmong is just one more
element contributing to the fragmentation of the Hmong language with
its several writing systems and two dialects.

The force and relevance of some of these arguments is not immediately apparent, however. **V̇** does not actually resemble any character
in the Russian alphabet (Chapter 7). The followers of Shong Lue who
stayed at Phou Bia to "organize people for resistance" did not act like
winners on the side of the victorious communists, but began resisting
the new communist government, suffering terribly in so doing. (Adherents to Geu Vang's point of view point out, on the other hand, that
political friends do sometimes become political enemies.)

Pa Kao Her did go to China looking for help after the Chinese
stopped supporting the North Vietnamese, but so did General Vang
Pao, and that is never considered an argument that the general and his
following are communist. And Pa Kao Her has received a little help
from non-communist governments as well.

The argument about the appearance of the Lao-script Pathet Lao
writing for Hmong about the same time as the Pahawh Hmong seems
puzzling. The Pathet Lao system actually appeared a few years later,
and so did the Whitelock system in Lao script. The latter would seem
to provide just as good an argument for the Pahawh Hmong being allied
to the Royal Lao Government, except for the fact that we know the details of its development.

Chia Koua Vang's reaction to much of this is that Geu Vang is unin-
formed or misinformed. He denies the implication of disloyalty, and
points out that many of the followers of Shong Lue Yang fought hard in
the war effort under General Vang Pao. Many died doing so.

According to Chia Koua, the healer mentioned by Geu Vang was a
famous shaman, Chua Xa Thao (Tshuas Xab Thoj ꘍ꘒ ꗖꗃ ꗥꗤ), a relative of General Vang Pao's mother. Chia Koua, who had studied traditional Hmong medicine at the suggestion of Shong Lue Yang, spent
several days observing the healer at work because he had such a great
reputation, to see if he was as good as people said. Chia Koua saw him
carving by hand the symmetrical tablets to which Geu Vang refers as
requiring Chinese technical assistance.[6]

According to Chia Koua Vang, also, the retreat of Yong Youa Her
from "La Plaine des Jarres" was a bloody defeat by the Vietnamese,

who used tanks in battle against the Hmong troops.[7] Other Hmong forces suffered the same fate as Yong Youa's troops. And Yong Youa continues doggedly to resist the communists at Phou Bia.

An Intellectual's Skeptical Perspective

A similar perspective to that of Geu Vang, but with different overtones, was expressed by Lysao Lyfoung (Lischoj Lisfoom [illegible]),[8] younger brother of the great Hmong leader, Touby Lyfoung (Tubnpis Lisfoom [illegible]). Lysao was educated in France in keeping with his membership in one of the elite Hmong families. He approaches the Pahawh Hmong and Shong Lue Yang with intellectual skepticism rather than the forceful certainty of Geu Vang. He couches his statements about the prophet with hedges like "in my opinion," "it should be possible to verify this," and "as I see it now," but he, too, does not accept much of what believers claim about Shong Lue.

Lysao differs from perhaps all other Hmong elite in that he has actually studied the Pahawh Hmong (Second Stage Reduced Version). This effort is in keeping with his interest in everything to do with the Hmong language. He has also examined the other systems for writing Hmong which were created in Laos.

Also unlike both of the other leaders whom we quote, Lysao met Shong Lue Yang on two occasions in Long Cheng, about 1966 or 1967. The first time, Lysao went to visit Shong Lue to learn about the writing system, but Shong Lue would not talk to him directly about it, referring him to some of his students to teach him. This was Shong Lue's normal practice at the time, but Lysao was not a normal visitor and considered the treatment inappropriate. He did consult with the students, however, and was able quickly to figure out the Pahawh Hmong system and record the values of its symbols in the Romanized system. He came to the conclusion that perhaps the origin of the Pahawh Hmong is Chinese rather than Russian.

The exchange with Shong Lue that Lysao remembers most vividly was when Shong Lue said to him, "All that you are doing is not even as important as a *nai kong* [a low-grade official, usually with little education]." Lysao was a candidate running for the Laotian Assembly at the time, a fact which Shong Lue knew. Lysao does not know whether Shong Lue was trying to ridicule the system, or if that was his true opinion of him personally.[9]

A year or so later General Vang Pao asked Lysao what he thought of the writing. Lysao replied that it was "bizarre" in the sense that it was completely different from other systems in the order of the consonants and vowels. From the standpoint of the formation of words it worked well, but was difficult to learn because the letters themselves were a mixture of many sources. Lysao also told Vang Pao that he believed the writing to be a communist subversion, something to be careful of, although he did not know what its purpose would be or how it would be carried out.

Now that Lysao is in the United States he has met Chia Koua Vang and has talked with him about these things. He finds Chia Koua and others here to be building Shong Lue up as some kind of a prophet and liberator, something like Christ.

Lysao believes that the whole issue is fundamentally a political one, revolving around the resistance against the present regime in Laos. He points out that allies change as political issues change, and onlookers have to change accordingly. The movement which was opposed to the former government turned against the new government with its North Vietnamese and Russian backing. Lysao therefore has considerable sympathy for the liberation movement led by Pa Kao Her and for the resistance center at Phou Bia.

Lysao commented on Shong Lue's reputed ability to communicate with the spirits and with people far away, to know what was happening elsewhere. He remarked that people said that Shong Lue could go out into the forest and bring back messages gained in this way. Lysao feels that the easiest explanation is that Shong Lue had a radio with which to do it. As for Shong Lue's persecution by the communists, Lysao believes that his escapes from their attacks could have been prearranged.

Lysao strongly prefers the Romanized system of writing Hmong because of the considerable amount of published material in it, the ease of using any inexpensive English or French typewriter, and the ease of learning. Like Geu Vang, he believes that the Pahawh Hmong is just one of many rivals to the Romanized Hmong system that serve only to add to the division and confusion already created by the dialect differences. He believes that unless it is part of a truly powerful political movement in Laos, the Pahawh Hmong will not gain ground.

Another Intellectual's Sympathetic Appreciation

Still a third perspective was expressed by Dr. Yang Dao, a prominent leader and intellectual among the Hmong.[10] As a strong proponent of the preservation of Hmong culture, Yang Dao considers the Romanized system for writing Hmong more useful than the Pahawh Hmong. He mentions the lack of typing and printing facilities and the fact that the Romanized is known by far more Hmong people. In the past he believed, as have many Hmong intellectuals, that the Pahawh Hmong must not be very good as a writing system.

But unlike Geu Vang and Lysao Lyfoung, Yang Dao emphatically does not believe that Shong Lue Yang was a communist. He sees no destructive elements in Shong Lue's teaching, nothing harmful. On the contrary, he says that Shong Lue always encouraged Hmong people to love each other, to learn their own language and preserve their own traditions. He said Shong Lue seems to have been a very wise man, always encouraging Hmong to do good, to respect life and each other, to serve people.

Yang Dao assumes Shong Lue was killed out of jealousy, because he was gaining so much influence. Perhaps the leadership was afraid he might build political power. Many people were coming to him for advice.

Yang Dao is puzzled about how a man like Shong Lue could have created the writing. He sees no reason for believing that Shong Lue went to Russia to learn a system created by the Russians, or that he got the writing from China, as some Hmong have supposed. He simply finds it astounding that this man could create a writing system without previously knowing any writing system at all.

The Views of One Western Analyst

As a Western scholar who has studied Shong Lue Yang, his movement and the Pahawh Hmong for two years, I, William Smalley, would like also to express my conclusions, to take the privilege of the "last word" in this volume. I am deliberately changing to the first-person singular because I do not here want the responsibility of writing something necessarily acceptable to my co-authors. They have agreed that just as they told Shong Lue's story from their perspective in the first chapter, I can now present mine.

From some standpoints my research on the Pahawh Hmong and Shong Lue Yang has been the most fascinating in which I have ever engaged. Some parts have been easy; the analysis of the stages in the writing system, for example, was relatively uncomplicated. Other parts have been less straightforward; in Chapter 7 I described some of the forces and factors which I thought might have contributed to the development of the writing system. In spite of obvious difficulties, I am also cautiously confident of the approximate historical accuracy of everything beginning with Chapter 2.

But the ideology of the system—of Shong Lue and his movement—is extremely complex, shrouded in myth and memories as well as in controversy. It has been tantalizing to try to interpret it. I am aware that my admiration for Shong Lue Yang and his writing system, and for my co-authors, has colored the way this book has been written. I know also that there are aspects of the story which have not been told to me as freely as have others.[11] I am intrigued by the world view manifested by Shong Lue and his followers, and by the problem of trying to understand it for myself.

I begin by summarizing what I feel are some solid conclusions, ones already developed throughout the book, based on my best judgment as an anthropological linguist whose specialties have included the development of new writing systems and the languages and cultures of Southeast Asia:

1. So far as I can see, the evidence strongly supports the contention that this writing system was created by Shong Lue Yang, a Hmong man who could not read or write any language, who had no education. All other theories offer nothing but speculation based on the assumption that Shong Lue could not have done it or that the writing was the product of a communist plot. Any evidence suggested to support such speculation is extremely weak. In addition, it cannot account for the four stages of the writing system or the lack of a zero in the Source Version. Such evidence also discounts considerable eyewitness testimony.

2. The writing does not give any evidence of being copied from any other system (although a few letters by chance look like letters in other languages). In fact, it is different in structure from all other writing systems. Such a feat is extremely unusual in the history of the world, but it is more easily understandable if the creator did not know any other writing system.

3. The few times in history when an illiterate person has produced a writing system, that writing system has almost always represented words (a logographic system) or syllables (a syllabic system) not individual sounds (a phonographic system). The writing system of Shong Lue Yang is more abstract in that it is a phonographic system in each of its recorded stages.

4. After the writing was produced in 1959, it was revised three times by Shong Lue, each version easier to learn and remember than the previous one. Some of the changes were also linguistically significant, manifesting growing insight into Hmong spoken language.

5. The Pahawh Hmong writing system at all stages matches the spoken Hmong language as perfectly as writing systems ever match

spoken language, and is adapted to both Hmong Daw and Hmong Leng dialects. Anything which can be said in Hmong can be written in the Pahawh Hmong just as accurately as in the Romanized writing.

6. Shong Lue also made a writing system for the Khmu' language, the birth language of his mother. I have not had an opportunity to examine that writing, but the fact of one uneducated and illiterate person making a writing system in two such different languages at the same time is probably unprecedented.

7. Shong Lue must have been a man of extraordinary intelligence to have done these things. Of course, if he did not do them, and the system in its successive stages was the construction of some cryptographer in Moscow or Peking, the case for the significance of the writing system collapses.

Aside from the fact that there is virtually no credible evidence for the theory of Chinese or Russian origin for the Pahawh Hmong or of its being a communist instrument, such a theory is not even plausible unless we assume that Shong Lue was a supporter of the communist faction, and for that we have seen contrary evidence (Chapter 2). Lysao's speculation that Shong Lue's escape from the Vietnamese was staged is of course possible if he was a communist agent, but there is no evidence for it, and the theory does not match other evidence.

Over all, the communist conspiracy theory smacks of rationalization by those who could not find any other way of accounting for Shong Lue, or who feared his influence on so many hundreds of people. It apparently became self-reinforcing as rumors proliferated, and it became a way of justifying action against him. Moreover, theories of communist plots provide easy self-justification for right-wing administrations which feel threatened anywhere in the world.

Locating the roots of Shong Lue Yang's work in Hmong messianism and the tradition of the foretellers makes much more sense. Shong Lue Yang was a unique individual, but there are patterns to his innovations; the patterns resemble the patterns of other messianic movements among the Hmong and other peoples and show significant similarities to the few documented cases when people who could not read or write any language invented a writing system.

There is one respect in which my assumptions have been significantly altered during the course of this investigation. I came into it assuming that Shong Lue was foretelling the coming of a Hmong king, and I continued to maintain that assumption for several months. It was based on a well-known form of the Hmong messianic myth, on the meager published information available on Shong Lue[12] and on my interpretation of remarks made by Chai Lee in an interview in Ban Vinai in 1985.

Chia Koua Vang has consistently denied Shong Lue's role as a fore-teller throughout our study. At first I thought the denial was part of a mythologization process to protect Shong Lue's memory, and to protect his disciples, against the accusation of subversion which had brought about his death. But eventually I realized that there was nothing in what I was learning which supported the assumption. I realized that my colleagues did not really see Shong Lue as a prophet who was foretelling a messiah (as I had assumed), but as a messiah himself, not one with political ambitions, but one who saw himself as bringing writing and a new understanding of cultural values to the Hmong.

This does not mean that none of Shong Lue's followers have dreams of a future Hmong state. I think some of them may. From what I have been able to find out, however, when outsiders attribute such ideas to Shong Lue Yang himself they are projecting upon him the larger Hmong messianic myth and memories of people like Pa Chai.

The stories of the revelation of the Pahawh Hmong are more problematic. My world view does not accommodate women impregnated by whirlwinds, ants and birds tending rice fields, twin fetuses emerging nightly from their mother as grown men to teach their father/brother the writing systems he had been sent from heaven to teach (but had forgotten), or letters from newborn babies.

The evidence indicates that Shong Lue both claimed to be one of the sons of God and was a person of phenomenal intelligence, leaving me with an intellectual dilemma because my world view does not easily reconcile the two. I am tempted to patronize his claims and the associated world view. Then again, if I heard about such a person in my own culture, someone with such unusual intellectual accomplishments who claimed to come from heaven, I would likely dismiss him as a very smart charlatan, who preyed on the gullible. But the testimony of the best-informed witnesses also seems strong that Shong Lue was a man with a deep concern for the plight of his people, and that he did not seek to capitalize on his enormous popularity for his own benefit. He remained poor to the end.

I am tempted also to wonder if Shong Lue Yang was deluded, but then I realize that this is a temptation to rationalize, to reduce the anomalies between what I hear and what I believe by substituting more acceptable explanations. Because I cannot believe what Shong Lue said about himself I skip from one "explanation" to another without any evidence, trying to satisfy myself with a model for his behavior which would be believable from within my own world view; and I am myself deluded into thinking that my ad hoc explanations using terminology from psychology are more "scientific" than Shong Lue's view of himself. Indeed, I am merely speculating, as I believe Shong Lue's opponents were speculating with respect to the writing system.

Much of the evidence on which I have based my understanding of Shong Lue and his movement comes from Chia Koua Vang, and maybe I have been conned. Maybe Chia Koua is the charlatan, or the deluded one, telling a story fabricated from faulty memories and notebook notations made long ago. Perhaps when I came along to express an interest in the writing system he saw an opportunity to use me to gain the credibility he has been denied by many of the Hmong elite. There is no doubt that I have been useful to Chia Koua and he to me, and certain Chia Koua must have his share of delusions, as I have mine. But the man I have seen at work on this book has been eager for documentation, not speculation; he has wanted the story verified, has wanted Shong Lue and the Pahawh Hmong vindicated through telling the facts as accurately as possible. He has shown great curiosity to know the truth where he lacks information.

There is certainly a process of myth-making taking place with regard to Shong Lue Yang, and Chia Koua is one of the centers of it. His memories must have been affected by filtering and restructuring over time, as are those of all of us. His memory together with his notebook, however, seems more legitimate as evidence than the speculations of people who were never even close to the events. But although that seems obvious to me when people doubt that Shong Lue created the writing system, it does not increase my own ability to believe the stories of its relevation, as when one of the pages of Chia Koua's notebook has a drawing of the footprint on the letter to Shong Lue Yang.

I hear these stories through my "incorrigible assumptions,"[13] assumptions so deeply held that they are not even shaken by contrary evidence. I explain away the evidence to keep the assumption. On the other hand, the evidence for Shong Lue's claims for supernatural origin is not very strong, either. It consists of his own account, reported to me second hand.

When I look at the accounts of other non-literate people who devised writing systems in Africa or Suriname, I find that most of them also claimed some kind of supernatural inspiration. Some reported that they got their stimulus from divine communication through dreams. And although Shong Lue was not a shaman in Hmong terms, accounts of shamanism all over the world are full of events like the events related in Chapter 1.[14]

Westerners have had a tendency not to take claims about dreams or other forms of communication with the supernatural (or the supernatural itself) seriously. Some scholars, for example, assume that those who invented the West African writing systems made up the dreams after the fact to give credibility to their systems. Although that is not impossible, it discounts the importance of dreams as sources of insight and directives to action in many cultures. It is a comfortable (that is, culturally biased) way of explaining away the mystery.

Although a modern secular world view rejects the possibility of revelation from spirits through dreams or any other medium, psychologically valid experiences (from a Western point of view) may well be understood in just such terms in some cultures. Flashes of insight, intellectual illumination, intuitive hunches and synthesizing leaps of intellect are experiences sometimes associated with rest, meditation and sleep. We use our secular metaphors for them, and we seek for mechanistic models to give us the illusion that we have control over their mystery. The fundamental world view of Western science rejects animism (power of spirits) as a world view, but its advocacy of all-powerful natural processes at work is equally primitive animatism, mana (power in matter). Scientists develop animatism into theories of evolution and of all the other processes of "nature" much as some other peoples develop their theories of powerful spirits, their theologies. So we talk accordingly, people using language in ways suitable to their different understandings of reality.

Visions, dreams and the voice of God are not restricted to non-Western cultures, of course. They occur frequently in our own cultural tradition also. The voice of God such as spoke to Jeremiah and others, calling them to be prophets or to perform some other task, and visions such as those of Ezekiel and even (much later) of Joan of Arc are distant enough from us so that the secular modern person shrugs them off as some kind of primitive delusion.

Closer to us, however, some people have considered William Blake (d. 1827) insane because of his visions and dreams (Gilchrist 1973: Chapter 35), which began when he was a child and continued through his life. But these experiences were inextricably interwoven with his brilliance both as a poet and as an artist. Indeed, in one of his visions Blake got the idea for an important advance in the technology he needed for reproducing his work. As a skilled engraver he had been puzzling over technical problems standing in the way of reproducing his highly original composite art (poetry and drawing created together as a single artistic piece). Then his dead brother Robert appeared to him and told him how to do it (Gilchrist 1973: 68–69). The technique worked, and Blake was able to publish his exquisite *Songs of Innocence and Experience*, as well as later works.

Even closer to our modern, scientific age, Friedrich Kekule, called "founder of structural organic chemistry," worked through one of his most important discoveries in a dream in 1865. He was puzzled by the fact that the substance benzine did not behave as it should in light of the fact that its molecules had a low ratio of hydrogen atoms to carbon atoms. Then he dreamed of the molecule of benzine as a whirling snake biting its tail. From that he developed the concept of the benzine molecule as a six-carbon ring, which suddenly clarified the facts of organic chemistry known up to that time (Inde 1984: 348; Britannica 1986: 787).[15]

In our own time, Helen Schucman is a scientifically minded person who heard an inner voice dictating a large book to her over a period of seven years. A professor of medical psychology at Columbia University College of Physicians and Surgeons in New York, she describes herself as "psychologist, educator, conservative in theory and atheistic in belief" (Inner Peace 1975: Preface).[16]

One of the metaphors of psychology is "incubation." This is a term for the process of unconscious problem solving which many people have experienced. It is sometimes seen as the second step in a creative sequence consisting of preparation, incubation, illumination and verification.[17] The person with a world view which does not allow belief in Shong Lue's story may speculate that the prophet had long been obsessed with the need for writing among his people (shown in his dream as a child), and with the myths and legends which categorized writing as a gift from God. He had long struggled with the problem of how to write, a period of preparation. Then in the confines of his small bedroom, with his family asleep, smoking his opium, the normal inhibitions to thinking in new patterns were relaxed, and a new perception of Hmong and Khmu' sounds and their representation developed in his mind (incubation), until suddenly, illumination.

Note that Shong Lue's presentation of the Pahawh Hmong was always in tables, with the vowels and tones, at least, arranged in a pattern rather than strung out in linear *a b c* fashion. One of the theories of incubation is that it allows the right hemisphere of the brain, the pattern hemisphere, to work with less interference from the linear left hemisphere.[18]

If Shong Lue did create his writing system by such a process, he would then have to explain it to himself, and his metaphors for self-understanding would, of course, come from his own world view. Assuming that his illumination came from God would no more be self-deception than would be the incubation explanation above. It would represent a rational conclusion based on assumptions which had long been a part of his culture.

Then, once he reached the conclusion that the writing system had been revealed, other events might be seen in relation to it. Insight can seem like a voice from the air, like the experience which some people in our literary culture have had when reading. They report "words leaping from the page" at moments of insight. Twins (an unusual phenomenon) were born right after the relevation/illumination. They died after the mother-in-law scolded the family, so they must have understood what she said. . . . They must have been supernatural. . . . They must have been the source of the revelation.

It would be easy to spin this speculation out into a full web. But speculation it remains, and as fragile as a web, not because it could not be true, but because there is not an iota of evidence that it is true. It is spun out of my world view and out of my habits of thought because I cannot believe Shong Lue literally at this point, just as I think the communist conspiracies are spun out of similar disbelief.

On the one hand I cannot help doing something like this if I seek to understand the truth of the story told in Chapter 1, but on the other hand I am guilty of intellectual one-upmanship through it. I establish my view as the standard, and I find ways of interpreting Shong Lue in my terms, even if I try to be charitable to him. I trivialize and demean his understanding, although it makes as much sense from his perspective as mine does from mine.

A fairer way of attempting to understand Chapter 1 may be through a model of "translation"[19] from Shong Lue's story, based on his world view, to a corresponding story based on mine. If I see myself as a literary artist in addition to a social scientist, my metaphors take on a different kind of legitimacy. Artistic and scientific truth have different bases, because scientific methodology seeks to eliminate from its purview what cannot be verified. Scientific truth is supposed to be subject to test, but who can test the truth of Hamlet? And whereas scientific truth is more useful for some purposes it is woefully inadequate for many parts of life, where artistic truth can bring insight, though not necessarily explanation.[20]

Perhaps the story of incubation I began to tell above does have equivalent truth to Shong Lue Yang's story. (There is never identical truth in translation.) Perhaps my metaphors are pictures of the same experience described by his metaphors. Perhaps both explanations really are metaphors even though we may each believe ours to be literally true. Psychologists have had a difficult time verifying incubation experimentally, although it remains a tantalizingly apt concept to many Westerners as a characterization of their experience.

Human beings are helpless without metaphors when we talk about experience or thought which goes beyond the usual, but the metaphors we choose affect our perception of the experience they articulate. Illiterate mountain villagers do not often come up with new writing systems. Shong Lue Yang knew it; we know it. He found his metaphors for telling his story, explaining the unusual occurrence, in terms of the messianic traditions of his people, and he proceeded to act out those traditions. We find our metaphors elsewhere, and act differently.

When we use metaphors we make associations. Shong Lue's title Theej Kaj Pej Xeem (ꕙꕘ ꕓ ꕔꕕ ꕖꗞ) literally means 'one who stands for, takes the place of, the common people'. The Hmong authors, after much discussion, chose 'Savior of the People' as our English translation. The expression *theej* 'one who stands for, takes the place of' is used in traditional religious contexts and has been adopted to Hmong Christianity.[21] Thus, in addition to the meaning of the metaphor in its original context, the choice of the English word 'savior' for Shong Lue probably implies that he is somehow analogous to another who is also called 'Savior'.[22] Metaphors refer to reality as we understand it in complex ways, deriving from and contributing to the reality which we create for ourselves as participants in a culture.

In trying to understand Shong Lue I find the metaphor of translation fairer and more honest than my previous rationalizations. At least it does not automatically assume my world view is the norm from which to judge Shong Lue's world view. It does not try to "explain away" or trivialize his self-perception. It leaves room for recognition that my world view may be as "unscientific," as "superstitious," as his, and that his may be as "rational," as "realistic," as mine, even though in my ethnocentrism I do not really believe that to be the case.

On the other hand, in seeking not to trivialize Shong Lue's self-perception by insistence on a scientific understanding, and in translating his metaphors into equivalent metaphors from my perspective, I may still be guilty of swallowing his world view up in mine. When the

Hmong authors translate the name of the great Hmong spirit Va Leng Tsi as 'God', and I write that Shong Lue claimed that he was one of the twelve sons of God, the Westerner cannot imagine Va Leng Tsi as my Hmong associates imagine that deity.

'Savior of the people' likewise takes on whatever meaning 'Savior' has to the reader.[23] When we look at metaphors from different cultures as equivalent we may have a tendency to whitewash differences between the thought systems with a sentimental "all truth is one," which for many people seems to mean, "down deep everybody really believes as I do." The process of rewriting the message, of recreating it in our own image, always plagues the translation of complex ideas between different cultures.

But that does not mean translation should not be done; it is still essential to communication. We expand our understanding of reality through the descriptions of other people's experience and imagination, in some cases even if we understand those other people very imperfectly. Westerners tend to be very open to this expansion in scientific and technological areas. Learning about the experience of astronauts walking on the moon was not particularly difficult for us. But those of us who have learned from people with very different world views also know that such expansion of our understanding can take place through translation across much more unfamiliar boundaries also.

There is an additional dimension to my own world view which contributes to my fascination with Shong Lue Yang. However, it is not one shared by most social scientists. My awareness of problems in understanding Shong Lue is sharpened because I see close analogies to the problems of understanding another poor man, who also had a message of love, of harmony, of concern for the disenfranchised, of hope for the future. He reinterpreted his cultural traditions in creative ways that have challenged people of many cultures ever since. He preached corrective nativism; he was a messiah at a time of political distress; and people called him the Son of God. The establishment found him a threat and accused him of being subversive to the ruling power, and he was executed. Maybe messiahs have to be killed; it would not do for a messiah just to fade away.

People have been trying to understand that man ever since. Multiple accounts of him exist, sometimes contradictory. On the one hand his miracles have been trivialized and explained away; and on the other hand stories like that of his being born of a virgin have been fossilized into dogma, stifling insight into what they might mean. It took his followers several generations to work out an "orthodox" understanding of him. Many people simply dismiss him, but others from many cultures have been profoundly challenged by him, and the stories we have continue to intrigue us through the fog of trivialization. Those who strain to hear him behind all that interference find elements in his story, too, which we understand as literary truth rather than scientific truth, truth that science cannot handle.

Tapp has suggested that Christian missionary teaching has reinforced the Hmong messianic myth.[24] That is very possible. So far as we know, Shong Lue himself was never exposed directly to Christian teaching, but it is very possible that Christian stories and ideas have been disseminated through large parts of the Hmong population and restructured within the world view of those who have had no contact with Christianity.

But whether or not Christian images account for some of Shong Lue's perception of himself and his role as messiah, maybe Shong Lue's metaphors are more closely analogous to my personal ones than they seemed at first. Maybe the surface differences hide similarity at a more profound level. For one of God's twelve sons to be born in a poor Hmong village in the mountains of Vietnam resonates well with God's son being born in a stable in Bethlehem.

I remain tantalized by Shong Lue Yang, and I feel I never will understand him. If I ever think I have done so that in itself could well be proof that I have not.

Final Irony

The heart of Shong Lue Yang's message was harmony, cooperation, elimination of division from among the Hmong people so that their culture could be preserved and their potential could be realized. But ironically, the message of harmony is deeply disturbing, and therefore divisive, to people in power, maintaining power by division. It is deeply disturbing, and therefore divisive to the wealthy, maintaining wealth by class. A message of harmony enrages the violent and denies the victim violent revenge against violence. So people reject harmony, though they may long for it. The rivalry between Shong Lue's Pahawh Hmong and the Romanized writing system has thus become one more source and symbol of division among Hmong people, as both Lysao Lyfoung and Geu Vang commented.

That I have made a contribution to both writing systems, symbols of division as they may be, is a personal irony. I am grateful to have had the opportunity to help provide the Romanized system for the Hmong people when they needed it. I am also very grateful to have had an opportunity to learn about and publicize the Pahawh Hmong and its remarkable author. I did not undertake this study and help write this book to promote the Pahawh Hmong, but I am eager to clarify the system and the way in which it developed.

I began this study out of curiosity, and I end it with admiration. I want my fellow Westerners to appreciate what this mountain villager did, what a remarkable human being he was. And as a friend of Hmong people, I want all of them to be proud of Shong Lue Yang and his writing system, regardless of how they choose to write their language. I believe the creation of the Pahawh Hmong was a major intellectual feat, in some ways unparalleled in the world. I would like all Hmong people to know that it was achieved by a Hmong.

Postscript

Chia Koua Vang reports an incident which I make no attempt to explain, but it reflects an apocalyptic vision worthy of the Old Testament prophet Ezekiel.[25] In 1971, for a few days after Shong Lue and his wife had been killed, his followers in the village were waiting for a sign from him, as he had directed when he was expecting his death. Then one night they heard a loud sound from the air and rushed out of the house to see a star falling right toward the round house used for worship.

When it reached the level of the treetops the star broke in two, falling to either side of the round house. In a few moments each of the two pieces flared up as high as the treetops. Then, becoming one star again, they rose together high in the sky. Finally, the united star broke up into four pieces flying off into the four directions: north, south, east and west. After they were gone everything was pitch black. Nobody knew what to make of it.

To Chia Koua, however, interpreting this event in the Nam Phong refugee camp in 1975, seared by the trauma of this people's loss of their country and of having killed Shong Lue Yang, this sign (metaphor?) was a prophecy. The Hmong people had broken into two politico-military factions which had fought each other bitterly. In 1974 a coalition government was formed by the two sides of the conflict in Laos; but in 1975 the coalition exploded, sending Hmong refugees all over the world. The Hmong had killed a son of God again,[26] and their disunity would now be all the greater.

Chronology

Note that months in the earlier parts of the following chronology are approximate because the Western calendar does not exactly match the Hmong lunar calendar.

1929

September. Shoua Yang (later named Chia Shoua Yang, then Shong Lue Yang) is born.

1959

April. Shong Lue Yang and Pang Xiong prepare their rice field for planting; Pang Xiong is knocked unconscious by a whirlwind; Shong Lue hears a voice from heaven with instructions, and obeys.

May 15. Two men begin to appear to Shong Lue nightly, and teach the Pahawh Hmong and Pahawh Khmu' to him.

September 15. Pang Xiong gives birth to twins, who die at seven-day intervals; Shong Lue finds a letter from Xa Yang, the younger twin, reminding him of his divine origin and commission to bring the writing; Shong Lue begins to teach the Pahawh Hmong and Pahawh Khmu' in Tham Ha and environs.

1963

Near end of year. Communists attempt to take Shong Lue, who flees to Fi Kha, while Pang Xiong and children stay at Tham Ha.

Next few weeks. Shong Lue builds the first communal round worship house, appoints the first group of leaders and teachers (including Pa Kao Her) and builds the first school; he sends a delegation to get protection from General Vang Pao.

1964

Early in year. Communists attack Fi Kha; Shong Lue escapes and hides out in the jungle near Tham Ha, where his family joins him; Wang Sao Thao and Pa Kao Her build a round worship house, reinstate worship and teach the Pahawh Hmong at Pha Bong.

February. Communists attack Pha Bong; General Vang Pao's troops (including Chia Koua Vang) arrive soon afterward and establish a new community for Shong Lue's followers at Kiaw Boua.

Later. Communists discover Shong Lue's hideout and capture Pang Xiong, but Shong Lue and Ge escape.

September. Shong Lue and Ge are brought to Kiaw Boua; Shong Lue appoints new leaders and teachers, and a school is built.

1965

January. Shong Lue marries Bau Moua.

April. Shong Lue introduces the Second Stage Reduced Version of the Pahawh Hmong and the Pahawh Khmu'.

1966

Early in year. Shong Lue Yang is detained at Long Cheng; Chia Koua begins to study with him; many flock to him.

1967

September 15. Shong Lue is imprisoned.

Later. Chia Koua and Kao Lee make wood blocks with which to stamp the Pahawh Hmong characters; Chia Koua produces the first alphabet book by use of the blocks.

1968

Chia Koua and Kao Lee work on making a typewriter.

1969

Shong Lue adds punctuation to the Second Stage Version.

1970

August. Shong Lue gives the Third Stage Reduced Version to Chia Koua for the first time.

Later. Shong Lue predicts his assassination.

November 8. Gnia Pha Her rescues Shong Lue from prison and takes him to a jungle hideout near Nam Chia.

1971

January 21. Shong Lue gives the Pahawh Hmong Final Version to Chia Koua for the first time.

Late January. Spies discover Shong Lue, who therefore moves to Nam Chia; Shong Lue gives a packet of papers to Chia Koua for safekeeping.

Mid February. Shong Lue and Bau Moua are assassinated; Ba Yang is wounded, but escapes.

Soon afterward. Yong Lee Yang builds a round worship house at Houi Kinin and teaches the Pahawh Hmong; teaching begins at Nam Theng.

November. Yong Lee Yang is killed with several others; round worship house is bombed.

1975

May 14. Chia Koua and his family leave Laos and go to Nam Phong refugee camp in Thailand.

Soon after. Gnia Yee Yang meets and joins with Chia Koua for teaching and developing the Pahawh Hmong; classes are conducted, tasks are divided among several students and booklets are written.

Some followers of Shong Lue (among others) hide out on Phou Bia Mountain in Laos, eventually becoming involved in resistance against communist forces.

1976

April 15. Chia Koua, family and students move to Ban Vinai refugee camp in Thailand; Gnia Yee Yang soon begins teaching the Pahawh Hmong.

1977

June 1. Friends of the Shong Lue movement hold a planning meeting concerning the development of the Pahawh Hmong.

Sao Yang establishes the Ban Vinai Hmong temple; Chai Lee begins teaching the Pahawh Hmong.

1978

June. Chia Koua and Gnia Yee and their families move to Honolulu, Hawaii, and St. Paul, Minnesota, respectively.

Later. Search for ways of making a typewriter begins again; Gnia Yee takes training as a machinist, tries to make typewriter slugs with Pahawh Hmong characters; Chia Koua has rubber stamps made of Pahawh Hmong characters.

Pa Kao Her leaves Phou Bia Mountain to get help, and eventually forms the Ethnics Liberation Organization of Laos.

1979

June. Chia Koua moves to St. Paul.

1980

March 3. Supporters of the Pahawh Hmong hold a meeting in St. Paul, and eventually form the Motthem Family.

Gnia Yee makes contact with a machine tool company, which agrees to make type slugs and mount them on the keys of an electric typewriter; Gnia Yee designs the keyboard (Final Version).

1981

The first book by Chai Lee (in Thailand) is printed (in the United States).

September 1. Gnia Yee moves to North Carolina; the first press-apply letters, designed by Gnia Yee, are produced (eventually including all versions of the Pahawh Hmong).

1982

May 11. The first typewriter is delivered (Final Version).

July 27. Motthem Family is incorporated as a non-profit organization.

Late in year. The first printed book is produced, composed with press-apply letters.

1983

September. Gnia Yee moves to California, where he eventually makes contact with IBM to produce a printwheel; he designs the keyboard (Third Stage Reduced Version and Final Version).

December 11. Chia Koua and Smalley meet and eventually negotiate a research project on the Pahawh Hmong.

1985

Pa Kao Her visits the United States; in consultation with him, policy decisions are made to use the Third Stage Reduced Version in Thailand as well as in the United States, and to standardize the order of tables of characters.

1986

April 25. The first electronic typewriter with printwheel is delivered (Third Stage Reduced Version and Final Version).

September 1. The Pahawh Hmong research project begins; Gnia Yee begins designing computer fonts for the Pahawh Hmong (eventually all versions of the Pahawh Hmong).

1987

The first book containing Pahawh Hmong computer fonts is published.

Appendix
Hmong Individuals Mentioned in This Book

Ba Yang (Npam Yaj ꘒꘈ ꘈ). Son of Shong Lue Yang and Bau Moua.

Bau Moua (Npaub Muas ꘒꘈ ꘈ). Second wife of Shong Lue Yang, assassinated with him.

Blia Kao Her (Npliaj Kaus Hawj ꘈ ꘈ ꘈ). Head teacher of the Pahawh Hmong at the camp of the Ethnics Liberation Organization of Laos.

Bruce Bliatout (Pov Thoj ꘈ ꘈ). Hmong student in the United States at the time the war in Laos collapsed. Helped Chia Koua Vang arrange the reproduction of Pahawh Hmong characters with rubber stamps. Hmong scholar.

Cha Yang (Tsab Yaj ꘈ ꘈ). Older of the twin sons of Shong Lue Yang and Pang Xiong.

Chai Lee (Lis Txais ꘈ ꘈ). Student of Chia Koua Vang. Leader in the Hmong temple at Ban Vinai refugee camp and a primary writer of texts in the Pahawh Hmong.

Chao Yang (Txos Yaj ꘈ ꘈ). Student of Chia Koua Vang at Nam Phong refugee camp. Helped prepare a notebook of anatomical terms written in Pahawh Hmong.

Cher Lee (Ntsawb Lis ꘈ ꘈ). Student of Chia Koua Vang at Nam Phong refugee camp. Helped prepare a notebook of traditional medicines written in Pahawh Hmong.

Cher Thao (Cawv Thoj ꘈ ꘈ). Teacher of the Pahawh Hmong and religious leader in the Phou Bia resistance area.

Chi Chang (Chij Tsab ꘈ ꘈ). Publisher of a cultural bulletin written in the RPA in China.

Chia Chue Yang (Txiaj Tswb Yaj ꘈ ꘈ ꘈ). Adult name of Chue Yang, older brother of Shong Lue Yang.

Chia Koua Vang (Txiaj Kuam Vaj ꘈ ꘈ ꘈ). Primary disciple of Shong Lue in his last years in the Long Cheng area. Leader in the promotion of the Pahawh Hmong. One of the authors of this book.

Chia Long Thao (Txiaj Looj Thoj ꘈ ꘈ ꘈ). Neighbor of Shong Lue Yang in his early years. Helped him when under attack by communist forces.

Chia Shua Yang (Txhiaj Suav Yaj ꘈ ꘈ ꘈ). Shua Yang's (Shong Lue Yang's) name as a young adult.

Chong Chi Yang (Txoov Cib Yaj **ᨠᨶ ᨯ ᨶ**). Father of Shong Lue Yang.

Chong Vang (Txoov Vaj **ᨠᨶ ᨯᨮ**). Teacher of the Pahawh Hmong at the Phou Bia resistance area.

Chong Yeng Yang (Txoov Yeeb Yab **ᨠᨶ ᨮᨶ ᨯᨶ**). Linguistic informant for Yves Bertrais when the RPA writing for Hmong was being developed in Laos.

Chua Xa Thao (Tshuas Xab Thoj **ᨶᨶ ᨯᨮ ᨶᨶᨶ**). Famous Hmong shaman and practitioner in folk medicine.

Chue Her Thao (Tswv Hawj Thoj **ᨯᨶ ᨶᨶᨶ ᨶᨶᨶ**). Linguistic informant for Yves Bertrais when the RPA writing for Hmong was being developed in Laos.

Chue Yang (Tswb Yaj **ᨶᨶ ᨯᨶ**). Older brother of Shong Lue Yang.

Diav Lor (Diav Lauj **ᨯᨶᨶ ᨶᨶᨶ**). Foreteller whose pseudowriting is reproduced in this book (Fig. 3).

Djoua X. Xiong (Xeev Nruag Xyooj **ᨯᨶ ᨶᨶᨶ ᨶᨶᨶ**). A leader of the Mong Volunteer Literacy Group, which uses a variant of the RPA.

Faydang Lobliayao (Faiv Ntaj Lau Npliaj Yob **ᨶᨶᨶ ᨯᨶᨶ ᨶᨶᨶ ᨶᨶᨶ ᨶᨶᨶ**). Top leader of the Hmong communist faction and official in the present Lao government.

Ga Va Her (Nkaj Vas Hawj **ᨯᨶ ᨶᨶᨶ ᨶᨶᨶ**). Leader of the Hmong group using the Sayaboury script.

Ge Yang (Zeb Yaj **ᨶᨶᨶ ᨯᨶ**). Son of Shong Lue Yang and Pang Xiong. Escaped captivity with Shong Lue Yang when Pang Xiong was taken by the communists.

Ger Yang (Ntxawg Yaj **ᨶᨶᨶ ᨯᨶ**). Linguistic informant for G. Linwood Barney when the RPA writing for Hmong was being developed in Laos.

Geu Vang (Ntxawg Vaj **ᨶᨶᨶ ᨯᨮ**). Military officer in the Hmong army. Outspoken critic of Shong Lue Yang's movement.

Gnia Chao Her (Nyiaj Txos Hawj **ᨶᨶᨶ ᨶᨶᨶ ᨶᨶᨶ**). One of three men who went to General Vang Pao seeking help for Shong Lue Yang and his followers when they were being hounded by communist forces.

Gnia Gao Yang (Nyiaj Nkaus Yaj **ᨶᨶᨶ ᨶᨶᨶ ᨯᨶ**). First president of Motthem Family, Inc.

Gnia Pao Lee (Nyiaj Pov Lis **ᨶᨶᨶ ᨶᨶᨶ ᨶᨶᨶ**). Hmong novelist who uses a variant of the RPA.

Gnia Pha Her (Nyiaj Phab Hawj **ᨶᨶᨶ ᨶᨶᨶ ᨶᨶᨶ**). Devised the plan to rescue Shong Lue from prison and hide him near Nam Chia.

Gnia Sau Her (Nyiaj Xauv Hawj **ᨶᨶᨶ ᨶᨶᨶ ᨶᨶᨶ**). One of three men who went to General Vang Pao seeking help for Shong Lue Yang and his followers when they were being hounded by communist forces.

Gnia Yee Yang (Nyiaj Yig Yaj **ᨶᨶᨶ ᨶᨶᨶ ᨯᨶ**). Student of Chia Koua Vang. Main person involved in working out ways of reproducing the Pahawh Hmong in the United States. One of the authors of this book.

Hang Sao (Ham Choj **ᨯᨶᨶ ᨶᨶᨶ**). Chief of the Intelligence Division in the Hmong Army. Formerly proponent of using Lao characters for Hmong.

Jonas V. Vangai (Na Vaj **ᨶᨶ ᨯᨮ**). Bilingual teacher in Merced, California.

Joua Pao Yang (Ntsuab Pov Yaj ⊓ⱪ ⴱⵉⵎ̂ ⴵⱳ). Villager who took care of Bau Moua after she was shot, and who arranged the funeral for her and Shong Lue Yang.

Kao Lee (Kos Lis ⴱⵉ ⴺⵊⴲ). Son of Ying Yang, Shong Lue's adopted sister. Helped Chia Koua Vang in efforts to reproduce the Pahawh Hmong. Teacher of the Pahawh Hmong at the Phou Bia resistance area.

Kao Yang (Kos Yaj ⴱⵉ ⴵⱳ). Teacher of the Pahawh Hmong at Nam Theng after Shong Lue was killed.

Kong (Koo ⴱ̇). Mother of Shong Lue Yang.

Koua Yang (Kuam Yaj ⱪⵒ ⴵⱳ). Older brother of Shong Lue Yang.

Lia Ma Vang (Liaj Mas Vaj ⱳⴲ ⱪ̄R ⴵⵛ). Colonel in the Hmong army. Gave Shong Lue Yang money which was used to buy a Lao typewriter to be adapted to Pahawh Hmong.

Lor Moua (Lauj Muas ⴲⴲⵉⴲ ⱪ̄R). Student of Shong Lue Yang at Kiaw Boua. Vice president of Ethnics Liberation Organization of Laos.

Lor Youa Vue (Lauj Ntxuam Vwj ⴲⴲⵉⴲ ⱪⱳ̀ ⴵⵛ). Religious leader in the Phou Bia resistance area.

Lysao Lyfoung (Lischoj Lisfoom ⴺⵊⴲ ⴲⵉⵊ ⴺⵊⴲ ⴱⴲ̇). Younger brother of Touby Lyfoung. Hmong intellectual who studied the Pahawh Hmong out of curiosity about all things concerning the Hmong language.

Mai Yang (Maiv Yaj ⱳⵉR ⴵⱳ). Sister of Shong Lue Yang.

Mi Yang (Mim Yaj ⴲ̇R ⴵⱳ). Typist for some of the Hmong published materials produced under the leadership of Yves Bertrais and at the Catholic center in Vientiane.

Mitt Moua (Miv Muas ⴲR ⱪ̄R). Translator of texts used in preparing this book.

Pa Chai Vue (Paj Cai Vwj ⴵⵉⵎ̂ ⱳⵉⴲ ⴵⵛ). Hmong messianic figure who led an insurrection in Laos, 1919–1921.

Pa Chia Yang (Paj Txiab Yaj ⴵⵉⵎ̂ ⱳⴲ̌ ⴵⱳ). Present name of Ge Yang, son of Shong Lue Yang.

Pa Kao Her (Paj Kaub Hawj ⴵⵉⵎ̂ ⱪ ⴲⵉⵔ). One of Shong Lue Yang's earliest students, then a teacher of the Pahawh Hmong. President of the Ethnics Liberation Organization of Laos.

Pa Yang (Paj Yaj ⴵⵉⵎ̂ ⴵⱳ). Sister of Shong Lue Yang.

Pang Xiong (Paj Xyooj ⴵⵉⵎ̂ ⴱⵉⵊ). First wife of Shong Lue Yang, captured by the communists.

Pao Chang (Pov Tsab ⴱⵉⵎ̂ ⴵⱪ ⴲ̇ⵔ). Teacher of the Pahawh Hmong and religious leader in the Phou Bia resistance area.

Sai Long Yang (Xaiv Looj Yaj ⱳⴲ ⴱⵉⴲ ⴵⱳ). Student of Chia Koua Vang. Taught a class in the Pahawh Hmong in a Christian church in St. Paul.

Sai Yang Vang (Ntxhais Yaj Vaj ⴲ̇ⴲ̌ ⴵⱳ ⴵⵛ). Wife of Chia Koua Vang. Went to Vientiane to buy a Lao typewriter for Chia Koua to adapt to typing Pahawh Hmong.

Sao Yang (Xauv Yaj ⱪⴲ ⴵⱳ). Foreteller who started the Hmong temple in Ban Vinai.

Shong Chai Yang (Soob Cai Yaj ᵐ ᵐ ᵐ). Friend and neighbor of Shong Lue Yang at the time the Pahawh was revealed.

Shong Lue Yang (Soob Lwj Yaj ᵐ ᵐ ᵐ). Messianic figure and creator of the Pahawh Hmong. "Mother of Writing" and "Savior of the People."

Shoua Vang (Suav Vaj ᵐ ᵐ). Teacher of the Pahawh Hmong at Nam Theng, sent by Yong Lee Yang.

Shoua Yang (Suav Yaj ᵐ ᵐ). Colonel in the Hmong army who became a leader in Nam Phong and Ban Vinai refugee camps. Sympathetic to the followers of Shong Lue Yang.

Shua Vang (Suav Vaj ᵐ ᵐ). Student of Chia Koua Vang. Helped prepare a notebook of comments on plant seeds and related matters in Pahawh Hmong.

Shua Yang (Suav Yaj ᵐ ᵐ). Shong Lue Yang's name as a child.

Touby Lyfoung (Tubnpis Lisfoom ᵐ ᵐ ᵐ ᵐ). Major Hmong leader and government official in Laos.

Tua Xiong (Tuam Xyooj ᵐ ᵐ). Linguistic informant for G. Linwood Barney when the RPA writing for Hmong was being developed in Laos.

Vang Pao (Vaj Pov ᵐ ᵐ). Hmong general and most powerful Hmong leader during the war, commander of the Second Military Region.

Wa Cha Xiong (Vam Tsab Xyoob ᵐ ᵐ ᵐ). Taught the Pahawh Hmong to a class of university students in Winona, Minnesota.

Wang Houa Ber Yang (Vam Huas Npawv Yaj ᵐ ᵐ ᵐ ᵐ). Leader of a home guard unit which led Shong Lue Yang to Kiaw Boua.

Wang Sao Thao (Vam Choj Thoj ᵐ ᵐ ᵐ). One of the earliest clan representatives taught by Shong Lue Yang. Wounded in a communist attack.

Wang Seng Vang (Vam Xeeb Vaj ᵐ ᵐ ᵐ). Colonel in the Hmong army who became a leader in Nam Phong and Ban Vinai refugee camps. Sympathetic to the cause of Shong Lue Yang.

Xa Yang (Tsab Yaj ᵐ ᵐ). Younger of the twin sons of Shong Lue Yang and Pang Xiong.

Yang Dao (Yaj Dos ᵐ ᵐ). The first Hmong to earn a doctorate. Official in the coalition government of Laos.

Yang Dia Inthamanivong (Yaj Diav ᵐ ᵐ). Typist for most of the Hmong published materials produced under the leadership of Yves Bertrais and the Catholic center in Vientiane.

Yer Vang (Ntxawg Vaj ᵐ ᵐ). Student of Chia Koua Vang. Wrote a poem in Pahawh Hmong about Hmong history.

Yi Vang (Yis Vaj ᵐ ᵐ). Developed a variant of the RPA used by some Hmong in France.

Ying Yang (Yeeb Yaj ᵐ ᵐ). Adopted sister of Shong Lue Yang.

Yon Yia Yang (Ntxoov Yias Yaj ᵐ ᵐ ᵐ). Taught the Hmong RPA for three months at the Institute of Southeast Asian Studies in Kunming China.

Yong Chue Yang (Ntxoov Tswb Yaj ᵐ ᵐ ᵐ). Colonel in the Hmong forces. Friend and benefactor of Shong Lue Yang.

Yong Lee Yang (Ntxoov Lis Yaj ᵐ ᵐ ᵐ). One of the twelve clan representatives at Kiaw Boua. Leader in rekindling the movement in Houi Kinin after Shong Lue Yang was killed.

Yong Nou Lee (Zoov Nus Lis ພຸ້ ñư ãໝ). Husband of Ying Yang.

Youa Vang Lee (Ntsuab Vaj Lis ເບໍ ວ່ຍ ãໝ). Officer sent with his troops to find and rescue Shong Lue Yang and his followers from communist forces.

Youa Ze Vang (Ntxuaj Zeb Vaj ຫັ້ ພຸ້ ວ່ຍ). Student of Shong Lue Yang who became the primary military leader of the resistance at Phou Bia.

Notes

Introduction: Background for the Alphabet

1. We have not been able to analyze the writing system for the second language (Khmu') because we have not been able to find samples of it.

2. Throughout this book Hmong names and terms will normally be spelled in Anglicized fashion in the text, but two other transcriptions will generally be provided also the first time the Hmong word appears in a chapter. One transcription is the Romanized Popular Alphabet for Hmong (Chapters 3, 11), and the other the Third Stage Reduced Version of Shong Lue Yang's writing system (Chapter 4).

3. Strecker 1987a.

4. Some sources on the history of the Hmong are Savina 1924; Mottin 1980a; Geddes 1976: Chapter 1; Yang Dao 1975, 1976; Dasse 1976; Tapp 1982; Bliatout et al. 1988.

5. On the stages and some of the processes by which the Hmong adapted to their new situation and new neighbors in Laos, see Smalley 1985, 1986. Modern published descriptions of the Hmong in English generally deal with the Hmong in Thailand: Cooper 1984; Geddes 1976; Lewis and Lewis 1984: 100–133; Tapp 1986. Publications in French on the Hmong in Laos include Larteguy 1979; Lemoine 1972b; Yang Dao 1975. Olney 1983 is a bibliography of resources about the Hmong.

6. Westermeyer 1982; McCoy 1972: 78–85, 264–293.

7. Mottin 1980a: 43.

8. Mottin 1980b: 82–121.

9. Tapp (1982: 119) reports a Miao chief in China proclaiming himself 'King of the Sky' and leading a rebellion in 1802. Bertrais (1978: Chap. 1, p. 8, n. 3) mentions an extensive succession of people claiming to represent or to be Huab Tais/Fuab Tais, the Hmong legendary ancient King or Emperor.

10. In Thai *Chao Fa* also means 'prince born to the queen', the highest-ranking level of princes. Smalley has not been able to attest this usage in Lao, but wonders if such a meaning could not have suggested to educated onlookers that Shong Lue's movement was advocating a new Hmong king. The Hmong authors are not familiar with the Thai usage and do not believe it is a factor in

the perceptions people had of Shong Lue. The term *Chao Fa* is now used for Hmong who are still fighting against the communist authorities in Laos.

11. The typology of movements sketched in this section is adapted from Linton 1943 and Wallace 1956. Kamma (1972: 231–319) and O'Connor (1974: 506–531) provide surveys of the extensive literature on movements of these kinds.

12. Tapp 1982 interprets Hmong messianism as a way of reconciling the contradiction between a state and a stateless society through myth. He also suggests that Christianity, with its messianism and its emphasis on writing has had a catalytic effect on modern Hmong expressions of the myth.

13. Bertrais 1978: Chap. 1, p. 3; Lee 1981: 301, n.4; Tapp 1982. Lemoine (1972a: 124–144) comes the closest to giving specific published evidence that Shong Lue's teaching was subversive to the Lao government or the Hmong administration in Long Cheng. Chia Koua Vang, however, puts a very different interpretation on these events (Vang, Yang and Smalley, 1990).

14. McCoy 1972: 78–85; Dasse 1976: 121–126; Mottin 1980a: 47–50; Chagnon and Rumpf 1983.

15. Yang Dao 1982: 7–8; Dasse 1976: 125–126.

16. Dasse 1976: 129–130.

17. In Hmong usage a clan name may be placed either before or after an individual's given name (either Yang Shong Lue or Shong Lue Yang), more frequently before. To make it easier for our readers, however, we will normally write the clan name last (as though it were a Western surname), as in Shong Lue Yang. In a few instances, however, the Hmong personage is well known by the other order in the West, as are General Vang Pao and Dr. Yang Dao. In those cases we will keep the order by which they are generally known here.

18. McCoy 1972: 268–293. For glimpses of General Vang Pao as military commander see Robbins 1987. This book also contains a detailed chronology of the war. Its perspective, however, is extremely narrow, reporting the views of the American pilots flying for the general in the war.

Chapter 1: How the Alphabet Began: A Believer's Perspective

1. Colonel Yong Chue Yang, formerly of the Hmong army in Laos, now lives in Sheboygan, Wisconsin, and was interviewed in St. Paul, Minnesota. Shong Lue stayed with him in Long Cheng, Laos, in 1966 after leaving Kiaw Boua, and they had considerable opportunity to talk.

2. Traditional Hmong months do not coincide exactly with months in the Western calendar, but they are close enough for readers not to be significantly misled by interpreting the Hmong 'fifth month', for example, as 'May'.

3. The Hmong term *Pahawh* (Phajhauj 𖬖𖬰𖬰 𖬖𖬰) applies to this particular writing system, not to writing systems in general. It is a neologism, coined by Shong Lue Yang. The writing system is known more widely to people outside the movement as *Chao Fa* writing (Ntawv Cob Fab 𖬂𖬰𖬲 𖬌𖬝 𖬓𖬰𖬲), a term followers consider erroneous and pejorative.

4. The Hmong and Khmu' languages are historically unrelated and radically different from each other, spoken by completely different minority groups in Laos. All we know about the form of the Pahawh Khmu' is that Chia Koua Vang has seen it, and that the letters were like the Pahawh Hmong letters, which leaves us no way of evaluating it as a writing system. It may not have been preserved.

5. Many of the events recorded here are reported to have taken place on the fifteenth day of the respective months. This day was especially auspicious in Shong Lue's understanding, and remains so among his followers. It is spoken of as one of the days when "God (Vaj **ꞡꞓ**) comes." Other auspicious days are the fifth and the twenty-fifth of the month.

6. The small (and sometimes temporary) Hmong villages mentioned in these first two chapters had names in both the Hmong and the Lao languages. Sometimes the Lao name (pronounced in Hmong fashion) was known more widely even to Hmong people than the Hmong name, especially if they were not residents of the community. The village names used in this book are those known to the Hmong authors and other sources of information. The names are sometimes Hmong, sometimes Lao, and sometimes both.

7. Ying Yang is now married to Yong Nou Lee (Zoov Nus Lis **ꞡꞌ ꞑꞣ ꞗꞟ**) and lives in Clovis, California. She was interviewed by telephone.

8. Shong Lue had two older brothers, Koua Yang (Kuam Yaj **ꞟꞌ ꞢꞤ**), who died when Shong Lue was still quite young, and Chue (later Chia Chue [Txiaj Tswb **Ꞡꞡ ꞓꞟ**]). He had two sisters, Mai (Maiv **ꞟꞢ**) and Pa (Paj **ꞡꞟꞌ**).

9. Chia Long Thao now lives in Madison, Wisconsin, where he was interviewed by telephone and on visits to St. Paul. He remembers clearly when the Pahawh appeared to Shong Lue, and he helped Shong Lue during the time when communist leaders tried to have him arrested and killed at Tham Ha. He helped him escape to Fi Kha and Fi Kham (Chapter 2).

10. Shong Chai Yang lives in Merced, California, and was interviewed by telephone.

11. As will be seen in Chapter 7, this does not mean that there was no literacy in the area. Larger villages would often have at least one person literate in Lao, Vietnamese or French. This seems not to have been the case in the villages where Shong Lue lived.

12. There is one source known to us, written by somewhat heretical "believers" (Chapter 9), which speaks of Shong Lue as a young man spending three years away from home in a school in Vietnam (Bertrais [ed.] 1985: 101–102). According to that report, he left his home at the village of Tham Hau (Thab Hauv **ꞡꞟꞌ ꞟꞢ** [note the difference from Thab Has **ꞡꞟꞌ ꞟꞢꞌ**]) for three years to get an education "to help the universe," and studied the Vietnamese writing system. The source gives no basis for this information, nor have we found any other indication of such education except for the speculations of non-believers (Chapter 12). This source presents much the same view of the origin of the Pahawh as does the account in this chapter, but differs markedly in detail (99–104).

13. According to Ying Yang, the sons were Nu (Nus **ꞑꞣ**), Ge (Zeb **ꞡꞌꞌ**) and

Ba (Npam ꞏꞏ). She does not remember the names of the daughters. Ge figures later in the story. He now has the name Pa Chia (Paj Txiab ꞏꞏ ꞏꞏ). Nu lives in Vietnam, the others in Laos.

14. The agricultural techniques mentioned are those of slash-and-burn temporary swidden ricefields on mountain slopes, not the permanent paddy fields of the lowlands.

15. Fields where crops were grown were located anywhere from one half hour's walk to two or more hours' walk from the village.

16. Chia Koua Vang thinks that the reason Shong Lue Yang was required to smoke opium for the visits of the two young men was to help him stay awake and concentrate.

17. Round houses were used by Hmong foretellers (saub ꞏꞏ) as places of revelation and worship. The significance of the round house in connection with Shong Lue Yang will be discussed in Chapter 7.

18. The kind of monument which Shong Lue Yang was required to build was a square structure made of wood, constructed in levels, with each level smaller than the next lower one, creating a stair-step effect, reaching to a peak. The size and number of steps varied in later years as Shong Lue and his followers continued to build such monuments. Nothing was contained within the structure, and no ceremonies were connected with it per se.

19. The process of making indigo ink was like that traditionally used by the Hmong to make the blue-black dye for their clothes. People in Southeast Asia also make paper from various organic substances. In the case of bamboo paper, bamboo shoots are pounded into a pulp and soaked in water. Then a screen or cloth stretched on a wood frame is lowered into the water and lifted up, letting the water flow through, but leaving a film of pulp on the screen. This is allowed to dry and then peeled off as a sheet of paper.

20. *Pulika* birds are light brown in color, somewhat smaller than a crow. They like to eat rice and corn from the fields.

21. Worship consisted primarily of praying aloud.

22. The bedroom in a traditional Hmong house is in one corner of the structure, divided off from the rest by a partition. It is almost completely filled by a sleeping platform on which father, mother and children all lie. The husband normally sleeps at the edge, nearest the doorway. The wife is next to him, and the children between them and the wall. The door has no closing.

23. The Hmong authors are aware of the fact that the dates would indicate a pregnancy of only five months, but they do not know how to account for the anomaly.

24. The implication is that if the illiterate Chia Shua Yang (Shong Lue Yang) can write, something miraculous has been happening, and the mother-in-law should shut up.

25. Following French practice, documents in Laos needed to be stamped with a rubber stamp to make them official. Chia Koua Vang speculates that the footprint may have had the function of such a stamp.

26. Note the discrepancy between the seven-month pregnancy mentioned

here and the five-month pregnancy implied in the dates given earlier. Chia Koua Vang points out that some pregnancies last only seven months, but cannot explain the differences in the account.

27. Shong Lue Yang taught that writing had been made available to the Hmong people at various intervals in the past seventeen hundred years, but that each time it had been thwarted, the messenger who brought it having been killed before it could be used (Chapter 11).

Chapter 2: Spread of the Alphabet

1. To have issues settled by contests of various kinds is a recurrent theme in unpublished Khmu' folklore collected by Smalley.

2. Communist authorities included Vietnamese, Pathet Lao, and Hmong (the latter under the leadership of Faydang Lobliayao).

3. Chia Long Thao was one of the sources quoted in Chapter 1.

4. Notebooks and writing implements were readily available in the valley market towns.

5. Pang Xiong, Shong Lue Yang's first wife, remarried and is still alive in Vietnam, at last report.

6. The hills of Laos were sprinkled with airstrips used in the war. Every military center had one. Civilians were allowed to travel on military aircraft if there was room.

7. Colonel Yong Chue Yang was one of the sources quoted in Chapter 1.

8. We have relied heavily on these notes in writing this book. Chia Koua Vang's account of the life and teaching of Shong Lue Yang is recorded in very much more detail in Vang, Yang and Smalley (1990).

9. Chia Koua Vang recorded the month, but not the exact date of the assassination. Bertrais (ed.) 1985 records it in one place as February 4, 1971 (p. 108), and in another as February 14, 1972 (p. 109). The year of the latter is clearly erroneous.

10. Shong Lue's oldest son, Ge Yang, is still in Laos and has been in touch with his mother (in Vietnam) in recent years. Chia Koua Vang hears from him from time to time.

11. The lead Hmong pilot in the raid was interviewed for details. One of the frequently told versions of Shong Lue's death is that the prophet was killed in this raid. Apparently some people have conflated two different events.

Chapter 3: The Sounds of Hmong

1. This chapter is based primarily on Smalley 1976e, which deals somewhat more technically with the sound systems of Hmong Daw and Hmong Leng, and with the Romanized writing system (as well as a Thai-based writing system) for Hmong. There is a relatively non-technical treatment which is fuller than the one in this chapter by the Center for Applied Linguistics (n.d.). For some recent technical discussions of certain features of Hmong Daw pronunciation,

based on acoustical measurements, see Huffman 1985 and Jarkey 1985a, 1985b, and 1987. These discussions are also incorporated in Ratliff 1986: 15–22.

All speech sounds vary in different contexts and sound different when pronounced as individual, isolated syllables than they do in the stream of speech. Such variations have not in general been included in this book, which represents deliberate pronunciation of individual syllables, not the rapid flow of connected speech.

2. Tone ↖ is here represented differently from the corresponding representation in Smalley 1976e: 101. There the tone was shown as low and breathy, an impression which was confirmed instrumentally in Huffman 1985. Here it is shown as high-falling and breathy. The difference reflects the fact that high-falling and breathy (↖) is the way the Hmong collaborators in this project pronounce it when they are reading individual syllables containing this tone in the tables. Ratliff (1986: 21–22) has also observed the high breathy fall, but only in women's speech, with the low breathy fall in men's speech. However, the co-authors, on whose pronunciation the high breathy fall noted in this chapter is based, are men. On the other hand, some people observed in the process of learning Pahawh Hmong recited the tone as low breathy. The class was led by a speaker of Hmong Leng.

3. On the ⱴ variant of L see Ratliff 1986. The examples are hers (p. 143).

4. When Hmong examples appear in running text (as opposed to tables and examples set off clearly by space or parentheses), consonant vowel and tone phonemes (distinctive sound units) will be placed between / /, phonetic detail or variant pronunciations will be placed between [ ], spelling symbols will be underlined, and Romanized transcription will be italicized. Thus, we will write: The Hmong Daw sound /d/ is pronounced [ʔd] and spelled d, as in *dev* 'dog'.

5. Some rare, sporadic and marginal vowel sounds occasionally show up in one Hmong dialect or another. Heimbach (1969) includes some, and some are described by Smalley (1976e: 109). They are not symbolized in the Pahawh Hmong writing system to be described in the next chapters.

6. /g/ [ŋ] is extremely rare in Hmong, and was not included in the initial stages of the Romanized or in Bertrais 1964. Because many Hmong learned the Romanized writing system as interpreted by Bertrais (Chapter 11), they think that the sound has been omitted from the Romanized system. It is, however, included in Heimbach 1969 and the whole situation is discussed in Smalley 1976e.

7. Jarkey 1987 disputes the analysis of /d/ as having associated glottal closure.

8. /ndlh/ is so rare that Barney (who studied Hmong Leng for several years and collaborated in the development of the Romanized writing system) did not discover it, and it was not included in Smalley (ed.) 1976. Lyman includes a place for it in his sound system for Hmong Leng, but could find no examples (Lyman 1974: 32, 258).

Chapter 4: The Writing System

1. On the problem of writing <u>hm</u>, <u>hn</u>, <u>hny</u> in Hmong Leng (in which they are pronounced /m/, /n/, /ñ/), see Chapter 11.

2. Statements in the chapter concerning the fit of the Pahawh Hmong to the spoken language refer to the basic inventory of significant sounds, including some very rare ones, as described in Chapter 3. However, as mentioned in the notes to that chapter, there are occasional sporadic vowel sounds in one local sub-dialect or another which are outside this basic inventory. They are not symbolized in the Pahawh Hmong any more than they are in the Romanized transcription.

3. There are also some demi-syllabic characteristics (Chapters 5, 10).

4. Catlin 1982, 1986; Bertrais 1978: Chap. 2, pp. 26–28.

Chapter 5: Evolution of the Writing System

1. Much of the information about details of the various stages of the Pahawh Hmong reported in this chapter is from Yang 1986a. A copy of this book and of all others we know of written in the Pahawh Hmong has been deposited in the Library of Congress in archives for research programs funded by the Indochina Studies Committee of the Social Science Research Council.

2. Shong Lue had created the ⁚ to indicate certain intonational contours (Chapter 6).

3. The forms of Pahawh Hmong reported by Lemoine (1972a) and Bessac (1982) are both Second Stage Reduced Version. Lemoine's presentation of the consonants has a few alternate forms, several gaps, missing diacritics, and other mistakes. The symbol 𝘼, which he records for <u>k</u> is really <u>hn</u>, which he does not list. <u>k</u>, of course, is inherent in the vowel symbol. He does not list any symbol for <u>rh</u> or <u>nkh</u>. For <u>ndl</u> [ntl] he has a variant of <u>tsh</u>. The placement of the diacritics on 𝐕 is irregular. Some of them are reminiscent of the Source Version, as when people substitute symbols from one version in writing another.

Bessac's report also has errors: <u>keev</u> has a diacritic reminiscent of the Source Version, <u>kuas</u> should be Ữ rather than Ữ, <u>kawg</u> should be 𝗶 not 𝗶, and <u>kib</u> and <u>kij</u> are reversed. The basic symbol for <u>hnau</u>, <u>khau</u> and <u>ntau</u> should be 𝘼. The symbol 𝗞 which is shown in the article is the numeral '100'. The accent on <u>nplhau</u> should be ˣ. The base symbol for <u>nchau</u>, <u>nrhau</u> and <u>npau</u> is ill-formed. The number for '6' should be 𝐂. There are a few errors in the Romanized transcription of the consonants as well: Ữ should be <u>nqau</u>, Ữ <u>nqhau</u>, 𝐄 <u>qhau</u> and m̐ <u>pau</u>.

Different people learned these systems to differing levels of competence. Use of the system also atrophied after it became dangerous to know it in 1967 (Chapter 2). From then on, most people did not keep anything with the writing on it for fear of holding evidence that they were connected with Shong Lue or the movement. Some maintained their fear even in the United States (Bessac

1982, 1987). It is not surprising, therefore, that Lemoine and Bessac recorded imperfect renditions of the Pahawh Hmong.

4. Vang 1967 and Chai Lee 1981a, 1981b, 1983, 1984a, 1984b are in the Second Stage Reduced Version.

5. Introductions to the Third Stage Reduced Version are Chia Koua Vang 1976; Yang 1976; Yang 1986b; Vang and Yang 1987.

Chapter 6: Punctuation, Numerals and Other Symbols

1. The names for the symbols ( ) ⟨ ⟩ are reversed in Yang 1986b from what is shown here. The names here are the ones originally coined by Shong Lue Yang. The reversal took place when Pa Kao Her sent a list of punctuation marks and terms from Thailand to the United States, to be included in Yang 1986b.

2. The alternative punctuation marks used by Chai Lee and his students are to be seen in any of his books (see bibliography), and are explicitly listed as part of the system in Lee 1981b and 1984a.

3. Logographs are sometimes known as "ideographs."

Chapter 7: How Did Shong Lue Yang Do It?

1. McCoy 1972: 80–81.

2. Strecker 1978b.

3. Johns 1987.

4. Lemoine 1972a: 124–125. Note also the important place of writing in Hmong messianic movements and mythology as outlined by Tapp 1982.

5. The point made about war goods stamped with writing from different parts of the world is from Lemoine (1972a: 145–146). He also assumes the Pahawh Hmong was influenced by the Tai languages of Vietnam and by the Pollard script used in the early part of the present century for a Hmong dialect in China (Chapter 10), but he gives no evidence for either influence.

6. The term "logo-syllabic" is from Goody 1987. De Francis (1984: 89–148) argues strongly against the Chinese system as being logographic in any straightforward sense, finding it to be based on a complex relationship between morpheme and syllable, with syllabic pronunciation predominant.

7. Tai languages in different areas are actually written in a number of different systems. What we refer to as the Tai-language writing system in this book is the type used in Shong Lue's environment, primarily Laos, Vietnam and Thailand.

8. Strecker (1987b) reminded me of this point.

9. Gelb (1963: 144), who analyzes the forms of writing systems, comments on how frequently writing systems without historical connection do have some similar symbols by coincidence.

10. Donald N. Larson suggested this idea.

11. For a linguist's account of glossolalia see Samarin (1972). Written glos-

solalia is discussed and exemplified on pp. 182–187. Herskovits and Herskovits (1936: 83, plate 15) also document spirit-inspired pseudowriting in Suriname.

12. Issues related to Shong Lue's claims of supernatural origin are discussed in Chapter 12.

Chapter 8: From Handwriting to Wordprocessing

1. Chia Koua Vang 1967. Copies of this book and the others listed in this chapter have been placed in the Library of Congress in archives for research projects funded by the Indochina Studies Committee of the National Research Council.

2. At the free market rate of five hundred kip to one dollar (QER 1967: 36; 1968: 38).

3. Vang and Yang 1975.

4. Vang and Lee 1976.

5. Shua Vang 1976.

6. Yer Vang 1976.

7. Yang 1976.

8. Chia Koua Vang 1976.

9. The manufacturer of the rubber stamps was Nikki Rubber Stamp, 1001 Dillingham Blvd., Suite 106, Honolulu, Hawaii. When no more orders were forthcoming, James Mack of this company gave the molds to the Bernice Pauahi Bishop Museum in Honolulu, who passed them on to the Southeast Asian Refugee Studies Project of the University of Minnesota, where they are now kept in the office of that project, 330 Hubert H. Humphrey Center, 301 19th Ave. So., Minneapolis, Minnesota 55455.

10. Motthem 1982: 1.

11. The manufacturer of the type slugs was the Product Manufacturing Co., 2515 Highway 61 N., St. Paul, Minnesota 55109. They were mounted on a Smith-Corona Coronet XL.

12. The manufacturer of the press-apply lettering was Pressure Graphics, Inc., 1825 Armitage Court, Addison, Illinois 60101.

13. Yang 1982.

14. Yang 1983.

15. The dealer who finally put Gnia Yee on the track of an acceptable typewriter solution was Tulare County Business Machines, Inc., 442 North M. St., Tulare, California 93274.

16. The electronic typewriter is the IBM Wheelwriter 5.

17. Dead keys, on which diacritics are placed, do not advance the type head, so that a diacritic can be typed first and then the letter below it before the type head moves on to the next space.

18. Yang 1986a.

19. Yang 1986b.

20. Smalley and the group in St. Paul were introduced by Dan Johnson, a

former linguistics student of Smalley, then working for the Product Manufacturing Company, which made the slugs for the electric typewriter. Funding was eventually obtained from the National Endowment for the Humanities, the Indochina Studies Program of the Social Science Research Council, and Bethel College.

21. The computer was a Zenith 158, XT-compatible, including a color graphics card, as required to produce the Pahawh Hmong characters. The printers ultimately used were Toshiba P321 and Epson LQ-800 and LQ-2500, all 24-pin dot matrix printers. The software was DTS, produced by International Computer Services, JAARS Center, Waxhaw, North Carolina 28173, for linguists and Bible translators of the Summer Institute of Linguistics. It makes possible wordprocessing with up to four different self-designed scripts at a time.

22. Microsoft Paintbrush.

23. Vang and Yang 1987.

Chapter 9: Contemporary Use of the Alphabet

1. The questionnaire was written in English, Pahawh Hmong and Romanized Hmong.

2. It was at this time that Hmong reports of attacks by chemicals ("yellow rain" among others) became persistent.

3. Kao Lee is son of Ying Yang, Shong Lue Yang's adopted sister, and was assistant to Chia Koua Vang in his attempts to make wooded type and brass typewriter keys for the Pahawh Hmong. Two other men round out the top leadership in the Phou Bia Mountain area. Cher Thao (Cawv Thoj [illegible]) and Pao Chang (Pov Tsab [illegible]) serve both as worship leaders and teachers of the Pahawh Hmong.

4. There are no people at all (so far as we know) who still use the Pahawh Hmong in Vietnam, although Shong Lue started teaching it there. The Vietnamese government reportedly adopted early on the practice of killing anyone who was thought to continue to use it.

5. Chai Lee was interviewed in Ban Vinai. He spoke English well, having worked in the home of Americans in Long Cheng. The most complete description of Chai Lee, his background and his ideas, seems to be Desal 1981: 85–119. It is unpublished, but a copy is on file at the Southeast Asian Refugee Studies Center, University of Minnesota. Desal lacked certain background and made some faulty interpretations, but her general description is helpful.

6. The published books are Chai Lee 1981a, 1981b. Unpublished ones we know about are Chai Lee 1983, 1984a, 1984b. All of these are included in archives (deposited in the Library of Congress) for research funded by the Indochinese Studies Committee of the Social Science Research Council. The original Pahawh Hmong manuscript of Bertrais (ed.) 1985 was also done by people connected with the temple.

7. Lemoine 1972a; Bessac 1982.

8. Vang, Yang and Smalley, 1990.

9. Lemoine 1986: 337.

Chapter 10: The Alphabet in History

1. Our definition of writing is more narrow than many others, those which include some other forms of communication (Gaur 1984; Sampson 1985; Harris 1986). The difference is not so much a theoretical one as a convenience, because such other forms are apparently not relevant to the Pahawh Hmong story.

2. The most up-to-date and linguistically sophisticated book on writing systems is Sampson 1985. Gelb 1963 (first edition, 1952) is the major previous study, and includes information on more and different writing systems. Diringer 1968 (first edition, 1948) is the most extensive historical and typological compendium of different types of writing systems. Goody 1987 has up-to-date sections very relevant to this chapter and book.

3. On the process of adapting writing systems to new languages in modern times, see Smalley (ed.) 1964, 1976, and Fishman (ed.) 1977. Writing systems are adapted not only to related languages, but also across language families. Vietnamese, Navajo, Swahili, Hmong (Romanized) and Western European writing systems belong to the same line or family, but the languages they symbolize belong to five radically different families of languages. That is, Romanized writing systems are all descended from the same written source, but the languages they represent may be descended from a variety of often unrelated spoken sources.

4. De Francis (1984: 89–130) has clarified the fact that Chinese characters are not the straightforward logographic symbols they are often described to be. See also Ramsey 1987: 134–137.

5. The term "phonemic alphabet" in this context does not mean exactly what it means in linguistic discussion. Here it simply means that in general the phoneme is the level of linguistic unit symbolized in the writing system.

6. The classification of some stages and parts of the Pahawh Hmong as demi-syllabic rather than phonemic depends somewhat on perspective. Hmong people seem to sense the initial Hmong spoken consonants, no matter how complex, as though they were single sounds, which could make the distinction between demi-syllabic and phonemic difficult to maintain.

7. The standard version of Sequoyah's story, followed here, has been told repeatedly. See, for example, Foster 1979, first published in 1885; Van Every 1966: 54–64, and major encyclopedias. A descendant of Sequoyah, however, claims that the writing was pre-Columbian, and to have documentary evidence that many Cherokee people already knew it when Sequoyah learned it as a child (Bird 1971).

8. Foster 1979: 92.

9. There was in fact a fifth new system invented during this period, but as

its developer was a well-educated doctor, we have not included it in our discussion. On the African writing systems discussed in the chapter see Dalby (1967, 1968) and Kotei (1977), in addition to brief references in Diringer (1968) and Gelb (1963). An important modern study of the Vai people, who use Vai, English and Arabic writing systems, is presented in Scribner and Cole (1981).

10. Huttar 1987a, 1987b; Gonggryp 1960; Gonggryp and Dubelaar 1963. Brenda Johns called the Ndjuka script to our attention.

11. A more recent writer (Goody 1987: 62) allows for syllabic writing as a first stage if the person who develops it is aware of the phenomenon of writing, but he considers going straight to a new alphabet too much of an abstraction for pre-literate people.

12. See the various views in Morais et al. 1979, 1986; Read et al. 1986; Mann 1986. Martha Ratliff called these articles to my attention.

Chapter 11: Other Hmong Writing Systems

1. Parts of this chapter lean heavily on Lemoine 1972a and Smalley (ed.) 1976. Not every system described by Lemoine is included here, however, since he covers some forms of communication which do not come under our definition of writing (Chapter 10), as well as some writing systems for languages probably not mutually intelligible with Hmong Daw or Hmong Leng. On the other hand, we include some systems that he does not mention. Lemoine gives more detail on the individual systems on which he reports than we do here, except for the Romanized and the Pahawh Hmong.

David Strecker helped us identify which languages in China are mutually intelligible with the Hmong languages of Laos, and which are not (see also Strecker 1987a). The writing systems in this chapter include only ones prepared at least in part for use by Hmong people, as opposed to ones used only by scholars to transcribe the language for linguistic or anthropological purposes.

2. D'Ollone 1912: 269–301; Lemoine 1972a: 137–142.

3. Lemoine (1972a) says that they were derived from Chinese cursive symbols, but Strecker (1987b) suggests that they look more like Chinese writing during the Zhou dynasty, 300 B.C., which would be most tantalizing, if true.

4. Tapp 1982. See also Chapter 7 in this volume.

5. Samples of the Pollard script may be seen in Lemoine 1972a: 146–147; UBS 1972: 294–295; and Smalley 1976b: 6. Information on the present use of the Pollard script in China and a copy of the A-Hmao primer (Yang and Wang 1983) came from Norma Diamond, via David Strecker.

6. Savina 1924. Our description of the Savina writing system is based entirely on Lemoine 1972a: 148–151.

7. Strecker 1987b.

8. Savina 1916.

9. Samples of the Trung Thai-character system may be seen in UBS 1972: 293, and in Smalley 1976b: 9.

10. A copy of the Homer-Dixon primer is in Smalley's possession. Informa-

tion on the other publications in this writing system is from Homer-Dixon 1941, supplied by John Sawin.

11. One of Bertrais's major early contributions using the RPA was his Hmong Daw dictionary (1964). See also Bertrais 1978: 8–10.

12. Results of these sessions were reported in Barney and Smalley 1952, 1953a, 1953b.

13. Bertrais 1978: 8–10; 1988. Bertrais (1988) mentions also that the person who typed almost all of this material (several thousand pages) was Yang Dia (Yaj Diav ꓦꓳ ꓮꓲꓼ) Inthamanivong, joined in 1972 by Mi Yang (Mim Yaj ꓮꓣ ꓦꓳ).

14. An important scholarly publication in RPA from this place and period is the dictionary of Hmong Daw by missionary Ernest Heimbach (1969).

15. Bertrais 1988. Bertrais had earlier been invited to do the teaching himself, but had deferred to a Hmong.

16. A major work by the Mong Volunteer Literacy Group is their dictionary (Xiong, Xiong and Xiong 1983).

17. Strecker 1987b.

18. This description of the Vietnamese Romanized system is based entirely on Lemoine 1972a: 149–151.

19. Schein 1986; Bertrais 1988. Systems were also prepared for other Miao languages closely related to Hmong. Sources often refer to these mutually unintelligible languages as "dialects."

20. Bertrais 1988.

21. This description of the Pathet Lao system is based entirely on Lemoine 1972a: 155–158.

22. For an exposition of the whole issue of minority languages in Thai script, and of the goals Whitelock was trying to achieve, see Smalley (ed.) 1976: 85–123 and 1–42.

23. Copies of these manuscripts have been deposited in the Library of Congress along with Pahawh Hmong manuscripts and publications, as part of archives collected by projects funded by the Indochina Studies Program of the Social Science Research Council. Information on the circumstances surrounding the discovery of the Sayaboury writing system is from Wimuttikosol 1987; other information comes from Lemoine 1987.

24. Sayaboury, n.d.

25. Jonas V. Vangay (Na Vaj ꓤꓵ ꓴꓳ) says there were three meetings of this kind in Long Cheng and five in Vientiane (Vangay 1987: 5). Information in this section comes from him and from Yang Dao.

26. The first two of these arguments were central again to discussions in 1982 when a conference was called by General Vang Pao in Minneapolis to try once more to settle the question of standardizing the RPA. The results of the conference, which were never implemented, are contained in Thao and Robson 1982.

27. Some of the arguments Hmong people made against the Lao-based alphabet are summarized in Lemoine 1972a: 161–163.

28. Bertrais 1988.

Chapter 12: Other Views on "Mother of Writing"

1. Lemoine 1972a. See the discussion of the problems with Lemoine's analysis of the Pahawh Hmong in the notes of Chapter 5.

2. Vangay 1987: 5.

3. A sampling of these can be found in Bessac 1982.

4. Among influential Hmong leaders, the only one who knew Shong Lue Yang well was the highly sympathetic Colonel Yong Chue Yang, whose views are incorporated in Chapters 1 and 2, along with those of other "believers." Still another leader whom we interviewed, the head of intelligence for the Hmong army in Long Cheng at the time of the events of Chapter 2, did not speak as freely as any of these others, and did not consent to having the interview with him reported.

5. Geu Vang was interviewed in Minneapolis, Minnesota.

6. According to Chia Koua Vang, although the man had skills in traditional Hmong medicine, he was in some respects a fake, pretending, for example, to give western-style intravenous infusions to villagers, who were fooled by air bubbles moving in the water to think that medicine was going into their bodies even though their skin had not been punctured.

7. He also speculates that the enemy may have been using chemicals.

8. Lysao Lyfoung was interviewed in St. Paul, Minnesota.

9. Chia Koua Vang interprets this as a typical enigmatic statement with which Shong Lue tested people. When people took Shong Lue literally, and did not probe his meaning, this was evidence to him of their lack of readiness to hear what he had to say.

10. Yang Dao was the first Hmong to earn a Ph.D. (in France) and was an official in the Lao Coalition Government, which ruled Laos for a period between the death of Shong Lue Yang and the collapse of Laos in 1975. He was interviewed in Minneapolis, Minnesota.

11. Some pages of Chia Koua Vang's notebook, for example, have been closed to me. He says Shong Lue told him it was not time yet for these things to be known.

12. Lemoine 1972a.

13. After Gasking's "incorrigible propositions" (1955); Mehan and Wood 1975: 9–11.

14. Eliade 1964; Halifax 1979; Lemoine 1986.

15. Geoffrey J. Huck called the Blake and Kekule cases to our attention.

16. Carol J. Smalley called this case to our attention.

17. Wallas 1926; May 1975. James Koch and Michael Roe called these concepts and this literature to my attention. Sahlin 1982 provides a brief survey of some of the issues.

18. Gowan 1979.

19. "Translation" is here a metaphor also. In a more literal sense, translating re-expresses in one language the concepts written or spoken in another language. The faithful translator tries not to alter the concepts in the process (with

varying degrees of success). What is being called "translation" here clearly alters the concepts because a world view is part of the conceptual system. This kind of cross-cultural communication is sometimes called transculturation.

20. "In most contemporary research . . . the analytical tools that have been developed have been less well-shaped to study the aesthetic, the emotional, and the spiritual, as well as alternative systems of rationality, which define much of human life, and which contribute importantly to social as well as to personal action.

"As a result of its analytical tools, the Western social sciences have often either ignored or found it difficult to deal with actions and constraints derived from transcendent systems of faith, belief and feeling, and their resulting imperatives" (Metcalf 1986: 5). Margaret Lindley Koch called the article to my attention.

21. Heimbach 1969: 338.

22. The comparison to Jesus is sometimes explicitly made by followers of Shong Lue.

23. For example, this metaphor used of Shong Lue Yang may strike some Christians as blasphemy.

24. Tapp 1982.

25. This incident was recounted to Chia Koua Vang by Joua Pao Yang (Ntsuab Pov Yaj [illegible]) and Gnia Pha Her (Nyiaj Phab Hawj [illegible]), and has been confirmed by other people present. They also said that the next day, when they went to the site where the two parts of the star flared up, there was nothing unusual to be seen.

26. According to Shong Lue Yang, God had sent sons to help the Hmong on four previous occasions, but they had always been killed (Vang, Yang and Smalley, 1990).

References

Entries marked with an asterisk (*) are publications or manuscripts in Pahawh Hmong or the Sayaboury script Hmong, copies of which have been placed in archives established by the Indochina Studies Committee of the Social Science Research Council and located in the Record and Sound Division, Library of Congress, Washington D.C.

Augst, Gerhard (ed.)
　1986　*New Trends in Graphemics and Orthography.* Berlin: Walter de Gruyter.
Barney, G. Linwood, and William A. Smalley
　1952　"Report of Conference on Problems in [Hmong] Phonemic Structure." Manuscript.
　1953a　"Report of Second Conference on Problems in [Hmong] Phonemic Structure." Manuscript.
　1953b　"Third Report on [Hmong]: Orthography and Grammar." Manuscript.
Basso, Keith H., and Ned Anderson
　1973　"A Western Apache Writing System: The Symbols of Silas John." *Science* 180.4090 (8 June): 1013–1022.
Berry, Jack
　1977　"The Making of Alphabets Revisited." In Fishman (ed.) 1977.
Bertrais, Yves
　1964　*Dictionnaire Hmong-Francais.* Vientiane, Laos: Mission Catholique.
　1978　*The Traditional Marriage among the White Hmong of Thailand and Laos.* Chiang Mai, Thailand: Hmong Center.
　1988　Personal communication.
Bertrais, Yves (ed.)
　1985　*Origin of the Hmong, according to Vinai "Confraternity"* [in Hmong: *Keeb Kwm Hmoob Raws Tsev Koom Haum Vib Nais*]. Javouhey, French Guiana: Association Communauté Hmong.
Bessac, Susanne L.
　1982　"The Significance of a New Script for the Hmong." Manuscript.
　1987　Personal communication.

Bessac, Susanne L., and Frank B. Bessac
    1982   "American Perceptions of Hmong Ethnicity: A Study of Hmong Refugees in Missoula, Montana." *Contributions to Southeast Asian Ethnography* 1 (September): 56–71.
Bird, Traveller
    1971   *Tell Them They Lie: The Sequoyah Myth*. Los Angeles: Westernlore Publishers.
Bliatout, Bruce Thowpaou, Bruce T. Downing, Judy Lewis and Dao Yang
    1988   *Handbook for Teaching Hmong-speaking Students*. Folsom, Calif.: Folsom Cordova Unified School District, Southeast Asia Community Resource Center.
Britannica
    1986   "Kekule von Stradonitz (Friedrich) August." *The New Encyclopaedia Britannica, Micropoedia* 6. Chicago: Encyclopaedia Britannica.
Catlin, Amy R.
    1982   "Speech Surrogate Systems of the Hmong: From Singing Voices to Talking Reeds." In Downing and Olney (eds.) 1982: 170–197.
    1986   "The Hmong and Their Music: A Critique of Pure Speech." In Kohler et al. (eds.) 1986: 11–18.
Center for Applied Linguistics
    n.d.   *The Hmong Language: Sounds and Alphabets*. Indochinese Refugee Education Guides, General Information Series 14. Washington, D.C.: Center for Applied Linguistics.
    n.d.   *The Hmong Language: Sentences, Phrases and Words*. Indochinese Refugee Education Guides, General Information Series 15. Washington, D.C.: Center for Applied Linguistics.
Chagnon, Jacqui, and Roger Rumpf
    1983   "Decades of Division for the Lao Hmong." *Southeast Asia Chronicle* 91: 10–15.
Cooper, Robert
    1984   *Resource Scarcity and the Hmong Response: Patterns of Settlement and Economy in Transition*. Singapore: Singapore University Press.
Cross, Frank M.
    1967   "The Origin and Early Evolution of the Alphabet." *Eretz Israel* 8: 8–24.
D'Ollone
    1912   *Ecritures des Peuples non Chinois de la Chine*. Paris: Ernest Leroux.
Dalby, David
    1967   "A Survey of the Indigenous Scripts of Liberia and Sierra Leone: Vai, Mende, Loma, Kpelle and Bassa." *African Language Studies* 8: 1–39.
    1968   "The Indigenous Scripts of West Africa and Suriname: Their Inspiration and Design." *African Language Studies* 9: 156–197.
Dassé, Martial
    1976   *Révoltes et Guerres Révolutionnaires en Asia du Sud-Est Continentale*. Bangkok: DK Book House.

De Francis, John
1984 *The Chinese Language: Fact and Fantasy.* Honolulu: University of Hawaii Press.
Desal, Christine A.
1981 "From Kweichow, China, to West Philadelphia: A Biography of Religious Change among the Hmong." B.A. thesis, Princeton University.
Diringer, David
1968 *The Alphabet: A Key to the History of Mankind.* New York: Philosophical Library.
Downing, Bruce T., and Douglas P. Olney
1982 *The Hmong in the West: Observations and Reports.* Papers of the 1981 Hmong Research Conference, University of Minnesota. Minneapolis, Minn.: SARS Project, CURA, University of Minnesota.
Driver, G. R.
1976 *Semitic Writing: From Pictograph to Alphabet.* London: Oxford University Press.
Eliade, Mircea
1964 *Shamanism: Arctic Techniques of Ecstasy.* New York: Princeton University Press.
Fishman, Joshua A. (ed.)
1977 *Advances in the Creation and Revision of Writing Systems.* The Hague: Mouton.
Fleming, Ilah (ed.)
1987 *The Thirteenth LACUS Forum 1986.* Lake Bluff, Ill.: Linguistic Association of Canada and the United States.
Flew, Anthony (ed.)
1955 *Logic and Language.* Garden City, N.Y.: Doubleday and Co.
Foster, George E.
1979 [1885] *So-quo-yah: The American Cadmus and Modern Moses.* New York: AMS Press.
Gasking, Douglas
1955 "Mathematics and the World." In Flew (ed.) 1955.
Gaur, Albertine
1984 *A History of Writing.* New York: Charles Scribner's Sons.
Geddes, William R.
1976 *Migrants of the Mountains: The Cultural Ecology of the Blue Miao (Hmong Njua) of Thailand.* Oxford: Clarendon Press.
Gelb, I. J.
1963 *A Study of Writing.* Chicago: University of Chicago Press.
Gilchrist, Alexander
1973 [1880] *Life of William Blake, with Selections from His Poems and Other Writings.* Totowa, N.J.: Rowman and Littlefield.
Gollasch, Frederick V. (ed.)
1982 *Language and Literacy: The Selected Writings of Kenneth S. Goodman.* 2 vols. London: Routledge and Kegan Paul.

Gonggryp, J. W.
1960   "The Evolution of a Djuka-script in Suriname." *Nieuwe West-Indische Gids* 40: 63–72.
Gonggryp, J. W., and C. Dubelaar
1963   "The Papers of Afaka in His Djuka Script" [in Dutch, with English summary: "De Geschriften van Afaka in Zijn Djoeka-schrift"]. *Nieuwe West-Indische Gids* 42: 213–254.
Goody, Jack
1986   *The Logic of Writing and the Organization of Society.* Cambridge: Cambridge University Press.
1987   *The Interface between the Written and the Oral.* Cambridge: Cambridge University Press.
Gowan, J. C.
1979   "The Production of Creativity through Right Hemisphere Imagery." *Journal of Creative Behavior* 13.1: 39–51.
Halifax, Joan
1979   *Shamanic Voices: A Survey of Visionary Narratives.* New York: E. P. Dutton.
Harris, Roy
1986   *The Origin of Writing.* LaSalle, Ill.: Open Court.
Heimbach, Ernest E.
1969   *White Hmong–English Dictionary.* Linguistic Series 4, Data paper 75, Southeast Asia Program. Ithaca, N.Y.: Department of Asian Studies, Cornell University.
Hendricks, Glenn L., Bruce T. Downing and Amos S. Deinard (eds.)
1986   *The Hmong in Transition.* New York: Center for Migration Studies.
Herskovits, Melville J., and Frances S. Herskovits
1936   *Suranam Folklore.* New York: Columbia University Press.
Homer-Dixon, Homera
1941   "Among the Meo in the Highlands." *The Call* (October): 30–31.
Huffman, Franklin E.
1986   *Bibliography and Index of Mainland Southeast Asian Languages and Linguistics.* New Haven: Yale University Press.
Huffman, Marie K.
1985   "Measures of Phonation Type in Hmong." *University of California Working Papers in Phonetics* 61: 1–25.
Huttar, George L.
1987a   "The Afaka Script: An Indigenous Creole Syllabary." In Fleming (ed.) 1987: 167–177.
1987b   "Afaka and His Creole Syllabary." Paper presented to the Linguistic Association of the Southwest.
Inde, Aaron J.
1984   "Kekule von Stradonitz." In *Encyclopedia Americana* 16. Danbury, Conn.: Grolier.

Inner Peace

1985 *A Course in Miracles*. 3 vols. Tiburon, Calif.: Foundation for Inner Peace.

Jarkey, Nerida

1985a "Consonant Phonemes in White Hmong." Manuscript.

1985b "Vowel Phonemes in White Hmong." Manuscript.

1987 "An Investigation of Two Alveolar Stop Consonants in White Hmong." *Linguistics of the Tibeto-Burman Area* 10.2 (Fall): 57–70.

Justeson, John S., William M. Norman, Lyle Campbell and Terrence Kaufman

1985 *The Foreign Impact on Lowland Mayan Language and Script*. New Orleans, La.: Middle American Research Institute, Tulane University.

Johns, Brenda

1987 Personal communication.

Kamma, Freerk Ch.

1972 *Korreri: Messianic Movements in the Biak-Numfor Culture Area*. The Hague: Mouton.

Keyes, Charles F. (ed.)

1979 *Ethnic Adaptation and Identity: The Karen on the Thai Frontier with Burma*. Philadelphia: Institute for the Study of Human Issues.

Kohler, Ruth de Young et al. (eds.)

1986 *Hmong Art: Tradition and Change*. Sheboygan, Wis.: John Michael Kohler Arts Center.

Kotei, S. I. A.

1977 "The West African Autochthonous Alphabets: An Exercise in Comparative Paleography." In Fishman (ed.) 1977: 55–73.

Larteguy, Jean (with the collaboration of Yang Dao)

1979 *La Fabuleuse Aventure du Peuple de l'Opium*. Paris: Presses de la Cité.

Lee, Chai

1981a *Hmong Cooperation* [in Hmong: [illegible] (*Hmoob Moj Them*)]. Jackson, Mich.: Pragmatics International.*

1981b *Grammar, Hmong Language Book 2* [in Hmong: [illegible] (*Txheej Txheem Moj Kuab Hmoob Phau 2*)]. Jackson, Mich.: Pragmatics International.*

1983 "Philosophy" [in Hmong: [illegible] (*Xeeb Ceem*)]. Manuscript.*

1984a *Hmong Language* [a reading book in Hmong about hunting techniques: [illegible] (*Hmoob Moj Kuab*)]. Tulare, Calif.: Motthem Family.*

1984b "Arithmetic Book 2, for Teaching Members of Project Family 59" [in Hmong: [illegible] (*Kob Cuj Phau 2 Siv Qhia Me Zeej Teej Num Hauv Yim Neej Tsib Caug Cuaj*)]. Manuscript.*

Lee, Gar Yia

1981 "The Effects of Development on the Socio-Economy of the White Hmong." Ph.D. dissertation, Dept. of Anthropology, University of Sydney.

Lemoine, Jacques
  1972a   "Les Ecritures du Hmong." *Bulletin des Amis du Royaume Lao* 7–8: 123–165.
  1972b   *Un Village Hmong Vert du Haut Laos*. Paris: Centre National de la Recherche Scientifique.
  1986   "Shamanism in the Context of Hmong Resettlement." In Hendricks, Downing and Deinard (eds.): 337–348.
  1987   Personal communication.
Lewis, Paul, and Elaine Lewis
  1984   *Peoples of the Golden Triangle: Six Tribes in Thailand*. New York: Thames and Hudson.
Linton, Ralph
  1943   "Nativistic Movements." *American Anthropologist* 45.2 (June): 230–240.
Lyman, Thomas A.
  1974   *Dictionary of Mong Njua*. The Hague: Mouton.
McCoy, Alfred W. (with Cathleen B. Read and Leonard P. Adams III)
  1972   *The Politics of Heroin in Southeast Asia*. New York: Harper and Row.
McMillan, Carol
  1982   "Women, Reason and Nature: Some Philosophical Problems with Feminists." Princeton, N.J.: Princeton University Press.
Mann, Virginia A.
  1986   "Phonological Awareness: The Role of Reading Experience." *Cognition* 24: 65–92.
May, Rollo
  1975   *The Courage to Create*. New York: Norton.
Mehan, Hugh, and Houston Wood
  1975   *The Reality of Ethnomethodology*. New York: John Wiley and Sons.
Metcalf, Barbara Daly
  1986   "The Comparative Study of Muslim Societies." *Items* 40.1: 2–6.
Morais, Jose, Paul Bertelson, Luz Cary and Jesus Alegria
  1986   "Literary Training and Speech Segmentation." *Cognition* 24: 45–64.
Morais, Jose, Luz Cary, Jesus Alegria and Paul Bertelson
  1979   "Does Awareness of Speech as a Sequence of Phones Arise Spontaneously?" *Cognition* 7: 323–331.
Morechand, Guy
  1955   "Principaux Traits du Chamanisme Meo Blanc en Indochine." *Bulletin de l'Ecole Francaise de l'Extreme-Orient* 47.2: 509–546.
Motthem Family
  1982   *Bylaw of Motthem Family Incorporation*. St. Paul, Minn.: Motthem Family 59.
Mottin, Jean
  1980a   *History of the Hmong*. Bangkok: Odeon Store.
  1980b   *Contes et Legendes Hmong Blanc*. Bangkok: Don Bosco Press.

Naveh, Joseph
  1982   *Early History of the Alphabet: An Introduction to West Semitic Epigraphy and Paleography.* Jerusalem: Magnes Press, The Hebrew University.
O'Connor, Gulbun Coker
  1974   *The Moro Movement of Guadalcanal.* Ann Arbor, Mich.: University Microfilms 74-14, 117.
Olney, Douglas P.
  1983   *A Bibliography of the Hmong of Southeast Asia and the Hmong Refugees in the United States.* Southeast Asian Refugee Studies Occasional Papers No. 1. Minneapolis: Center for Urban and Regional Affairs, University of Minnesota.
Ong, Walter J.
  1982   *Orality and Literacy: The Technologizing of the Word.* New York: Methuen.
QER
  1967, 1968   *Quarterly Economic Review: Continental Southeast Asia: Annual Supplement, Intelligence Unit.* London: Economist.
Ramsey, S. Robert
  1987   *The Languages of China.* Princeton, N.J.: Princeton University Press.
Ratliff, Martha S.
  1986   "The Morphological Functions of Tone in White Hmong." Ph.D. dissertation, University of Chicago.
Read, Charles, Zhang Yun-Fei, Nie Hong-Yin and Ding Bao-Qing
  1986   "The Ability to Manipulate Speech Sounds Depends on Knowing Alphabetic Writing." *Cognition* 24: 31–44.
Robbins, Christopher
  1987   *The Ravens: The Men Who Flew in America's Secret War in Laos.* New York: Crown Publishers.
Sahlin, Claire L.
  1982   "Theoretical Accounts and Clinical Studies of Incubation." Manuscript.
Samarin, William J.
  1972   *Tongues of Men and Angels: The Religious Language of Pentecostalism.* New York: Macmillan Co.
Sampson, Geoffrey
  1985   *Writing Systems: A Linguistic Introduction.* Stanford, Calif.: Stanford University Press.
Savina, F. M.
  1916   "Dictionnaire Miao-Tseu-Francais." *Bulletin de l'Ecole Francaise d'Extreme-Orient* 16.2.
  1924   *Histoire des Miao.* Hong Kong: Imprimerie de la Société des Missions-Etrangères.
Sayaboury
  n.d.   "First Alphabet Book in Our Hmong Writing" [in Sayaboury script Hmong]. Manuscript.*

Schein, Louisa

1986   "The Miao in Contemporary China: A Preliminary Overview." In Hendricks, Downing and Deinard (eds.) 1986: 73–85.

Scribner, Sylvia, and Michael Cole

1981   *The Psychology of Literacy.* Cambridge, Mass.: Harvard University Press.

Smalley, William A.

1954   "A Problem in Orthography Preparation." *The Bible Translator* 5.4 (Oct.): 170–176; reprinted in Smalley (ed.) 1964.

1959   "How Shall I Write This Language?" *The Bible Translator* 10.2 (April): 49–69; reprinted in Smalley (ed.) 1964.

1962   "The Use of Non-Roman Script for New Languages." *The Bible Translator* 13.4 (Oct.): 201–211; expanded in Smalley (ed.) 1964.

1969   Introduction to Heimbach 1969.

1972   "Problems in Writing Thailand Minority Languages in Thai Script." In Jimmy G. Harris and Richard B. Noss (eds.), *Tai Phonetics and Phonology:* 133–136. Bangkok: Central Institute of English Language.

1976a   Review of *Dictionary of Mong Njua, a [Hmong] Language of Southeast Asia,* by Thomas Amis Lyman. *Linguistics* 174: 107–112.

1976b   "Writing Systems in Thailand's Marginal Languages: History and Policy." In Smalley (ed.) 1976: 1–24.

1976c   "Bases for Popular Writing Systems." In Smalley (ed.) 1976: 25–42.

1976d   "The Problem of Vowels: Northern Khmer." In Smalley (ed.) 1976: 43–84.

1976e   "The Problems of Consonants and Tone: Hmong." In Smalley (ed.) 1976: 85–123.

1985   "Adaptive Language Strategies of the Hmong: From Asian Mountains to American Ghettos." *Language Sciences* 7.2: 241–269.

1986   "Stages of Hmong Cultural Adaptation." In Hendricks et al. (eds.): 7–22.

Smalley, William A. (ed.)

1964   *Orthography Studies: Articles on New Writing Systems.* London: United Bible Societies.

1976   *Phonemes and Orthography: Language Planning in Ten Minority Languages of Thailand. Pacific Linguistics* Series C, No. 43. Canberra: Department of Linguistics, Australian National University.

Strecker, David

1987a   "The Hmong-Mien Languages." *Linguistics of the Tibeto-Burman Area* 10.2 (Fall).

1987b   Personal communication.

Street, Brian V.

1984   *Literacy in Theory and Practice.* Cambridge: Cambridge University Press.

Tannen, Deborah

1982   "Oral and Literate Strategies in Spoken and Written Narratives." *Language* 58: 1–21.

Tannen, Deborah (ed.)

1982   *Spoken and Written Language: Exploring Orality and Literacy.* Norwood, N.J.: Ablex Publishing Corp.

Tapp, Nicholas

1982   "The Relevance of Telephone Directories to a Lineage-based Society: A Consideration of Some Messianic Myths among the Hmong." *Journal of the Siam Society* 70: 114–127.

1986   *The Hmong in Thailand: Opium People of the Golden Triangle.* London: Anti-Slavery Society.

Thao, Chue, and Barbara Robson

1982   "Interim Report: Mhong Language Council Conference, Aug. 12–14, 1982, University of Minnesota." Washington: Center for Applied Linguistics. Xerox.

UBS

1972   *The Book of a Thousand Tongues.* New York: United Bible Societies.

Van Every, Dale

1966   *Disinherited: The Lost Birthright of the American Indian.* New York: William Morrow.

Vang, Chia Koua

1967   *Hmong* [unique copy hand-printed in Hmong: ᮀᮬ (*Hmoob*)].*

1976   *Grammar: Hmong Language, Beginning Book 1* [unique copy hand made in Hmong: ᮁᮁ ᮁᮁ꞉ ᮁᮁ ᮁ ᮀᮬ, ᮁᮁ ᮁᮁ ᮁᮁ, ᮁ ᮁ (*Txheej Txheem: Moj kuab Hmoob, Ntu pib ib, Phau ib*)].*

Vang, Chia Koua, and Cher Lee

1976   [No title. A copy book listing of Hmong herbal medicines and their use, in Pahawh Hmong].*

Vang, Chia Koua and Chao Yang

1975   [Untitled manuscript on anatomy, in Pahawh Hmong].*

Vang, Chia Koua, and Gnia Yee Yang

1987   *Hmong Alphabet: Pre-primer for Learning Vowels, Consonants, Tones* [in Hmong: ᮁᮁ ᮁᮁ ᮀᮬ ᮁ ᮁᮁ ᮁᮁ ᮁᮁ ᮁᮁ ᮁᮁ (*Phajhauj Hmoob Phau Pwv Xyaum Yub Las Cim*)]. St. Paul, Minn.: Motthem Family 59, Inc.*

Vang, Chia Koua, Gnia Yee Yang and William A. Smalley

1990   *The Life of Shong Lue Yang.* Minneapolis: Southeast Asian Refugee Studies, University of Minnesota.

Vang, Shua

1976   [No title. A copybook of comments on plant seeds and related matters, in Pahawh Hmong].*

Vang, Yer

1976   "Actions of Hmong Leaders" [handwritten poem in Hmong: ᮁᮁ ᮀᮬ ᮁᮁ ᮁ (*Nom Hmoob Lub Keeb*). It describes fateful events beginning with the split between Hmong leaders in the Nong Het area of Laos].*

Vangay, Jonas V.

1987   *Hmong Language Development.* Merced, Calif.: Bilingual/Bicultural Dept., Office of the Supt. of Schools. Xerox.

Wallace, Anthony F. C.
    1956   "Revitalization Movements." *American Anthropologist* 58.2 (April): 264–281.
Wallas, Graham
    1926   *The Art of Thought*. New York: Harcourt Brace and Co.
Westermeyer, Joseph
    1982   *Poppies, Pipes and People: Opium and Its Use in Laos*. Berkeley: University of California Press.
Whitelock, Doris
    1982   *White Hmong Language Lessons*. Southeast Asian Refugee Studies Occasional Papers 2. Minneapolis: Center for Urban and Regional Affairs, University of Minnesota.
Wimuttikosol, Nina
    1987   Personal communication.
Xiong, Lang, Joua Xiong and Nao Leng Xiong
    1983   *English-Mong-English Dictionary*. Milwaukee, Wis.: Mong Volunteer Literacy.
Yang Dao
    1975   *Les Hmongs du Laos Face au Developpement*. Vientiane, Laos: Siaosavath Publishers.
    1976   *The Hmong of Laos in the Vanguard of Development* (translation of Yang Dao 1975). Vientiane, Laos: Siasavath Publishers.
    1980   *Dictionnaire Francaise–Hmong Blanc*. Paris: Comité National d'Entraide.
    1982   "Why Did the Hmong Leave Laos?" In Downing and Olney (eds.) 1982: 3–18.
Yang, Gnia Yee
    1976   *Hmong Language Primer, Beginning Book 1: Hmong Cooperation* [handmade in Hmong: ꓕꓵ ꓪꓮ ꓦꓮ ꓟꓠ ꓵ ꓴꓰ, ꓠꓵ ꓥꓵ ꓥꓮ ꓘ ꓩ: ꓴꓰ ꓟꓠ ꓴꓵ (*Pwv Ntuas Nyeem Moj Kuab Hmoob, Ntu Pib Ib Phau Ib: Hmoob Moj Them*)].*
    1982   *Hmong Language Primer: Beginning Book 1* [in Hmong: ꓕꓵ ꓪꓮ ꓦꓮ ꓟꓠ ꓵ ꓴꓰ: ꓠꓵ ꓥꓵ ꓥꓮ ꓘ ꓩ: (*Pwv ntuas nyeem Moj kuab Hmoob: Ntu pib ib Phau 1*)]. Merced, Calif.: Pahawh 59.*
    1983   *Grammar, Hmong Language, Book 1* [in Hmong: ꓦꓣ ꓦꓣ ꓟꓠ ꓵ ꓴꓰ ꓘ ꓩ: (*Txheej Txheem Moj Kuab Hmoob Phau 1*)]. Merced, Calif.: Pahawh 59.*
    1986a   *History of the Hmong Alphabet* [in Hmong: ꓦꓕ ꓮꓘ ꓣꓲꓕ ꓴꓰ (*Keeb Kwm Phaj Hauj Hmoob*)]. Visalia, Calif.: Pahawh 59.*
    1986b   *Hmong Language Primer, Beginning Book 1, Elementary* [in Hmong: ꓕꓵ ꓪꓮ ꓦꓮ ꓟꓠ ꓵ ꓴꓰ, ꓠꓵ ꓥꓵ ꓥꓮ ꓘ ꓩ, ꓴꓣ ꓕ ꓴꓵ (*Pwv Ntuas Nyeen Moj Kuab Hmoob, Ntu Pib Ib Phau Ib, Txhooj Kawm Fem*)]. Visalia, Calif.: Pahawh 59.*
Yang, Zhongde and Deguang Wang
    1983   *A-Hmao Primer*, vol. 1 [in A-Hmao: *Ad Hmaob Ndend, Ib Nanck*]. Zhaotong Minorities Commission.

Index